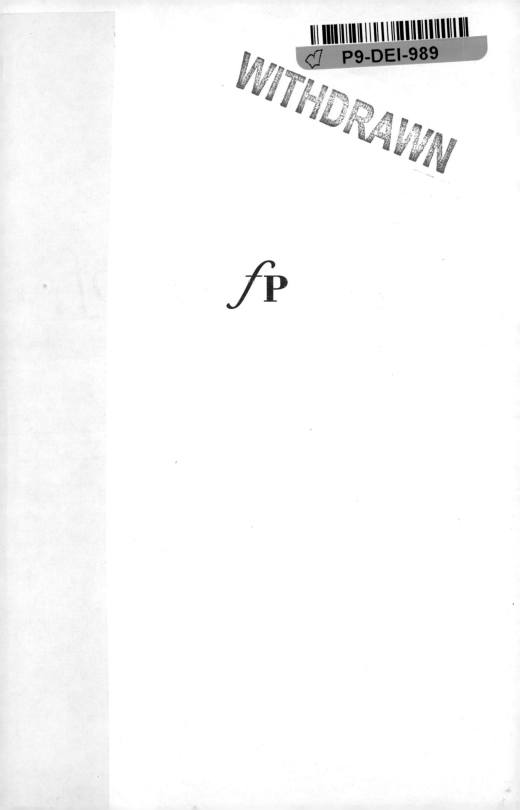

_f_ **P**

Nelofer Pazira

a Bed of

Red Flowers

IN SEARCH OF
MY AFGHANISTAN

FREE PRESS

NEW YORK   LONDON   TORONTO   SYDNEY

*f*P

FREE PRESS
A Division of Simon & Schuster, Inc.
1230 Avenue of the Americas
New York, NY 10020

First Free Press trade paperback edition 2005

Originally published in 2005 by Random House Canada, a division of
Random House of Canada Limited.

FREE PRESS and colophon are trademarks
of Simon & Schuster, Inc.

For information about special discounts for bulk purchases,
please contact Simon & Schuster Special Sales:
1-800-456-6798 or business@simonandschuster.com

Manufactured in the United States of America

2   4   6   8   10   9   7   5   3   1

Library of Congress Cataloging-in-Publication Data

Pazira, Nelofer.
A bed of red flowers : in search of my Afghanistan / Nelofer Pazira.—1st Free Press
trade pbk. ed.
p.   cm.
Includes bibliographical references and index.
1. Pazira, Nelofer. 2. Afghanistan—History—Soviet occupation, 1979–1989—Personal
narratives, Afghan. 3. Afghanistan—History—1989–2001. 4. Afghanistan—Description
and travel. 5. Motion picture actors and actresses—Biography. I. Title.
DS371.2.P42 2005
958.104'092—dc22
[B]
2005043781

ISBN-13:   978-0-7432-8133-1
ISBN-10:   0-7432-8133-0

To Habibullah, Jamila, Robert,
Hassib and Mejgan, for their
prayers, courage and love

CONTENTS

PROLOGUE

ON ONE LATE AFTERNOON in September 1978, our family driver took me to the detention centre in Baghlan, where my father was imprisoned. My purple velvety trousers were brushing the dust from the unpaved road as we walked to the compound. I was holding the driver's

hand, forcing him to go faster. I wanted to see my father. For a child, whose world consisted of family—parents, a younger brother and a baby sister—not seeing my father for three days was a great deal of missing. I was three months short of being five years old.

At the prison, all I could see of my father was his face—striped with the lines from the shadow of the metal bars. He looked desolate. I wanted to hug and kiss him. But he was boxed in a small room. A thick wall, iron bars and several policemen stood between us. I was sitting on the ground, pushing my feet against the soil and crying, my trousers disappearing into a cloud of dry dust and hardly looking purple or velvety any more.

I shall never forget the angry voice of my father. "I didn't raise you to cry on such a day," he shouted at me. His words shook the compound. I stopped crying. Holding the driver's hand, I stood embarrassed, head down, listening to my father. At times his voice grew thicker, as if he himself was going to cry, but he paused and continued. "You mustn't cry," he said.

"You have to be strong and help your mother." He told me to tell her that he was fine and that they had no reason to keep him imprisoned. He'd be home soon.

"Your ten minutes is up," a voice announced coldly. There was a silent goodbye as my father shook his head. I had no tears, and my father faded from view.

I walked back to our car with the driver. There was a revolution inside me. I wanted to be strong, to break all those walls and bars and set my father free. I kept fighting the desperate need to burst into tears. My eyes were burning, much like my father's. But his were inflamed with anger, mine with helplessness. I wanted to arrive home without tears, even though I knew my mother wouldn't mind. She had shed many of her own tears in the last few days. I heard her cry at night, quietly in her bed.

That night I hated my mother's sobbing. I wanted to scream at her "Stop it!" But I felt sorry for her. I knew she was crying from the pain of missing my father, and it was not the only thing. I also heard her talking to a friend in the living room as she described how men were verbally abusing her. She spent her days going to various government offices to see if she could obtain my father's release. The governor of the city had told her she was "too young and beautiful to waste her life with a criminal" who was against the "rightful government." A police officer had told her "there were plenty of men who would be happy to please" her. The principal of the school where she was teaching said he was going to report my mother to the "higher authorities" if she missed another day of work to follow up on my father's case. But if she reciprocated his "keen affection," she would be nominated that year's best teacher.

* * *

3

My mother was not nominated any year's best teacher, and my father was released after nearly five months in prison. "He had a brave lawyer and lots of luck," as one of his best friends put it. It took me a while to grasp the gravity of my father's crime in refusing to support the communist government. The full extent of its meaning did not become clear until later in my life. In some ways, to this day, the child in me still asks "Why?" Why was my father, who in his daughter's view was a kind man and a good medical doctor, locked up away from us? Children see everything through the injustices they've suffered. In the perfect world that every child expects, this episode left a crack in the wall of my innocence.

I

ESCAPE

Let's mourn—
Orders come from abroad, like death itself;
The guns are free,
So are the bullets,
And this year is the year of dying young,
The year of departures,
The year of refugees.

Qahar Ausi, 1989

AT DUSK, THE DOWNTOWN Kabul district of Dehe Afghanan is cloaked with grey clouds and grey smoke. The early spring rain has left dirt and water across the paved roads. For over a decade now the highways have not been maintained, and the potholes have become deeper, the city's drainage system more derelict each year. It's not cold, but we all hug our arms around our bodies as if shivering from fear. We all walk fast, very fast—hoping to get away from everything and everyone. It's been ten years since the beginning of the war. Who started it? Who will end it? These days, we are so tired that we wish to forget. But is it possible to forget about war when minute by minute, hour by hour and day by day we feel that something bloody and terrible is about to happen?

The curfew starts at 10:00 every night. But there is another unspoken curfew that is imposed not by the communist government but by fear, a curfew that sets in much earlier. Which is why, at this hour, a cocktail of bicycles, motorbikes, pickup trucks, white-and-blue buses, red-and-orange minibuses and yellow taxis, all overcrowded, are merging into a river of traffic. People flood along the main road between the vehicles to reach the two bus stations. Vendors scream their hearts out in a desperate attempt to sell their apples and beans, spinach and meat. Fabrics are measured and cut at speed, four customers at a time. Even the clouds are racing over my head.

I move with the crowd. Meeting familiar eyes means a nod, stepping on someone's muddy shoes means a whisper of "sorry," hitting someone on the shoulder brings a shrug. My only thought is of reaching the bus station. Upon a pedestal a uniformed officer stands with a hand-held stop sign and a whistle, controlling the traffic, his eyes almost invisible beneath the white peak of his hat. I can see only the tip of his nose and his narrow chin. He appears to be smiling, but it could be fatigue. He is dressed in a grey uniform with white collar and cuffs, and black military boots. There used to be streetlights at the intersection, but there are now so many power cuts in the city that we hardly remember them. People are fighting to board the buses, standing in rainwater and dirt so thick they can't see the ground under their feet. There are few buses left and little fuel. So people stuff themselves into the vehicles, three times as many as the rules permit, hanging from the front and back doors, teenagers climbing through the windows, their bodies still dangling outside the bus when it moves away.

Chaos is normal for us. Fear, anger, panic and waiting—always waiting—is our life. Ten years, and we've been watching the gradual deterioration of life, not just seeing it, but living it. To protect ourselves from thieves, we young women have to be ready to nearly throttle a total stranger, to punch his arm, back or face, to shout an obscenity at him. Physical and verbal harassment on the streets is so common that we don't even talk about it any more. It's an accepted part of the war.

An empty bus arrives, and we circle like bees around the doors, breathless in our efforts to push them open. Suddenly a massive explosion makes the ground tremble beneath our feet. The shoving and pushing stop. There is silence after the clap of sound. I move my arms and shake my legs to make sure I am in one piece. Thank God! I'm untouched. I begin to hear screams and cries of pain. The explosion, it turns out, was at the bus station across the street, more than a block away. We barge our way towards the doors of the bus. All that matters is the hysterical, unstoppable desire to escape. As the semicircle of people gets larger and more frantic, I hesitate for just a moment, and I'm pushed out. I decide to try the driver's door, and go to the other side of the bus. Just then, there's another terrific explosion, followed by a third. I cannot move. The detonations feel closer this time; the ground under my feet shakes even harder. I see things flying through the air. There is more screaming. The bus, moving slowly away, has quickly filled with passengers.

The three explosions were from rockets landing a couple of metres from each other in the bus station. I walk with a few people from this side of the street towards the scene of the explosions. A tide of blood is running over the paved road, over the dirt and mud. I see a purse hanging from one of the bus station's destination boards and, next to it, a single arm, cut off at the elbow, upside down, blood dripping from fingers moving in the breeze, a sudden terrible goodbye. People are running, crying. An elderly man is trying to comfort a wounded boy buried waist-deep in a mass of body parts, mud and torn clothes. A cart lies on its side, wheels still turning. Hundreds of yellow and green prunes are lying on the road. It's only now that I begin to smell the blood and flesh, a butcher's shop of corpses.

I turn around and walk back along the pavement. Something lying in the dirt looks like a single finger. Yes, it is a finger. It has a ring on it. I walk backwards. The sound of people screaming mixes with car horns. The traffic circle is empty. The white peak of the officer's hat, stained with blood, lies on the muddy ground. I walk faster to get away. How many more rockets may yet land here?

An ambulance arrives. Policemen are pushing the crowd away. I return to my bus stop, where another bus is filling with panic-stricken passengers. We are sheep, our heads down, pushing towards the door. No words, no tears. The conductor, an elderly man, pulls a few people off the packed bus before he hops on. The passengers are mute. There is only the sound of the engine, the windshield wipers and heavy breathing. The driver pulls a folded greasy cloth from under his seat and, while steering the wheel, reaches to clean off the fog that is building on the windshield. I notice a crack in the glass that runs all the way to the top. Someone has tried to patch it with green duct tape. "Tickets, please." We act as if it's perfectly normal to see men, women and children in pieces, quite natural to walk through their blood and body parts, then get on a bus for home. "Tickets, please." The rain washes our memories. How many have just died? No one knows. Given the bleak state of things in Kabul, no one will have the right number. "Tickets, please." There will be a rough estimate, but the government can't keep up with the statistics when there are so many rockets and bombs exploding each day. Only the families of those who died—if they still had families—will know who's lost. For us on the bus, all that matters is to reach home and discover that it was not our friends, not our families who had died.

But I do know someone who was killed on this day in March of 1989. Ibrahim was a classmate in a mathematics course I used to take outside school hours. He was a tall, lean boy, about my age, around sixteen, in grade eleven in one of the boys' schools. I noticed him because he used to get good grades in our biweekly exams. Girls used to giggle when he and his friends passed by. He was a shy boy who didn't talk much. But I had seen him a couple of times, and he had nodded his head in a silent "hi," with just the touch of a smile on his face. I had heard that his family wanted to send him abroad, but death caught him too soon.

I can't bring myself to go to Ibrahim's funeral. I want to forget about those who die, not remember them. Otherwise my life is going to be dominated by dead people. My mother and father attend lots of funerals: family, friends, neighbours. I admire them for their courage—facing all that misery and pain, listening to each individual's story of loss. My mother, Jamila, is the one who tells me about Ibrahim. She was attending another wake in the same funeral home when she heard about him and saw his mother and sisters. "The two sisters, one with a baby, were crying," my mother says. "But his mother was like a wooden stick—dry and silent."

My mother goes on talking about how many funerals were held in that one place that day. The city's few funeral homes were built for ordinary times, not for war. The two funeral homes downtown are packed each day, with several services going on at the same time. My father, Habibullah, has only Fridays off from his work as a doctor to visit neighbours and friends to offer his condolences. But my mother, who works half-days as a teacher in one of the local schools, has more time to attend the ceremonies. Dressed in grey, brown or black suits, Jamila arrives home each day from funerals, looking more tired, more upset. Each evening begins with her words "God forbid! No family should go through this." But God doesn't forbid—and the Afghan government and its opposition forces, the mujahidin, the "holy warriors," make sure it is not forbidden. The funerals continue.

In the spring of 1989, Kabul is a city under siege. It has been this way for months. The mujahidin have encircled Kabul, launching rocket attacks. The communist government, helplessly holding on to power, responds with counter-attacks. The fear of dying is more real than ever. Starvation and mines, rockets and bombs are a sentence of death, a final conviction for the innocent. Explosions are frequent, happening at any time, at any location: marketplaces, bus stations, residential areas, schools, government offices, parks, streets, even graveyards. Nowhere is safe.

March 22 marks the beginning of the school year in the city. Streets, buses and sidewalks are crowded with students, teachers and professors. It rained last night, but the sun is out now, spreading a warm glow over the trees and grass. It's a beautiful day.

I walk with happiness to meet Dyana. She is taller than I am and has whiter skin, brown eyes and dark brown shoulder-length hair. To go to school or to go shopping or just for a walk, we always meet at the bus stop near our homes in the east Kabul district of Taymanie. We greet each other in the same way, saying "Salam" [peace] at the same time, with a handshake and three kisses on the cheek.

We manage to get on a crowded bus. As soon as it starts to move, a rocket passes over our heads. The driver is so scared he hits the brake. The bus shudders to a stop. We are packed and squeezed too closely to fall, but we all lean over each other, struggling to find something to hold on to. From the back, guys shout at the driver, "Move, move. Don't stop." A voice says, "It is just a rocket. Why on earth would you stop?" The driver finally steps on the gas and heads on up the road. There is a sigh of relief. We survived this one, but we know there are more to come.

Although we have grown used to these attacks, there is always a moment of panic and confusion when a rocket explodes. A missile is intrusive, impartial in its cruelty, impossible to dismiss or ignore. Each time I hear an incoming missile—the hiss and scream of its flight—I tremble with fear, for my life and for those of my family and friends.

Perhaps some of us are better at hiding our fear. But my mother never claims to be brave enough to remain indifferent. No Hollywood lighting expert could capture the paleness of my mother's face, the quivering of her colourless lips when she hears the rocket fire. She says her heart gets weaker with each explosion, each death and each funeral.

She is not the only one. In a barrage that has lasted months, the missiles come in unprecedented numbers. And so do the casualties, the burned cars and smashed homes. Of course, the war was always real to us, but until now the battles were in the countryside and in other cities. Before this, we used to hear news of the fighting; now we see its victims, bloodied, burned, broken and dead. For years we lived a fantasy war, but now it has invaded our lives. On the streets, inside our buses—even in classrooms—people get into arguments and fistfights quickly. We are losing our collective nerve. The war has come to *our* homes.

People have been fleeing the country for the past ten years, but the rate seems to have doubled in the last year. For months, every night around our dinner table, we have had this same conversation. We usually have dinner at eight, after my father is back from work. Each night, about midway through the dinner, my mother starts in on the topic. "Zarena-jan brought a set of golden bracelets to school today." The name of the teacher and the kind of jewellery change every few days. We all listen patiently, knowing where this is going to end. "She said she trusted only the few of us." And my father always replies, "If you like them, why don't you buy the bracelets?" At first Jamila is calm. "That's not the point—it's not about the jewellery, it's about our lives." Then she goes on to list all the people we know who have left the country. We roll our eyes, nodding as she pauses after each name to catch her breath. We know all the names of her fellow teachers and of Dad's colleagues who've escaped or who are about to flee Afghanistan.

By the time the table is being cleared, the conversation becomes more overt, more ferocious.

"So, how long do you think we should stay in this country, in this terrible war?" asks Jamila.

"Forever," my father replies. "Until only one other person is left in this land, I will remain here."

Irritated, she says, "What is in this stupid place that keeps you here, putting all our lives at risk, for what?"

"My people, my country, my job. What am I going to do if I go anywhere else? These people, they need me." He gets up angrily from the table.

There is a Socratic touch to my father's approach. He always wins my admiration for his persistence. I imagine him in a robe, after his trial, standing in the middle of a crowd, declaring that he is who he is because of Greece. Outside Greece, he is nobody—he'd rather die than run away. He sounds noble, but Habibullah is condemned. He can leave the table, but not the discussion.

"You want us all to starve to death." My mother follows him to the hallway.

A moment of rage. "Lady!" my father shouts. "Leave me alone—for God's sake, let us be." Then the voice of logic prevails. "We are not going to starve." Habibullah is calmer, sitting in the living room, sipping his tea. "Have a little faith. We are lucky. We have enough food and money."

In reality, we are among the few fortunate people in Kabul. We are not in danger of starving to death. In barrels stored under our stairs we have more than fifty tons of flour, nearly sixty kilograms of rice and gallons of cooking oil. Even

Four months before leaving Afghanistan. Hassib and Nelofer, in the Panje-shah mountains, 1989.

on cold winter days, my father manages to purchase enough wood for the antique steel chimney that heats the living and dining rooms, and enough gas to keep the stoves in our bedrooms running. Each autumn, my father buys a whole sheep that is prepared, smoked and stored for the winter. There are occasions when we don't have milk or sugar, but that's because there is nothing in the market to buy. Otherwise, my father will pay any price for anything we need. The fruit and vegetables in the market are not the best quality, but we can afford to buy them. My father shares this food with others and my mother is the first to make sure our maid's family receive their portion.

We hear and know all of this, but we also know that, in the absence of security, it doesn't mean much. It may even expose us to more danger at a time when poverty is driving

people to crime. People who dress well—or appear wealthy—
are robbed and killed in broad daylight. Wealth doesn't protect anyone from lawlessness and war. But my mother has a
more damning argument.

"What about your son?" she asks.

"What about him?" My father knows what is coming.

"Look how tall he's grown," Jamila says. "One of these
days, the soldiers will take him away, and he will be forced to
join the army. What are you going to do then?" She has scored
a point.

"I have enough contacts to guarantee him a safe military
service—perhaps as a security guard in the city." This is what
he always says, but we all know it is becoming increasingly
difficult to be safe in the city—as a civilian, let alone as a
security guard.

Since 1984 the Afghan government has been aggressively
conscripting all men between the ages of eighteen and forty
into the army. But in the past two years, the situation has
grown worse. Under the pretence of the "national emergency,"
boys are taken by force from the streets—sometimes from outside their schools—to join the army. Squads of soldiers check
the IDs of young boys, but they no longer care about their real
ages. If a boy of fourteen appears tall or strong enough, they
will take him to their military base. Bringing in a new conscript
can earn a soldier a half day off, or a night at home with his
family. Young men are on the run and there are few places to
hide. Houses are searched, day after day. Unless one is the son
of the president or a top intelligence man or a Communist
Party member, it is impossible to avoid military service. The
sons of the ruling party, of course, go to one of the countries
in the Communist bloc to "study." For the rest, the only escape
is to run away from Afghanistan.

Yaghen was a tough boy on our street. Well built, tall and attractive, temperamental and a bit arrogant, he was, perhaps, fifteen—a couple of years older than my brother. They played football and flew kites together until Yaghen was taken by soldiers. That winter, the boys in the street played kite games without him. I saw Yaghen come home one day to visit his mother. His military uniform suited him, from his new crew-cut to his neatly tied polished boots. Above his upper lip were the beginnings of a moustache, which made him look more handsome. But he looked smaller.

Three weeks later, Yaghen's body was brought home in a coffin. Both my parents attended the funeral. It was a Friday. I watched from behind our wall as his uncle and cousins carried the coffin from their shared home for burial. His mother, crying and shouting, would not let go of the wooden box. Some family members were trying to cover her head with her white scarf, which was constantly falling over her shoulders as she writhed in agony. Finally a couple of women pulled her inside the house as the men took away the remains of her son. She went on screaming, calling to him. "Yaghen! Yaghen! How I raised you, my boy," she shouted in a broken voice. "This wasn't the time of dying, leaving your mother fearful like this—if only I were going to the grave instead of you." The coffin was taken away; the wooden door of their home was closed. For the next few hours, there came an occasional sound of grief. By nightfall, I could hear her again, crying. Then it was quiet. Yaghen was gone.

The following week, another boy's body was brought home to our street—another conscript. His family lived farther down the road. I didn't know them, couldn't recall ever seeing him. But my parents once again paid their respects to the family. They returned with their usual sighs, broken spirits and the same old story. The boy had been taken from the street and sent at once to the front line, and—before his family could even get used to his absence from home—his coffin was brought to them. This was the third death in a month on our street. All were young boys. The son of an elderly woman who lives across from our home was injured. He is home now, recovering from a shrapnel wound. Everyone breathed with relief that he was alive. He gives a little hope to all of us.

Our dinner-table argument over leaving the country is gradually shifting. My father, in his nightly monologue, would insist the five of us must remain in Afghanistan. I used to take my father's side, asking my mother who would free Afghanistan from occupation—who would rebuild it—if we all left. But now Jamila argues about the need to survive, about our future and, more important, our education. The mention of the word "education" disarms Habibullah. "As long as one nail is left in my wall, I will pay for the education of my children," he says. He wouldn't object if my brother and I alone went to India to study—a plan my mother has put forward—but my father himself refuses to abandon his country. My mother, however, wants all of us to leave. I'm starting to take her side. Is there any other way out?

About four months earlier, I had tried to find a solution. In the beginning of winter, as soon as the school year ended, I started to stand in a line, not for food or fuel but for passports. If we managed to get passports and make the arrangement to go to India, my father just might be convinced to join us. India was still one of those destinations to which one could travel freely; it was, at least nominally, "non-aligned."

Once there, it was possible to get refugee status and eventually go to a Western country. We needed proper documentation, passports, visas, return tickets—and clearance from the KhAD (Khadamat-i Ittila'at-i Daulati, the State Information Service). It wasn't easy, but it was worth a try. After all, my mother's younger sister had recently managed to take her family to India. So I went to join the line. It was my birthday wish the December that I turned sixteen that I would get us all passports so we could leave the country legally.

With false IDs and applications for the whole family, I arrived at the passport office early one winter morning. It hadn't snowed yet, but a cold wind was blowing angrily, moving everything it found in its way. A couple of weeks of preparation had gone into this first visit. I had learned about the procedures and regulations by talking to a family friend who had a high-ranking position in the municipal government. My father respected him because he was a dedicated nationalist but never a member of the Communist Party. Through him, I learned that new laws forbade medical doctors, professors, teachers, nurses, engineers, students and all men of conscription age from obtaining a passport. The Afghan government was doing everything it could to stop professional people from leaving the country. Our false IDs looked as good as the real ones. The only difference was that my mother was marked down as a housewife and my father was listed as a shopkeeper. As for me—newly graduated from high school—I was now a girl without any education. Both my brother and my sister shared this status with me.

Carrying these documents as if they were precious stones, I walked with care. With a heavy heart, I arrived at the big, grey-walled, iron-gated compound. A security guard was standing at the gate, searching all who entered. A series of one-storey buildings had been constructed along the interior walls. I managed to find the door with "Passport Office" painted above it in black. I stepped inside. There was a tiny corridor, dark as a dungeon. The walls hadn't seen paint in decades. At one end was a room divided by a wooden counter and a thick glass wall, officials on one side, passport applicants on the other. The officials moved between papers and typewriters and heaps of files; they looked like comic, exotic creatures behind the glass. I was told to wait in line in the next room.

When I made it to the counter, I presented the documents to a man with a thick moustache. The officer took the papers, opened a big log book and painstakingly entered each name with the date and time of registry. Then he listed the applications and gave me a piece of paper with a reference number. "Come back next week," he said. Before I could ask a single question, the next person in the line was pushing in front of the counter. I felt triumphant.

I returned early in the morning the next week. All the way to the passport office, voices in my head competed against each other: they will tell me the documents are fake; they will call me in for questioning about the false IDs; they will tell me to leave and never come back.

It must have been noon by the time I made it to the counter. The officer took the number from my slip of paper and disappeared. Those few minutes felt longer than a day of waiting. He returned with our applications, handed them to me and told me to go and pay in the next room. I couldn't believe it. I took the papers and joined another line. So far, all was going well. While I waited, I was thinking of how to look innocent. I should try to act more like someone without any education—I shouldn't sound sophisticated.

Finally, I arrived at the payment counter, where the officer took the applications and examined them carefully. Worried that he might know something I didn't, I put on a silly smile. He asked me to pay. Then he gave me a form to sign. I pretended I didn't know how to hold a pen or sign. He gave me a look. "You don't expect me to believe that you—with your looks and your clothes—have no education," he said. "Come on!" I looked down, still pretending I didn't know what he was talking about. Exasperated, he pulled out a small ink pad, forcibly took my hand, pressed my thumb against the soft wet sponge and then pressed it hard onto the form. The purple lines—my fingerprint—looked like a puzzle. "Kid! Don't lie—no one will believe you," he said, handing me the papers. "Take them to the next room." I quickly moved away, my face burning—this was not just embarrassing, it was dangerous. By the time I made it into the next room, all the counters had closed. I couldn't submit the documents.

I walked home against a bitter wind. There were still some leaves scattered on the sidewalks; it hadn't yet started to snow. Cars and people went by, seemingly in silence. All I could hear were my own thoughts and my own footsteps on the pavement over the broken leaves. My mind was locked on the documents, the passports—our tickets to freedom.

The following day I submitted the documents without any problems at the proper counter and was told to check back in a week's time. One week became two. Before the end of the third week, I went to see the family friend who had furnished me with the earlier advice. His workplace was in the same compound, opposite the passport office. The corridor in his building was carpeted, and there were leather-covered seats. Warmth and the smell of burnt wood came from the chimney that stood in a corner. Here, too, there was a lineup. But our family friend, realizing I was there, came out and invited me to his office. A clerk and another man were there too. He got rid of the man, but the clerk was looking through some files in a cabinet. I managed to tell him—between phone calls and the clerk's questions—about the delay in our applications. He didn't deal directly with the passport office, he told me. I heard the nervousness in his voice and began to understand that the clerk was a spy. It took me a little while to realize that it would seem very suspicious for our friend to do anything. Helping someone escape the country was not part of his job description as the mayor's deputy. He could go to prison for it. But the next morning, outside his office, he introduced me to a long-haired man in a striped shirt, a man who was supposed to have good contacts in the passport office. The man in the striped shirt walked me there, made me wait in that dungeon-like corridor, went in with our file number and came back after thirty minutes. "It's being processed," he said. "Come back next week."

And so I did. It was snowing. A crowd had gathered in the yard. A man with a school notebook was standing on a stone in the middle, reading names aloud. Inside, an officer told me that our applications had gone to the KhAD for security clearance. It could take weeks or months to get an answer, he didn't know. All successfully returned files were listed in the book the man was reading from outside. "You have to wait there to see if your name is on the list," he said, pointing at the crowd. "We update the book every two days."

For the next five weeks, I went back every Saturday, Monday and Wednesday to stand in the yard, with hundreds of others, waiting for an officer to arrive and read from that notebook. There were different officers on different days. They stood on one of the steps or on a stone—slightly higher than the crowd—to read the file numbers and names. Being on the list meant you had obtained the KhAD's approval and would get a passport. It was so cold we could see the officer's breath, a white vapour that unfolded in the air. As he read, the officer would place one hand in his pocket to warm it up and hold the notebook with the other. Every so often, he switched hands. If he stopped for a moment, the crowd would grow uneasy and urge him to continue. It was a ritual.

We all stood to attention as he read, despite the cold. We kept moving closer and closer to the officer as he turned each page— a thread by which he pulled us towards him. Our cold-battered faces would light up as he began at the top of the page, but our hopes would be extinguished when he reached the bottom. Those who heard their names had to push their way out of the crowd. We returned faithfully, day after day. I listened with such concentration that all I could hear was the officer's voice, the numbers and the names. The cold gradually became hard to bear. My red winter boots, once fashionable, let in the icy water. There were days when I'd lose all feeling in my toes. It was only when I put my numbed feet in front of the gas stove at home that I would begin to feel the pain. I had a fur coat, which kept me warm. But a few people, including a couple of guards, started to pass close enough to stroke the fur with their elbows or arms. A few times, they poked the soft hair of the coat. After I heard someone call me a "dirty bourgeois," I stopped wearing it.

The cold eased and the snow began to melt. The tree in the yard near the passport office started to bud. The spring wind blew into our open jackets and coats. But those of us who still waited to hear our numbers and names didn't move an inch as the ritual went on. Each day, the officer started from the top of the list, reading yet again all the names that were not crossed out—meaning no one had claimed the forms. God knows, some names were now months old, and so engraved in our memories that we murmured restlessly, "next, next." Some of these people must have been dead. Or else they had fled Afghanistan without a passport. But no one said a word; no one knew whether the next person was a spy. We rolled our eyes, but listened attentively.

One day that spring, the family friend told me there was no point in standing there any more. Our applications were being held at the KhAD, he said. It would be better to find some contacts and bribe someone at the KhAD to get them out. He was going to look into it.

So my mother and I have given up hope. We have done everything. I waited in the line, we bribed anyone who could get our papers through the KhAD, we even started another set of applications. And now the government has added to its restrictions. Passports with visas, even if originally approved for security clearance, must go back to the KhAD for further verification.

My mother is looking frail. The rockets send her blood pressure through the roof—180/100 or 190/110, as recorded by my father on several occasions. As soon as the rockets start, she reaches for something to hold on to for support. The other day, she grabbed my arm and, for the first time, I could actually feel the vibration from her body as her heart pounded faster and faster.

My father still says he wants to stay as long as the last person remains in this land, albeit with less passion. I know his heart is bleeding too, but he's stubborn, as unbending as an oak tree. He says his roots are here, right in this city. He says the life of this country is in his blood; the history of his generation lives inside him, its hold too strong to let go. "I cannot leave," he says over and over again. "I cannot leave."

2

SLEEPING WITH WOLVES

My life
Was just a knapsack
That I carried from house to house.
And at the end
It was lost in the narrow old alleyways of the city.
Partaw Naderi, 1990

MY FATHER, HABIBULLAH, was born in Chindawal in September 1938. Part of the old city of Kabul, Chindawal was home to poor and lower-middle-class families. My grandmother, Sobera, had had two miscarriages, so Habibullah's birth was a relief. The family was surviving on a small income from a *kar khona-e shawlbafi* (weaving work-shop). But life was so difficult that after the birth of a second son, Asadullah, Sobera scarcely had the money to feed and clothe her new baby.

"We were poor and disenchanted," recalls Habibullah. On good days the family could afford to have tea with bread for breakfast and a watered-down potato soup for lunch or dinner. "We celebrated the day on which my mother could cook a meal of meat or rice as a special occasion."

My father recognizes himself and this early period of his life in the mirror of Chindawal's past. The grandson of a merchant involved in the import/export of silk and tea from China and Bokhara in Central Asia, he had heard about his grandfather, Ghulam Hossein, and his financial success, but never saw his money. By early 1900, the Silk Road between China and the Mediterranean had declined as merchants traded more and more by sea. Ghulam Hossein could not make the transition. Upon his death, his depleted estate was taken by the eldest of his three sons, my father's uncle.

Habibullah's father, Agha Jan, an unsuccessful businessman, divided his time between Afghanistan and Iran, travelling for both business and pleasure. Few tales of his life ever got passed down, other than the story of his famous sixty-day ride by horse from Kabul to Mashad. The older he grew, the more debts he incurred. His first wife died while giving birth, leaving him with two teenage children—a son and a daughter. He married my grandmother when he was approaching sixty and she was barely thirteen. The only thing he did right was to buy out his two brothers' shares in the family home to secure it for himself.

The Second World War intensified Afghanistan's poverty. The Afghan government had declared its neutrality

*Sobera, Habibullah's
mother, shortly
before she died in
1979.
Agha Jan
(Habibullah's
father), late 1950s.*

the year after my father was born, in September 1939, following the Nazi-Soviet non-aggression pact. But that didn't
stop the Germans from exerting pressure on Afghanistan to
provoke unrest in the North-West Frontier Province, along
the Afghan/Indian border, by declaring a jihad (holy war)
against the British. Although the Afghan government welcomed economic assistance from Germany, and even
allowed the Germans to train the Afghan army, it would
campaign against neither the Soviets nor the British. The
Third Reich offered Afghanistan aircraft, tanks and artillery
in return for its support in an anti-British resistance movement in India. Prime Minister Hashim Khan, King Zahir
Shah's uncle, who effectively ran the country on the king's
behalf, turned the Germans down. Neither the king nor the
prime minister wanted to risk a Soviet or British invasion of
their country

Habibullah didn't know that a war was engulfing the world
until, as a seven-year-old, he heard from an uncle who came
by for tea that the United States had dropped an atomic bomb
on Japan. For Habibullah, the family workshop, the small
yard with its well and its black mulberry tree, were his life.

"At the time, I'd accepted poverty, deprivation and inequality as normal," he told me years later.

In the post-war years, he learned about Europe in school. Indian independence had been achieved in 1948, and a new country called Pakistan was created. Habibullah remembers hearing about the British "defeat" in India while attending the Lycée Habibia, an all-boys school thirty minutes' walk from home. His shoes were so old and had been repaired so many times that nails stuck out of them, causing his feet to bleed. But ten-year-old Habibullah found a solution. His uncle Moama Qandi, who was employed by the ministry of transportation as a driver, went to work from 6:00 A.M. to 5:00 P.M. He wore a pair of shoes during the day and slippers at home. So every day at 6:30 in the morning, after Moama Qandi had gone to work and while the rest of the household was still asleep, Habibullah would sneak into his uncle's house, quietly put on his uncle's slippers and walk to school. In the early afternoon, he would return the slippers as discreetly as he'd picked them up, putting his own shoes on before going home. It was several months before the family could spare ten afghanis to buy him a pair of cheap shoes known as *charm-e chapa* ("upside-down leather") to relieve him of his agony and subterfuge.

By the time my father was twelve, his father was in his early seventies, and growing weak. At the workshop, where there were three weaving frames—*karga*s in Dari—Habibullah had to take his father's place. He had already spent two years learning to fill thread and to weave silk handkerchiefs and turbans. Now he had his own *karga,* three times his height, the frame standing against the wall with coloured threads running across the board to balls of silk. A square bar called a *nourd* was as high as his chest. After running the threads horizontally, he had to push the heavy *nourd* with both hands. For hours he would thread, pull and push on the machine to separate the bundles of silk. His young hands became so tough that a knife could not cut through his skin.

Every day, returning from school, Habibullah would rush into the workshop, leaving just before midnight to finish his homework and sleep before setting off again at six in the morning for school. But he was becoming a professional. In two weeks, he could weave twenty metres of silk, which sold in the market for fifty afghanis a metre. Deducting his expenses of buying the silk thread and paying for it to be dyed, he would be left with three or four hundred afghanis. His stepbrother, Ghafour, who lived on the second floor of the house with his wife and children, was working as a clerk in the ministry of education. His income also helped the family survive. Asadullah, the younger brother, had quit school after grade two. Refusing to learn the weaving trade, he joined a tailor's shop. But at the end of the day, it was twelve-year-old Habibullah's income that supported the family and paid for the medical needs of his aging father.

The winter of 1950 was brutal. It snowed heavily. The black mulberry tree, dressed in white, hung over Habibullah's young mother as she broke the ice around the well. She sat in the snow to wash clothes that, seconds after being hung out to dry, froze into thin cardboard sheets. Sipping lukewarm tea in front of the weaving board and frame, Habibullah would squeeze his toes together to fight off the cold, and pull and push in rhythm, watching his silk fabrics grow, centimetre by centimetre. During school holidays, he could work all day. But the family was still short of money, with debts to pay off from his father's unsuccessful business ventures. Habibullah didn't have the money for school clothes and shoes. This time, Sobera took out the very last of her precious things—her

Indian bridal shawl—to sell. With the two hundred afghanis she received, she bought him a pair of trousers, a shirt, a jacket and new shoes.

It was his father's cousin Abdul Ali who encouraged Habibullah to study. A university student, Abdul Ali also wove silk fabric, using the second frame in the workshop, and he talked to young Habibullah about life, education and politics as he wove. Abdul Ali was also part of a young anti-monarchist movement called the Student Union.[1]

A number of intellectuals demanding political change were raised on what were called "the steps of Chindawal's pulpits." The area was a mainly Shia Muslim ghetto and had always been at odds with the governing Sunnis. The rulers of Afghanistan have always been Pushtuns, the majority of whom are Sunni. With a couple of brief exceptions, they have dominated the political landscape of Afghanistan's modern history. Tajiks, the second-largest ethnic group after Pushtuns, are also Sunni, but they too were disenchanted with the ruling dynasty. However, grievances remained suppressed.

Chindawal was home to the Qizilbash, one of Afghanistan's prominent Shia ethnic groups, who trace their ancestry to the Iranian armies who came to Afghanistan in the eighteenth century. Several Tajik families also lived there, and shared a common language—Dari—with the Qizilbash.[2] Although both Dari and Pushtu were official languages, Dari was the language of the people and the administration in Kabul. The Qizilbash were proud of their literary heritage in a country where few could read. For decades, the Qizilbash provided bookkeepers, secretaries, administrators and teachers to the kingdom, which welcomed their services but not their religious practices.

Shias, who made up about a quarter of the population, faced discrimination. Once a year, during the Arabic month of

Muharram, Shias commemorate the massacre of the Prophet Mohammad's grandson Hussein, his family and his companions in the Iraqi town of Kerbala in 680 A.D. Many Afghan Sunnis saw this anniversary—involving acts of self-flagellation, the re-enactment of the burning of Hussein's camp, the killing of his eleven-month-old son and the capture of seventy-two members of his family—as bizarre. The Kerbala massacre was the bloody result of a split between the two Muslim groups, following the death of Prophet Mohammad. Since Shiism was, at heart, a protest movement, the government regarded it as a political threat, and had banned Shia religious practices. But Chindawalis continued to observe their rituals, away from the gaze of intolerant rulers. During Muharram, for thirty consecutive days, at sunset, four large stones were placed behind the four gates of Chindawal, with two people guarding each entrance. Some families had their place of worship and rituals in the basement, or rooms that were built halfway into the ground. Others had a hidden door that led to the next house, an escape route in times of trouble, to secure the safety of the Shia preacher and his congregation if the authorities arrived to arrest them. My father's home had a room in the corner of the yard for worship and religious gatherings, called a *takyee khona* in Dari, meaning a "house of prayer." Inside was the *alam,* a symbolic religious flag banner: a thick wooden stick wrapped and decorated with coloured fabrics, with a model of a human hand in aluminum on the top.

My father grew up with stories of Chindawal's oppression. Early preachers of the Shia faith encouraged people to practise *taqiya* (concealment), which meant they could deny their religion if they feared persecution. At the start of the twentieth century, government agents and spies roamed Chindawal. One day during the month of Muharram, so the story goes, the mayor of Kabul arrived in the area after hearing that, despite a government ban, Shias were still practising their religion. In a meeting with the leaders of the community, he demanded an explanation. They denied the existence of any *takyee khona*—their code of concealment allowed them to do so. The mayor, acting on intelligence he had received, walked into a tunnel and through a set of interconnected doors, where he found a *takyee khona* belonging to Khan Shreen Khan, a respected elder. The mayor immediately ordered its destruction. Shreen Khan arrived at the scene as the mayor was leaving. "We ruined your temple," the mayor said triumphantly. "To purify the place, we've ordered a Sunni mosque to be built in its place, and a Sunni imam will make sure you pray properly."

Stories like these were told and retold in my father's childhood as a reminder of Chindawal's minority status and continued suffering. But by the time Habibullah was growing up, the attitude of Chindawalis towards oppression was changing. The culture of concealment and secrecy was disappearing as Shia imams spoke about the need for active involvement in the political life of the country. The seventh-century Imam Hussein, once regarded as a mere victim of oppression, was now promoted as a symbol of resistance to injustice. By the late 1940s and early 1950s, Chindawal had become the seat of opposition to the monarchy. It was also emerging as a place of progressive ideas, a centre of religious reform and of university students who were calling for the rule of law, free elections and equality. Similar sentiments were being echoed in other corners of Kabul.

Although it took a while for politics to affect Habibullah's life, there were new movements he could not ignore. The Student Union was becoming a popular voice of freedom.

Underground groups were surfacing with demands for reform. By 1949, about 50 of the 120 seats in the Afghan seventh parliament were occupied by political reformers, liberals and leftists. There was a fragile new culture of religious tolerance. In the remote corner of the workshop, Habibullah heard the news from an excited Abdul Ali, who believed that Chindawal could soon have its own elected representative in Parliament.

Every Wednesday, the Student Union took centre stage at the Kabul Theatre with dramas and musicals about corruption in the country's administration. At Abdul Ali's suggestion, young Habibullah attended the Union's events. At fourteen, he became an enthusiastic spectator. The Union got away with its theatrical critiques until a play overtly criticizing Prime Minister Hashim Khan was staged, and the government shut down both the theatre and the Student Union. But the Union had aroused its audiences, provoked them into a freedom they would not abandon. A more reflective, questioning Habibullah would return to his home in Chindawal, which was itself now a centre of reform in Kabul. In 1953, King Zahir appointed a cousin, Daoud Khan, prime minister. Accusing his predecessor of developing too close a relationship with the West, Daoud launched into a new campaign of political oppression. By then, a group of intellectuals and reformers from Chindawal were already in prison. Daoud crushed all opposition, releasing only those prisoners who promised to abandon politics.

In the winter of 1955, just as he was turning eighteen, Habibullah completed his high-school education. He wanted to be a pilot and had even passed the first entry exam for a pilot training course in the southwestern city of Kandahar.

But his friend Abdul Ali talked to him of reality: he might succeed in becoming a pilot, but as a member of a minority group
he would never be trusted enough to be promoted. His second choice was medicine. He was accepted at the medical
college at Kabul University in 1956. Education, including university studies, was provided free of charge by the Afghan
government.

Meanwhile, the family home in Chindawal was falling
apart. For years now, there had been no money to pay for its
repair, and it had sunk gradually into decay. Habibullah had
also watched his young mother age through hardship and deprivation, more of a caretaker than a wife to her fading husband.

Habibullah considered his father a kind man but a failure.
Too old to walk without a cane, he was white-haired and
white-bearded. His deteriorating health, his weakening spirit
and eventually his inability to hear or speak were sad. Once a
family storyteller who could recite hundreds of verses of
poetry, he had become a shadow, waiting in an upstairs room
for his own disappearance. One sunrise, when Habibullah
went to check on him, he discovered a peaceful, cold and very
dead Agha Jan. The family had no written record of his age.
But since he had married my grandmother when he was in his
late fifties, he must have been eighty when he died.

Soon after Agha Jan's death, the family sold their house for
forty thousand afghanis, which paid the outstanding debts.
The remaining few thousand was divided among the three
sons, the daughter and the widow. Moama Qandi, the uncle
whose slippers Habibullah had secretly worn to school, had
already moved to a modern concrete house in the newly
developed area of West Kabul, and asked Habibullah and his
mother to move in above his garage. On a winter's day of fresh
snow, Habibullah walked for the last time through the empty

rooms and the family workshop, paying his last respects to the *alam* in the *takyee khona*. He touched the rough trunk of the mulberry tree, tucked his few medical books under his left arm and kissed the thick wooden door of the home before closing it behind him. A few hours earlier, he had helped take his mother and their few belongings—some blankets and cushions, clothing and rusty cooking pots—to his uncle's house.

His mother was in tears when she left Chindawal, but Habibullah had pride in his heart. Seeing the medical books under his arm, a neighbour gave him some advice. "Words alone won't feed you, young man—get to work, that's what I tell my sons." But Chindawalis are men of words rather than swords, and they like to wear this as a mark of distinction, something for which they are both admired and feared. That's what they taught from the pulpit of the *takyee khonas*. Habibullah pushed his books under the cover of his jacket to protect them from the wind and the snow that had started to fall. A shopkeeper, who had loaned the family brown sugar and tea when they had no money to pay, wished him luck.

From a world of misery and grinding work and poverty, from the decaying place of his birth, Habibullah took away with him a new outlook on life. He would often talk, in later life, about social democracy. As far as he was concerned, its roots had been sown in Chindawal. No wonder that later, in the most terrifying period of his life, my father would not want to leave his country; no wonder he resisted the government's pressure to join the Communist Party. I understood why, when I prepared our false IDs to try to obtain passports, he insisted I write the word "Qizilbash" next to the question in the document about ethnicity. It didn't make any difference to me which Afghan ethnic origin we adopted, but for my father, being a Qizilbash constituted a unique identity that reconfirmed his connection to his birthplace, Chindawal. He was happier to assume the position of shopkeeper than to give up his origins. For the rest of his life in Kabul, he returned each year at Muharram to his former family home, to their *takyee khona,* to make donations, to ask about neighbours and friends. He always went on his own, as if it were a date with the past.

One person whom my father always visited on special holidays was his uncle Moama Qandi. In the years that followed their departure from Chindawal, Habibullah and his mother continued living above his uncle's garage. My father calls a story he tells of that time "Sleeping with Wolves":

In the spring of 1958, when Habibullah was twenty, Moama Qandi was going on a New Year's Day outing to Mazar-e-Sherif, in northern Afghanistan. March 21, the first day of spring, is celebrated in the Afghan solar calendar as the first day of the New Year. Originally a Zoroastrian tradition, the event has been given an Islamic colouring by attaching it to Ali, the fourth caliph and also the first of the Shia imams. On New Year's Day, Ali's banner is raised across the country, celebrated by both Sunnis and Shias. However, the largest and most memorable celebration takes place in Mazar. It is called *melie gul-e sorekh*—"the picnic of the red flower."

That year, Habibullah decided to join Moama Qandi on the trip. A few friends came along, and they left Kabul early in the morning. The Salang Pass over the mountains had not yet been built. The old road out of Kabul ran through the Sheber Pass, a treacherous journey the drivers called the "engine killer" because the road over the mountain was high and rough, running along a sheer precipice. But the view, according to

Habibullah, was worth the risk. Adventurers at heart, both
Moama Qandi and Habibullah liked travelling. The Kabul sky
seemed clear when they started their journey in a minibus.
Yet, by the time they made it to the top of the pass, a heavy
snowfall had blocked parts of the road. A strong wind lifted a
mass of snow into the air and hurtled it around like a tornado.
An avalanche had stopped their vehicle. So Moama and
Habibullah got out of the bus with a couple of rusted shovels,
taking turns to try to clear the road. In vain. Moama, who had
travelled the road many times, suggested they would be better off spending the night inside the bus and setting off again
the next morning. Someone had a few *roats*—a kind of sweet
bread baked especially for the New Year. They shared the
roats and melted snow on the engine of the bus to make tea.
Then they each curled up on a seat, pulling a jacket, coat or
sweater over them to keep warm, and slept.

"Just as I'm dozing off," recalls Habibullah, "I hear a
wailing sound in the distance." He ignored the noise,
assuming it was the wind or a lost animal. "But the sound is
growing and getting closer, to the point that I can no longer
fall asleep." As he lifted his head from under his jacket, he
noticed that a couple of other friends were also aware of the
sound. They looked out. In the dark, they saw two wolves
dancing in the snow, perhaps from the excitement of
smelling humans. They are playing, Habibullah concluded.
No need to worry.

But after a few minutes, they heard a scratching sound. It
was very close. My father, curious and impatient, looked out
the window. He couldn't see the wolves any more. They must
have gone. Another scratch, and he looked down. The
sparkling eyes of a hungry animal shone in the dark as a wolf
brushed his furry head and body against the side of the

minibus. Startled by the sight of a wolf just below the window where he'd been trying to fall asleep, Habibullah screamed, "Moama Qandi, Moama!"

Moama Qandi, who had been asleep, sprang from the front seat. He saw several sets of terrified eyes: by now everyone was up and staring at him for help. "Wolves!" they cried. Moama Qandi turned the engine on, and the wolves ran away. Everyone sat still for a few minutes, then a cool and calm Moama Qandi turned the engine off, instructing them to try to get some sleep. "They are gone," he said.

A short time went by. Habibullah was still thinking of the hunting eyes he had seen so close to him when he heard the wolves baying again. Moama Qandi got up, turned the engine on again, switched on the headlights, spat a couple of swear words at the mother wolf and returned to his seat, leaving the lights on. Habibullah could now see the wolves. Their silvery bodies and dangling tails left a trail over the snow as they moved away from the bus. The engine was turned off again once they disappeared into the dark. But they returned. Moama Qandi was worried they would run out of fuel if they kept the engine running all night. Habibullah heard the wolves sniffing, their noses moving over the cold iron of the bus, their claws scratching as far up as their paws could reach. They all pretended they could tolerate the wolves' closeness, but no one was sleeping now. The tribe of wolves was gathering.

"They are working out how to open the door," one of the passengers said. "Maybe they've left their tools in another car."

"Do you think we can negotiate a truce if we offer to take them to the cars stuck behind us?" asked another.

"They'll take your offer and you at the same time," someone else answered.

The humour was wearing thin.

Moama Qandi turned the bus lights on and off a few more times. "Bastards!" he shouted. "They're no longer even afraid of the lights."

The wolves simply waited and returned, tossing and turning in the snow, cheerful and excited, getting closer and closer to the bus again. Each time, the distance they ran away got shorter. What did the wolves think about the weary and terrified eyes staring at them from behind the bus windows? Just before first light, the last of the wolves left. Exhausted, the travellers fell asleep for a couple of hours before the sun was fully up. Each must have had a *gurg* (wolf) dream.

Nearly two decades later, my father kept a female baby wolf as a pet in our home. Some farmer he'd helped had given it to him as a gift. The wolf, which had no name but Gurg, was a restless creature. Habibullah was captivated by the beauty of the animal because of the night he had spent on top of the Sheber Pass. Our *gurg* showed great friendship when we fed her and stroked her thick fur. But she grew up fast, faster than we would have liked. In a few months' time, a larger, stronger cage next to the garage replaced her small wired fence. Soon, we couldn't feed her with our hands or stroke her any more. It was too dangerous, my father said. He fed her with a spade, putting the meat on the blade and lowering it inside the cage. In a single move, the *gurg* would grab the meat. Ever more beautiful, she stared at us longingly, tempting us to pat her back. But we kept a distance at my father's suggestion; once he had nearly lost a piece of his own flesh while feeding her. I loved looking at the mysterious eyes of the *gurg*, her flat, long nose and furry ears with their sharp sense of hearing. "Gurg, Gurg!" She would look immediately in the direction from which she had been called.

Then the sound of her moaning, once soft and friendly, began to change to longer, louder cries, especially at night. Was she crying for help? Was she sending a message home, to tell her family her whereabouts? Was she talking to us? One day, Habibullah sent her away to the countryside, or so he told us. She would be happy with the rest of her clan. We

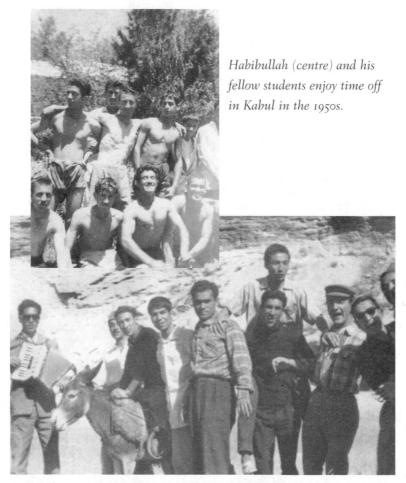

Habibullah (centre) and his fellow students enjoy time off in Kabul in the 1950s.

Before the communist takeover. Habibullah (third from left) and friends visiting Bamiyan.

never saw or heard her again. The gardener planted mint where her cage used to be. I always thought the little green leaves had the shape of her eyes, if not the colour. I missed her dearly. "Were you really afraid of the wolves that cold night?" I asked my father, each time hoping he'd say no.

An entire album of pictures in black and white is a testimony to the moments that Habibullah calls the good-time days. There are photos of him with a crowd of laughing faces, all friends from the university, in a swimming pool—jumping into it or climbing out or just sitting on the edges. There is one photo in which everyone is craning his neck to be included in the shot. Habibullah looks malnourished in these pictures. I can count his ribs—that's how skinny he is. But he's having a great time. Or do these pictures lie, like so many pictures of peaceful, calm and beautiful Afghanistan?

There is a shot of my father posing for the camera in his sports club jacket, a reminder of his days playing tennis on the university team; another of him in a trilby, with a shadowy background out of a Humphrey Bogart movie. Another shows

Habibullah at a farewell gathering of Kabul University classmates.

him on a dance floor with several men and women, knees bent, bodies slightly twisted and necks tilted. It is probably a classmate's engagement or wedding celebration. In another group shot—the girls in his class sitting, the men standing— everyone is smiling except for Habibullah, who seems to have been caught off guard as he's saying something. We tease my father. How is it, we ask, that in each shot that includes female classmates he's almost always close to an attractive woman? "I happened to be very popular," he replies with mischievous laughter.

There are a few snapshot reminders of more serious times. One photograph shows my father among his student friends. None of them are smiling; they might even be frightened. My father's hair is greased back. He is in his late twenties, skinny with a long nose. The picture is witness to an event that Habibullah knows is historic, called "Bloody October."

It would have been an ordinary day in late October 1965 were it not for the two thousand people who had gathered in front of Kabul University's administration building. Holding banners and placards, they were protesting a government ban on political parties, demanding free elections and the recognition of the Student Union. Habibullah was one of the speakers. Although he had already graduated from the university with a degree in medicine, he was still involved with the Student Union—which was illegal but remained active. For years now, the Union had been his second home, where friendships were put to the test and loyalties formed or betrayed. More to the point, the Union provided a framework within which young Afghan reformers expressed their demands. The government of Muhammad Yousuf, who had replaced Daoud Khan as prime minister, had just held general elections. Yousuf, who like my father was a medical doctor, was the first Tajik to be prime minister, a post usually held by a member of the royal family or one of the other Pushtun tribes. He passed the Afghan constitution of 1964, which gave all Afghan citizens the right to vote. But opposition parties were still not legal. Angry students were calling for the recognition of all political groups, for new elections and for an end to the monarchy.

On the fourth day of demonstrations, an even larger crowd gathered at the university—a mix of liberal, nationalist, socialist, communist and Islamist parties. The administration was becoming more and more nervous as the protesters' slogans echoed louder across the campus. A contingent of soldiers had been called in to isolate the demonstration and prevent it from spreading to other parts of the city. Around ten in the morning, the students decided to march to the prime minister's house in the Karte Chor district, a thirty-minute walk from the university. They broke through the army cordon, but found more soldiers blocking the way. So the crowd used side streets to reach a road leading to Dr. Yousuf's home.

As the crowd grew, the army was ordered to disperse the marchers. First they used tear gas, then gunshots rang out and several people fell to the ground, covered in blood. An ambulance siren brought Habibullah to consciousness. He'd been hit by a bullet that had left a hole in his left ankle. Pressing on the wound with his hands, screaming in pain, he could see his blood dripping onto the road as he tried to leave the scene. A friend helped him to the nearby Aliabad Hospital.

By noon, his wound was dressed and he felt well enough to return to the university to find out what had happened to the others. He found a few of the organizers, who told him that four people, including two students, had been killed and several others wounded. Some of the organizers were already trying to inform the families of the deaths of their loved ones. Others wanted to continue the protest. After a short meeting, they decided that the crowd should divide into small groups, walk casually along a trail that runs across the Sakhi Mountain and thus reach the king's palace. An exhausted Habibullah returned home at dusk, hoping to hide his injury from his distraught mother.

That night, as a result of the protests, Dr. Yousuf resigned his post as prime minister. The king appointed Hashim Maiwandwal as his replacement, but the riots continued for days, and Maiwandwal finally sent a message that he would come to the university to meet with the demonstrators. The crowds were now dressed in black to mourn the four dead; those who had no black clothes were asked to wear a black scarf or armband. At 10:00 A.M., Maiwandwal and his entourage of military officers and guards walked to the podium to deliver his speech. He had just started to speak when Habibullah—in the front of the crowd—took a black scarf from his classmate Soraya, limped towards the prime minister and hung the scarf around his neck. There was uproar and applause. My father told Maiwandwal that he should show a little respect for their mourning, and then walked away from the podium, leaving a stunned prime minister and his nervous guards behind. In his speech, Maiwandwal told the students that he "understood" their concerns. Of course, he asked them to end their protests, and Habibullah concluded to himself that the new leader was making more promises than he could fulfill.

As Maiwandwal made his way out of the crowd, he

passed my father. Pausing, he took Habibullah's hand, held it and then shook it. Was the gesture intended to show that the prime minister was a man of peace who felt genuine admira tion for the courage of a young man? A few days later, Habibullah was informed by the state health ministry that he was to be posted to a town outside Kabul as a trainee doctor. Maiwandwal may well have thought he'd saved the young man from ruining his career, but Habibullah saw it differently. He believed he had been made to pay the price for his action by being ditched in a backwater. He packed a bag, said good-bye to his mother and left for the small hospital in Katawaz, in southeastern Khost province. Decades later, during the 1980s, Khost became one of the mujahidin strongholds against the communist government, the place where Osama bin Laden built his military camps. At the time, Habibullah couldn't have imagined that Katawaz would one day be a bloody battle-ground. He promised his mother he would visit her as frequently as possible. Sobera convinced herself it was better to watch Habibullah leave than to lose him to a prison cell.

Katawaz was about three hours' drive from Kabul. With a few books, a white coat, his medical equipment and empty pockets, Habibullah found himself in a predominantly Pushtu-speaking Sunni town where doctors were a new phenomenon. The news of his arrival soon spread. The mayor invited him to his home for dinner, and then the tribal leader in the area invited him to be his guest. Though hardly an experienced physician, he cured a few people, which made him popular. He had, they said, a "good healing hand." Over time, he became famil-iar with the customs and traditions of the town, some more challenging than he'd expected.

"My wife is sick," said a tall, broad-shouldered young man, standing in front of Habibullah's desk. "Can you help us?"

"Bring her in," he replied.

Confused, the young man asked, "Bring her where?"

"To the examination room." Habibullah pointed towards a curtain. A small room with a bed and table and basic medical equipment, the examination room was an extension of Habibullah's office, separated by a set of beige curtains.

"Here?" the man asked. Assuming he had failed to communicate properly in Pushtu, Habibullah called in the young male secretary who usually sat at a desk just outside his office, with a registry book and a cup of green tea. "Can you ask this man to call his wife into the examination room? He says she's ill."

There was a fast conversation outside. Then the secretary turned to my father. "Sir—he says his wife is at home."

"Well, ask him to bring her, then," exclaimed Habibullah.

"He cannot bring her, sir," the secretary tried to explain.

"Does he live far away? Is she too ill to be moved?"

"He'll not bring her." Pause. "She is very ill." Longer pause. "And you cannot visit her—that's it, sir," said the secretary.

"But why not?" asked Habibullah. "If she is ill and needs help, then I must go and see her at their home."

"You're a doctor, right?" asked the young man.

"Yes, I'm a doctor."

"Then cure her," came the reply.

"But how can I help her if I don't know what is wrong with her?" asked Habibullah, frustrated.

"I can tell you what she suffers from," said the young man with pride.

"I have to examine the patient before I can suggest any prescription," replied Habibullah.

"You're a doctor," the young man kept repeating. "They told me in the village that you can heal patients. How come you cannot heal my wife?"

For the next half hour, Habibullah reasoned with the young man, using up every word of Pushtu he'd learned in school, both of them losing their patience. No man other than himself, the young husband insisted, was allowed to see his wife.

Finally, Habibullah and his secretary persuaded the young man to take Habibullah to see the patient. The three men walked up to a ramshackle village, just outside the town. As they arrived at the door of his clay hut, the young man was clearly troubled. Caught between the need to help his wife and the pressure of tribal traditions, he asked Habibullah if talking to the patient from behind a *pourdu* (a curtain) would suffice. Habibullah insisted that if she was in pain, he must examine her.

Habibullah and the secretary waited in the barren yard until finally the young man opened the door and invited Habibullah inside. The room had no air circulation, and not much light. A slim body lay in a corner, with knees pulled up to her stomach. She was covered with several blankets. She'd been unwell for months now, said the young husband. They had tried homemade remedies, but for the last two weeks there had been a steady deterioration in her health.

After more negotiations, the husband agreed to let Habibullah carry out a physical examination. He asked her a few questions, and in a weak, frail voice she answered. The examination took place with her face covered the entire time, which was the compromise that the young man had made. No one would see her face, but the doctor could examine her body. A contradiction, thought Habibullah, but he managed to diagnose the patient. She had an advanced form of malaria.

* * *

In the beginning, Habibullah was not terribly sensitive to what he termed the "cultural backwardness of the place." Slowly, however, he began to understand things better. In his mind, it could be blamed on decades of failed leadership, on self-serving kings who either brutally abused ordinary people with extreme reform projects or totally ignored them, but did little to address their needs. He discovered that these people were not so much against change as suspicious of how it would be implemented. They listened to the mullah, the religious leader in the community, who had spiritual but not political power. The mullah, however, was economically dependent on the few influential tribal leaders, who were in turn paid by the government for their services to the king. This cycle of reciprocity served the rulers and their acolytes rather than the poor and deprived. The closer Habibullah looked, the more he found fault with the government and its policies.

One afternoon, as he was walking with the secretary in the hospital yard, he noticed the young husband whose wife he'd visited. Habibullah smiled, remembering the difficulty with which they had convinced the man to let him examine his wife. "I have some trees and bushes, a cow and several chickens," the young man now offered. "I'd like to present them to you as a gift for what you did for my wife." Habibullah assured him that he didn't want any of his belongings. Two days later, the husband returned with an embroidered handkerchief and a small ball of fresh butter. "A gift from my wife," he said.

Slowly, it became acceptable in this otherwise very conservative town and its surrounding villages to let Habibullah examine female patients, even without their faces covered.

They made an exception for the doctor when it was needed, attaching a spiritual context to his work. He must be a faithful, spiritual man to have Allah's help in curing the patients. He was therefore an agent of God on earth, someone who had been given the miracle of curing the sick. Soon, he was welcomed in every household.

A year later, the Student Union in Kabul was planning a rally to mark the first anniversary of the deaths of those killed in the October 24 demonstrations. The Union and other groups were still seeking legal recognition and wished to remind the government of its promises. Habibullah wanted to help organize the protest, and took ten days off work in Katawaz, ostensibly to visit his family in Kabul. He was one of the speakers at the rally, where he passionately attacked the government's repressive policies and demanded an impartial investigation into the army's killing of the four.

By this time, there were a number of new and independent newspapers in Kabul, and the forces of opposition seemed stronger. They didn't speak with one voice, though. The Islamist parties blamed the country's problems on the lack of Muslim values; corruption was caused by people who forgot their religion. The leftists claimed the government was a tool of the aristocracy. The papers, almost all nationalist and anti-monarchist, were either Pushtun, Tajik, Marxist, Maoist or Islamist, separated by the politics of language and religious sect. According to Habibullah, the king could hold a symbolic role as head of state but the majority of Kabulis wanted a freely elected parliament and national assembly. Yet the entire opposition was a clique of the educated elite, with little support outside Kabul. The leaders knew each other—they had been classmates at school or university—but they were few in number, a fatal weakness.

Habibullah favoured the social democrats. Mainly brought up on the ideas of the *takyee khonas* in Chindawal, he wanted the religious men to help form a government—but not a theocracy. How you could bind all these contradictory forces together was a mystery, but Habibullah, like the rest of the opposition, concentrated on getting the government to recognize the parties so that they could participate in a democracy. Years later, he would remember those days with an almost naive affection: "There was a real belief that we were going to make a difference, that we could change things for the better. The eradication of poverty, equal treatment, elections—can you imagine it? This was hope for us."

On the evening after he spoke at the rally, Habibullah arrived home to find eight police officers waiting for him at his uncle's door. "Are you Dr. Pazira?" one of them asked. Habibullah could see his mother's face—full of fear—staring at him from the window of their room. "You must come with us." One of the policemen showed Habibullah a piece of paper. It was always the same in Afghanistan. A policeman claiming to represent the government, which claims to represent the people, a piece of paper and a prison cell. After twenty-four hours in custody, his stepbrother, Ghafour, secured bail. After he was released, he received a letter signed by the interior minister, Satar Sholezee, dismissing him from his work as a trainee doctor at the hospital in Katawaz.

For months, Habibullah waited and waited, under surveillance by the government, restricted in his movements and activities, without work. He spent most of his time reading, occasionally meeting the religious reformer Isma'il Balkhi and other friends, though with caution, since he did not want to further complicate his situation. For hours he would sit in his room above the garage, watching the street, the carts pulled by donkeys, carrying sheets of steel and iron, fruit and vegetables. Sometimes he would see his mother buying a bundle of leeks or radishes from a cart in front of the house. He absorbed his mother's silence as he waited for his trial.

It turned out to be a remarkable affair. In his opening speech, the government lawyer accused Habibullah of "disrupting social order" and of provoking a crowd whose actions resulted in the deaths of four innocent people. So now it was Habibullah—not the government—who was to be held responsible for the deaths. My father was charged with treason and the government requested the death sentence. Habibullah was not surprised, but he was now a desperately worried man. He turned to Isma'il Balkhi for help. Balkhi, in turn, introduced Habibullah to a legal scholar called Talib Kandahari, who helped him prepare a defence. With the courage of a Thomas More—though with none of More's knowledge and wisdom—Habibullah decided to defend himself.

On the day of the next stage of his trial, Habibullah and his mother left the house at the same time. He headed downtown, to the courthouse. Sobera walked to the Shrine of Sakhi, not far from home. Habibullah arrived in court wearing his best clothes, with his head full of arguments for his defence. His mother arrived at the shrine's door with two small candles and many prayers. Court was called to order, the charges were read again and a fearful Habibullah took the stand. "I'm not guilty." He heard those words echo across the courtroom. There was silence. Sobera lit the candles, said all her prayers but was afraid to go home. She sat huddled against the turquoise-tiled wall in a corner of the shrine, too weak to move, too sad to cry, too tired to fall asleep. She stared in silence at the clock above the donation box. Men, women and children passed her, all with their own requests to God. At midday, she finally worked up the courage to take a last turn around the holy flag banner. She kissed the copies of the Quran and made her way towards the door, repeating her prayers. All this she was to tell her son later.

In the courtroom, Habibullah had run out of breath, simply insisting that "Article 38 is obsolete in the face of the 1964 constitution."

Article 38 had been passed into law during the early years of Zahir Shah's rule as a direct response to the 1933 killing of his father, Nadir Shah, at the hands of a student. Anyone who was educated with government funding and who spoke or acted against the government would face execution. Since the government provided all education, the law ensured that no student could oppose the monarchy. The student who had shot Nadir Shah, during a school parade, was a young boy named Kholid. He was taken into custody, but Nadir Shah's family and supporters wanted to execute him in style. So Kholid died in stages, with the executioner hacking off body parts one by one in the same order in which Kholid had admitted using them to shoot the king. First was the eye that he'd aimed the shot with; it was gouged out. Then the finger that had pulled the trigger was cut off. Then the hand that had held the pistol. He was slaughtered bit by bit.

The bloody, painful execution was designed to discourage people from ever attempting other assassinations, and set a horrific precedent for official cruelty. Many had done worse in history—but could this be forgiven in the twentieth century? Even the guilty deserved human dignity, Habibullah told the court. What were future generations supposed to learn from this brutality?

The prosecution in Habibullah's trial had turned to Article 38 in the hope of silencing opposition. "But the new constitution annulled all previous constitutions and their laws, including Article 38," Habibullah argued. He had merely exercised his constitutional right to express his criticism of the government in a legal public forum, a civil protest. Uproar filled the court. The judge agreed that Article 38 could not be used in his case, and gave the government time to prepare for a second trial.

Habibullah took a long walk home, thinking about the fate of Kholid, the other people who had been involved in the plot to assassinate Nadir Shah, and how far the country had come under the new constitution. He discovered his mother at the door, still murmuring prayers. He had never told her that the government was seeking his death. It was better that she didn't know.

A new government lawyer was appointed. Sayed Ibrahim Noseri was a young man with little court experience but a lot of ambition. In his opening speech at the second trial, he argued that Habibullah Pazira was an ordinary criminal involved in acts of public unrest that had resulted in the deaths of four people. He requested a seven-year prison term. A more confident Habibullah snapped back that the young lawyer was presupposing his guilt by calling him a criminal in front of the judge. A defendant was innocent unless proven guilty in a court of law, he said. "In his enthusiasm to see me behind bars, he's already sent me there." Noseri was forced to restart his prosecution.

On the last day of the trial, the court decided that Habibullah was guilty and should be fined three hundred afghanis. My stubborn father claimed he was not guilty. The supreme court of justice had not yet been established, but a government-appointed committee of three ministers and two judges could review the case and announce their own decision. Thus, Habibullah went on to confront the ministers of justice, the interior and health. He insisted that he had acted within his constitutional rights, but realized this would not convince the committee. "If you think I'm guilty for criticizing the government, then so be it. But in the spirit of democracy that your government is claiming to promote, can it be that bad to set a single criminal free after years of unjustly executing, imprisoning and fining hundreds of innocent people for crimes they never committed?" After a short discussion, the committee announced that Habibullah was free to go. All charges had been dropped. He could return to work.

Good fortune, the force of logic, the right historical moment, courage or his mother's prayers—what saved my father? A year after he was freed—he was working as a fully qualified doctor at the Mastorat Hospital in Kabul—the Afghan parliament approved the legalization of political parties. But since King Zahir Shah refused to sign them into law, the reforms never came into force. To protect his throne and dynasty, the king destroyed the dreams of a generation. Refusing to give his people their rights had perverted the natural course of justice, redirecting his country's history. His denial set in motion the forces of unrest. Did it help sow the seeds of the violence, extremism and hatred that came to harvest years later? That same year, 1967, the export of natural gas from northern Afghanistan began, through a ninety-seven-kilometre pipeline to the Soviet Union. The strengthening of Soviet-Afghan relations came only a few years after Zahir Shah's first visit to the United States. The

Soviet and American governments continued their friendship with the king.

Not long after his trial, Habibullah travelled with some friends and classmates to the Bamiyan Valley to explore Afghan historic sights. They had dreams of a bright future, and were members of a new professional class that believed in respect and dignity for all Afghans. They travelled in a pickup from Kabul to Bamiyan, where they walked in the valley at the feet of the two giant Buddhas. A few pictures in my father's album bring that day to life: a group of cheerful young men picnicking on the mountaintop. They are sitting in a circle, with one man playing a harmonium. In one photograph, taken from a distance, the group is on top of one of the Buddha statues, part of the mountain visible in the background. In another, they are happy faces in front of the high cliff where the statues were carved between the first and the fifth centuries. The tribes of the Hazara, who lived in the caves under the feet of the Buddhas, are nowhere to be seen in these enthusiastic pictures, since Habibullah and his friends wanted to mark their presence at the site, not document the lives of the inhabitants. They were there not to celebrate the past but to rejoice in the future, the newly won tolerance and respect for their generation.

When, in the spring of 2001, the Taliban announced that they would destroy the Buddhas, Habibullah searched his album for those few snapshots of the past. And on the day when tons of explosives brought the great and ancient Buddhas crashing to the ground, debasing both history and culture, Habibullah arrived home with two enlarged photos in his hand. The first shows him and a friend, Hashim Askeryar, in front of

Hashim and Habibullah at the giant Buddha statue in Bamiyan.

the statues. The second is a picture of the giant Buddha in full, from a distance and out of focus, as if it is disappearing into the clouds. Enlarging the photos provided a kind of emotional relief for my father, who now lives thousands of kilometres away, in Canada. Is engraving the past in the form of enlarged photos all that's left of the future he once dreamed about?

ON A HOT SUMMER DAY in 2002, I find myself heading towards Chindawal, where my father grew up. The paved roads of the new city run through old Kabul as if a knife has cut through the place in five different directions. The district of Chindawal, once a closed circle and society, now chopped up, lies violated and dismantled, spread open under the midday sun before me, long forgotten by the architect of its disfiguration. Someone may have intended to resurrect the old city, but the plan, if one ever existed, didn't succeed.

On the side of the paved road, I walk into an opening that looks like an abandoned alleyway. A little girl, playing with the collar of her dress, stares at me with dark, curious eyes. A boy, slightly taller, steps out of hiding, tucking something into the pocket of his trousers. A female voice echoes in the darkness: "Don't forget to bring *yak desta gandana, yak paw chaka* [a bundle of leeks, a few grams of pressed yogurt], and don't be too long." He runs past the little girl; then, playing the caring-older-brother role, he stops to wait for her to catch up. He holds her hand and they turn onto the paved road, walking out of my sight. I walk a little farther and see the wooden frame of a tunnel. This is where the voice was coming from. Two steps into the tunnel, I encounter a pond with just a few centimetres of dry bank on either side. Mosquitoes and flies dance above the water. With my scarf pressed to my nose, I squeeze by, leaning against the mud wall; it is home to spiders' webs. Standing on dry ground again, I notice ancient wooden doors sunk halfway into the earth.

When I emerge from the tunnel, actually a covered alleyway, I'm in a different world: clay houses, heavy wooden doors—some with engravings, others with dark steel circular or rectangular ornaments hanging on them—traditional door knockers. The upper storeys have thick oak and pine window frames and cracked glass that hasn't been cleaned in decades. I pass a small mosque with a minaret painted blue and white. Near the entrance, a circular bar of rusted iron runs as a security barrier around an ancient tree. From its few lower branches hang pieces of green and red fabric. Not too far from the mosque is a bakery, a wooden structure with a large window and a ledge that hangs over the pavement. On the ledge are a few loaves of thin *non-e kosa* bread.

Once a city within the city, Chindawal is now like a bandage over an old wound. Its basements, underground rooms, interconnected houses, covered alleyways, heavy doors and mud walls are still intact. But there is no sign of the four infamous gates that once shut it off from the outside world, or the fierce, desert-like spirit of its activists that once enraged the government—the spirit I've witnessed in my father. Poor, overcrowded, rundown, it's not a place in which I'd choose to grow up. But I find the house where he lived, a patched-up building with clay and straw walls, looking much as it did in his youth. The lonely black mulberry tree has been cut down; its neatly sawed stump, rooted in the ground, is all that is left. But the well still provides water, and still there is the *takyee khona* in the corner room where Habibullah's family and neighbours would gather to worship and celebrate. The *alam* is there too, with its coloured fabric and its silver hand. A candle stands next to it, with a match for visitors to light it when they offer prayers.

3

THE PILGRIMAGE

One morning early I met armoured cars
In convoy, warbling along on powerful tyres,
All camouflaged with broken alder branches,
And headphoned soldiers standing up in turrets.
How long were they approaching down my roads
As if they owned them? The whole country was sleeping.

Seamus Heaney, 1979

THE BAGHLAN–MAZAR-E-SHERIF HIGHWAY
is a road of great beauty, and we are not in a hurry. We stop
from time to time to buy fruit from farmers' stands at the side
of the road, to take pictures of sheep grazing in the valleys and
to fill our flasks with cold water from a stream. Our caravan

of four families is driving north for a three-day holiday. Uncle Sultani is leading the way in his long black Chevrolet. We are following him in our orange Passat, behind us is Uncle Hatiq in his pale blue Beetle, and the last car is Uncle Bokhtari's navy blue hatchback.

Uncle Sultani pulls over. "Should we go straight to the port?" My father nods. In a short time we arrive at Sher Khan Bander—the Afghan-Soviet border. We children run as fast as we can into the open fields, arms stretched on each side of us like an airplane's wings. My father and his friends, all of whom we call "uncle," pull the picnic carpet from the car.

All doctors from Kabul, my father and my uncles have been posted to Baghlan to work in the city's only hospital. The wives of Uncle Hatiq and Uncle Sultani are also doctors; Uncle Bokhtari's wife stays at home.

Just months before the communist coup, on a road trip with friends in Baghlan, 1978.

Other than the three sons of Uncle Bokhtari and Uncle Hatiq, who are in their teens, we are between four and six years old. While the older children have to help set up the picnic, we dance in circles, holding hands. We pick yellow flowers that are scattered around the field like tiny stars and bring them to our mothers.

My father takes me to a precipice and helps me hold on to an iron balustrade from which we can peer far down into the gorge at the great river. My father tells me that we are looking at the Amu Darya, a silver, moving line that separates Afghanistan from the Soviet Union. At this side of the border, a diminutive ship is being loaded by a crane. My father points far down into the valley at the little boat, holding me from behind. Matchstick men are tying a net over the cargo; I watch the ship move slowly, cutting across the flow of the water. "Habib!" I hear my mother calling. "Habib! Don't let her go farther." I hold tighter to the iron bars, worried that the wind might throw me into the river. "The river is the border," my father carefully explains. "And that"—here his hand points to the other shore — "is the Soviet Union."

We stood and looked across into the Soviet Union on New Year's Eve of 1978. No one could have imagined that in just a year's time, the people on that other shore would invade our country; nor could we have foreseen that in four years' time a bridge called Pole Dostee—Friendship Bridge—would be built across the Amu River. And when the Soviets built the bridge, they could not have imagined that their soldiers would one day retreat across it in humiliation. The last Soviet soldier crossed the Friendship Bridge, which by then had become the enemy bridge, in 1989.

When I watched that cargo ship with such excitement as it crossed the waterway frontier, the river looked so gentle, and the surrounding world was at peace.

We play in a restaurant garden, the Amu River behind us with its ships crossing. My father and uncles have gone fishing. When they return, each carrying several fish, they brag about their catch. The frying pans and oil stoves are brought from the car. I run to the corner of the garden, where the women are stretching their legs over the picnic carpet. They're cooking fish, I tell my mother. "Good!" says Uncle Sultani's wife. "Tell them to hurry—we're hungry." Soon, we're settled around the tablecloth, eating the freshly fried fish. I cover the fish head and skin with a piece of flat bread. Fish heads always look scary: the ever-open eyes, the dry mouths, the gills pressed against the plate; the skin is greasy and wrinkled from burns. Uncle Sultani complains that he has to force his daughter and son to eat. "This is the time of their growth; they should eat well," he says. Uncle Bokhtari, who is very skinny, lifts each of us up by the shoulders, telling us we are so light that the strong border wind could blow us to the other side of the river. What would it be like to land suddenly in the Soviet Union?

Before we leave, we wave across the frontier. There is no one we can see from our Afghan cliff, but we say goodbye anyway. We throw the remains of the fish into the river, watching them as they dive and tumble through the air currents towards the water. Their clan may be relieved to have their bones, skulls and skins back, albeit broken, crooked and burned. We drive away slowly through a small shabby town, leaving the river, the dead fish and the frontier behind.

* * *

The next day, March 21, 1978, is Now Rouz, our New Year. We stop in the city of Mazar-e-Sherif. It is crowded with hundreds of visitors from across Afghanistan, all wanting to watch the raising of the flag at the famous Ali shrine. We take pictures in front of a fountain that splashes water over a large rectangular pond. For my parents, this is one of the best times of their lives. They have their wishes and plans for the New Year: buying a new car, visiting family and relatives in Kabul. They even talk of going to another province once my father's three-year term in Baghlan is over.

As we drive on, we pass through hills that look like mountains of green velvet. Thousands of red flowers called *gule dokhtaran* (girls' flowers) stand across the landscape like an impressionist masterpiece, a mass of red dots. This is *meli guli sourkh*, the red flower picnic everyone comes to Mazar to see. We stop to pick a few of the flowers, but they soon wither.

Every few weeks we go on a journey by car, frequently travelling to Puli-Khumri, which has a large movie theatre. Our parents like to go to concerts and films there. We also visit Kunduz. Like a snake coiled around the body of a mountain, with a frothing river under its shale, the Baghlan-Kunduz highway is a dangerous two hours' drive. I hear my father and my uncles talking about a recent accident in which a family of five, returning from holiday, crashed down the precipice to the river. Uncle Sultani, who's a surgeon, had to examine three bloated, bruised bodies that were brought to the Baghlan hospital. The two others were never found.

Whenever we go to Kunduz, I sit in the back of the car with a stack of my favourite magazines, the *Children's*

Companion. This is my mother's way of distracting me—I used to make my father nervous by standing behind his seat, saying, "Look, another car coming." Now I sit quietly, turning the pages of the magazine. It keeps my eyes off the road, but not my mind. My father is not the most careful driver. My family once told me the story of his accident in Kabul, when I was three years old. We were going to the wedding of one of my father's cousins late one afternoon. My mother had given birth to my brother several months earlier and was looking forward to showing up at the wedding party wearing something in her original size. But instead of attending a party, they had to spend hours in a hospital emergency room. Turning a corner at high speed, my father hit a light pole on the university road. Habibullah was slightly injured when the steering wheel pressed against his chest. I had only a few scratches, but my mother had a cut under her chin; its scar is still visible. She doesn't like to see it in the mirror. Like a crack in a glass, she says, once your skin bears scars, it will never be the same again.

On weekends when we don't travel, there is almost always a party. When I see Aushur, my father's *peyoda* (valet), bringing in large bags and helping our servant, Hussein-dod, set up a temporary kitchen near the veranda, I know that we are to be host this week. Hussein-dod, originally from Bamiyan, lives in our home and shops, cooks, cleans and watches over us when my parents are at work. Aushur is from Badakhshan, in northeastern Afghanistan, but has moved to work in Baghlan after a dispute over a land deal with his uncle and brothers. He wants to make his own life, he told my father when he was being interviewed for the job.

Both Aushur and Hussein-dod are in their late twenties and single. Hussein-dod cannot read or write. His parents didn't send him to school, he says, because there was no school near the village in which he grew up. Aushur has beautiful handwriting. "Like pearls on paper" is how my parents describe it. He studied up to grade eight, he says, but after failing to pass the entry-to-high-school exam, he couldn't continue. All students are required to pass a national exam before they can graduate to grade nine. Those who fail become dropouts without the chance of return. "It is totally stupid," my father says in fury. "It's part of President Daoud Khan's new plan for a country that needs more schools, not more entry exams." The president claims that the entry exam will raise students' level of intelligence. "But in effect, he's depriving thousands of teenagers of education altogether," says my mother, who teaches Dari literature at the local school. She says she's seen very intelligent students fail the exam. "And they have no choice but to work at low-paid jobs, without any future or hope for further education."

My father asks Aushur to register patients at his private clinic since he has such good handwriting. To help him save money, my parents let him stay in one of our spare rooms. During the summer, he sleeps on the veranda. "I'm a son of the mountains and rivers," he says. He wears a circular bead-decorated hat all the time, but his most striking features are his sharp pointed nose and the chickenpox marks scattered all over his face. My brother and I like Aushur because he is nicer than Hussein-dod, who, when our parents aren't around, makes us stand in the snow in our bare feet or run around the yard three times if we get into a fight or don't finish our meals.

On April 20, exactly a month after our trip to the Afghan-Soviet border, we are hosting a goodbye party for Uncle

Bokhtari. His term in Baghlan has ended, and he's going to Mazar for the next two years. Earlier in the day, Hussein-dod was talking about the stores in Baghlan, which have been painted white. President Daoud Khan is expected to visit in the next few weeks, and the mayor is trying to prepare the city for his arrival. Uncle Bokhtari wonders if Daoud Khan will still travel to Baghlan—there is unrest in Kabul. "He's probably not that concerned about the protests," says my father.

"Protests? Where?" asks Uncle Sultani, looking puzzled as he walks into the room. He is the tallest and handsomest of my uncles. He has a good sense of humour, but doesn't care much about politics. Uncle Bokhtari and my father explain that some ten thousand people have taken to the streets in Kabul, demanding an investigation into the death of one of the city's leftist leaders, Mir Akbar Khaibar. My father and his friends knew him—as they know most of the leadership of the various Islamist, socialist, Marxist and Maoist parties. Most of the educated professional class knew each other in school.

"Thirty years of struggle, and at the end you're dead, without much of an achievement," says Uncle Bokhtari.

Aunt Breshna thinks differently. "Bringing out so many people onto the streets, that's an accomplishment," she says.

My father is philosophical. "Khaibar's death has broken five years of silence, but who knows what it will all mean?"

Uncle Hatiq wants to know who might have wanted Khaibar dead.

"There were rivalries within the leftist parties," my father says. "But I don't think they could've sunk so low as to kill him for power."

Khaibar was shot on April 17, just three days earlier, near his home in the Macrorayn district of Kabul. His body was carried from his home to the graveyard in a long ceremonial march. Various leftist groups have taken advantage of the moment to express their fury with the government.

"No matter who did it, it's Daoud Khan's government that's being blamed for the assassination now," says my father.[3]

"Talking of the devil," says Uncle Sultani, referring to Daoud Khan, "they've cleaned up those filthy windows in the hospital."

Uncle Samemi is laughing. "I've even got a new tree planted in front of my window," he announces. His wife suggests he may lose the tree if Daoud Khan's visit is cancelled.

"They wouldn't take the tree away, would they?" he asks.

"No," says Aunt Breshna, "but they should also give one to Hatiq-jan for the help he gave a woman in prison."

Uncle Hatiq is a dentist and a very soft-natured man. Other than the affectionate name Hatiq-jan, our family also calls him *doctare dandon,* the tooth doctor. Khaibar's death and Daoud Khan's visit become irrelevant when compared to the tale of Uncle Hatiq's achievement. Urged on by the others, he recounts the whole story: "During my monthly visit to the women's prison, I saw an inmate with a disfigured face. She told me her husband had accused her of having an affair with someone and, while she was asleep, had taken a knife and cut off her nose." There's an expression among village elders when talking about unfaithful husbands and wives: *beni boreda*—a cut nose. This man had taken that literally. "She seemed to have been a real beauty," he says, "but without a nose she looked like a tragedy. I felt sorry for her. So I made her an artificial nose from the putty I use to measure teeth for fillings."

Aunt Breshna, who has also seen the woman, adds, "The poor woman is very young and terribly attractive, with the most lively eyes I've ever seen. God punish her stupid husband for his cruelty. She says her husband was in prison for the crime but has bribed some officers and has been released."

The next weekend, we arrive at Uncle Hatiq's house for our usual dinner and party. The topic of conversation is still the woman whose nose was cut off. Her husband is furious about the artificial nose and has sent a message to the hospital warning that he'll punish the doctor who helped his "adulterous" wife. A shaken Uncle Hatiq is lost in thought.

"So what are you going to do?" asks my father.

"I'm afraid she might have to live without the nose," says Uncle Sultani.

Uncle Samemi is smirking. "You can't deal with a mad husband," he says. "So before she suffers any more and you put your life in danger, it's better to undo your creation." And I'm sorry to say that that is what Uncle Hatiq admitted he would have to do, out of fear of the husband's revenge.

At the dinner table, one of my uncles gives us the news that Radio Afghanistan, the only radio station in the country that broadcasts from Kabul, has been announcing unbelievable reports of a revolution. All conversation stops. Our attention is turned to the small brown leather-covered radio that's been brought into the room. Low, ominous and sinister music replaces the laughter of our party. As if in a mystery movie, as if they want to prolong the suspense, Radio Afghanistan is playing one nationalist song after another. There is no information. We sit with our plates, quietly chewing our kebabs. The music stops and an announcer—his voice shaking at first—says that the revolutionary guard, with the help of "freedom-loving" people, have "uprooted decades of tyranny" by bringing an end to Daoud Khan's regime. The people have taken over the presidential palace.

The euphoria in the room is overshadowed by a sense of disbelief. What does this mean?

"God keep our families safe in this chaos," says Aunt Breshna.

Aunt Mirmun is in the corridor, looking for something among the half-empty glasses. "I'm looking for some water," she says to my mother, looking frantic, as if in pain. "By mistake I drank some alcohol. My mind was so taken up with the news that I didn't realize until I was sipping the damn thing what it was." After drinking a full glass of water, she says her mouth is still burning from the sensation of the alcohol, which is forbidden in Islam.

The news of Aunt Mirmun's mistaken drink spreads faster than that of the government change, and brings laughter and jokes back into the room despite the heavy music playing once more on Radio Afghanistan. Then the announcer returns with more news. Daoud Khan and thirty members of his family have been killed while trying to escape, he says. We are stunned.

Events have unfolded at such speed they are difficult to follow. At eight o'clock that morning, Afghanistan's 4th Armoured Division, commanded by General Watanjar, moved towards Kabul from its southern base at Puli Charkhi. With the support of the Air Force, led by Colonel Qader, the palace was surrounded at the very time when the president was meeting with his cabinet to determine the fate of several recently arrested leftist leaders. By late afternoon, after an air strike of rockets and a barrage of 20mm shells, the palace guard surrendered.

My father cannot believe what he is hearing. "A powerful

man who established a republic of fear is gone in a matter of a few hours."

Then Colonel Qader comes on the radio. "For the first time in Afghan history," he says in a pompous voice, "the sultanate of the Mohammadzai dynasty has come to an end.[4] Power has passed into the hands of the masses." He declares that, for the time being, a "military revolutionary council," headed by him, of course, will exercise power.

By the time tea is served, everyone is congratulating each other, cheering the end of Daoud Khan's reign. In 1973, Daoud Khan staged a coup against his cousin Zahir Shah.[5] He ended decades of monarchy and became the first Afghan president. At the time, Daoud Khan was supported by the leftist parties. But after consolidating his power, Daoud declared the republic a one-party state—with no prospect of elections or introduction of a party law. His Marxist allies felt betrayed; they concluded that Daoud had been seduced by Arab and Iranian gold and was distancing himself from the Soviet Union. In April 1977, during a state visit to Moscow, Brezhnev warned Daoud Khan about the increasing number of "Western spies" in Afghanistan. Daoud bluntly replied that Afghanistan would remain free, and that Russia would never be allowed to dictate how the country should be governed. He personally offended Brezhnev by refusing to meet with him again the next day. The following month, Moscow began a successful campaign to reunite the two Afghan communist parties of Khalq (Masses) and Parcham (Banner) as the People's Democratic Party of Afghanistan (PDPA), which had split into two competing factions shortly after their formation in 1965. In order to further silence opposition, Daoud Khan arrested several leaders of the PDPA; the most prominent among them were Babrak

Karmal, Nur Muhammad Taraki and Hafizullah Amin. A rumour spread that Daoud Khan was going to execute them all. But the PDPA had secret members within the military with orders from the Party that—if the situation got worse—they should launch an attack on Daoud. To everyone's surprise, on that day in April 1978 when we were all gathered at my uncle's house, the PDPA succeeded in taking power.

The so-called Afghan Revolution, also known as the Saur Revolution—April 27 coincides with the seventh of Saur in the Afghan calendar—was a one-day affair. The entire operation took about twelve hours, and even in the height of the battle, one visitor to Kabul observed, "people queued up for buses, taxis honked for tanks to move over. The traffic policemen motioned the tanks to pull over to the curb."[6]

The next day there is a march. A lot of people gather around a podium in Baghlan's park. After each speaker there is loud applause and cheering. My father reads a poem and speaks for a few minutes. Aushur and I stand among the crowd watching him. He's very emotional and looks truly pleased.

The following day, my parents go to work. Hussein-dod says there was another march at noon, but this time fewer people showed up. That evening, our neighbour Mofatish comes over. He has a big smile and gives my father a strong hug. His two eldest sons, both political prisoners, have been released. He used to work as an inspector for all-boys schools, but in recent years—after being labelled a communist—he lost his job and his whole family was ostracized. They are very poor and, according to my mother, they sleep without food many nights. When my father saw the children for the first time, he realized that they were starving, yellowish skin

71

pressed tightly to their bones, their black eyes sunk in their skulls. Mofatish and his children are my father's patients, and he treats them for free. When we have a party, my mother often quietly asks Hussein-dod to take a large pot of rice to Mofatish's house.

My parents go to our neighbours' house to congratulate them and see the sons. They tell my father that, in Kabul, the bodies of Daoud Khan and his family have been left on the floor of the palace. People are going to look at Daoud Khan's body, to spit at it and kick it as they walk by. Mofatish calls the communist coup a "workers' revolution." These stories trouble my father, who worries that exaggerating the importance of the event and encouraging the pillage of the palace while people walk around the dead bodies might prompt a backlash.

The radio tells us that a Revolutionary Council is now ruling the country, with Nur Muhammad Taraki as its leader, and that the word "Democratic" will be added to the Republic of Afghanistan. The new rulers and their supporters claim that Afghanistan has joined the list of communist revolutions.

The new authorities of the Democratic Republic of Afghanistan (DRA) have asked Uncle Azahar to relinquish his position as the director of Baghlan Hospital. It's part of the political change in the country. Uncle Azahar has already returned to Kabul. But the rest of the doctors don't feel any threat and want to work normally.

We no longer go on car journeys, but we still have parties. We have not seen Mofatish and his family in a while. Aushur says Mofatish and his two sons have been given leading positions in the Democratic Republic and now speak at all the important gatherings and marches. Every few days, there is a march in support of the new regime. My father doesn't attend any more; he says he's done enough cheering, that it's time for the government to get to work.

My mother's school has a new principal. The elderly head teacher, whom all the teachers and students liked, has been replaced by a revolutionary, a tall man with a thick moustache. He is ill-mannered and stares at all the female teachers in an inappropriate way.

The PDPA government has shown little interest in accommodating other Afghan leftist, nationalist or Islamist parties. Taraki, a Khalqi and a Pushtun, is both president and prime minister; Karmal, head of the Parcham Party and a Tajik, is first deputy prime minister. The rest of the cabinet is made up of PDPA members. My father says this is a weakness that will haunt the government later.

The Khalq and Parcham parties had both claimed to propagate Marxist socialist ideology, but they had become arrogant and elitist. Parcham was often mocked as the "royal" communist party because of its close ties to the monarchy. The leadership and membership of both came from the five percent of educated, urbanized Afghans, with little or no support in the countryside. A further splinter group, Shoulee Jawed (Eternal Flame), adapted Maoist ideology and succeeded in influencing some rural areas of Afghanistan. For this, Shoulee Jawed could not be forgiven, and was ruthlessly denounced by the new government.

By August 1978, less than four months after the establishment of the Democratic Republic, the old animosities between the Khalq and Parcham parties have begun to resurface. Once again we hear the ominous sound of national music on Radio

Afghanistan. This time, it's the Khalq Party that accuses Parcham members of plotting a countercoup. The plot has been uncovered and the "American agents"—as Parcham Party members are now branded—have been punished for their crime. Parcham members and sympathizers are imprisoned; the party's leader, Babrak Karmal, has gone into hiding in Moscow. The same men who were earlier held up as heroes and exemplary revolutionaries are now wanted on criminal charges against the very government they helped bring to power. There is yet another shuffle in the cabinet, and the ruling Khalq government, with its leader, Nur Muhammad Taraki, adopts a new red flag and a Soviet model of governance for Afghanistan.

For my father and uncles, the excitement of "revolution" is long gone. They are worried about the increasing Soviet influence. At our family gatherings, there are more stories of mismanagement in the hospital. Apparently, the newly appointed director has been fired before he even arrived for work, complains Uncle Sultani. Uncertainty and contempt have replaced euphoria. "How much more injustice and political chaos can this country handle?" my father asks.

It's late in the afternoon when Mofatish's younger son, Mohammad, comes by to visit. I follow my mother to the yard, where he is standing, constantly smoothing his dark, greasy hair to the back of his head with his right hand. He takes my mother aside and speaks with her for some time. She turns pale as she listens to him, her hands moving nervously. My mother walks to the door of my father's office, where several patients are waiting for his arrival. "Aushur, tell all the patients to go home," she says. "The doctor won't be here to see them today." Like a sparrow sticking his neck out of the nest, Aushur peers from the office, puzzled. My mother comes inside the house. "They've taken your father," she says, bursting into tears, holding my baby sister in her arms. Taken my father? Where? Why?

A couple of government agents visited my father in his office that afternoon, searched his desk and then took him away for questioning. Someone had reported that my father was "anti-government." Mohammad told my mother that they found a picture of Daoud Khan in his desk drawer and that he's held on charges of being a supporter of the old regime. "It's absurd," my mother keeps saying to Uncle Sultani. "He's always denounced Daoud Khan passionately."

Uncle Sultani tries to explain. "The people in charge are not a reasonable bunch. This could be personally motivated." As he is leaving, he turns to my mother and asks if there can possibly be anything else the agents could use to implicate my father. My mother assures him that my father has not been involved in politics for years. "He's not a member of any party," she says. "Once, he had his own party, but he gave all that up a long time ago."

And he did. Almost ten years ago, when Habibullah fell in love with my mother, Jamila, he decided it was time to give up smoking, politics and flirting with other women. My parents met one bright spring afternoon outside the Mastorat Hospital, where my father worked. Jamila, about eight years younger than Habibullah, had finished university and begun work as a teacher. That afternoon, after school, she was visiting her sister, who was a nurse. On her way out of the building she ran into her sister's colleagues, and Habibullah was introduced to her.

My father still fondly recounts their first meeting as if it were yesterday, his story like a script from a romantic movie.

A young woman with long blonde hair, dressed in a miniskirt with a stylish sweater over her shoulders, smiled at him, and Habibullah's heart was bound up with the ringlets of her hair— as he made clear in a verse he composed to mark the occasion.

But as in so many classic love stories, he was a poor young man and she was one of the spoiled daughters of a well-to-do family. Her family opposed their union on the grounds that

Jamila and Habibullah, shortly after their engagement.

My parents' wedding day, Kabul, 1969.

Habibullah and Jamila at a party, mid-1970s.

even his medical degree wouldn't ensure sufficient income to pay for the comfortable life they wished for their daughter. Jamila insisted she would be happy despite his poverty. The family warned of hardship. "Your toes will get caught in the loose threads of his old carpets," Jamila's aunt said. A cousin predicted that her fingers and their painted nails would turn into "logs" after washing dishes and clothes at his home, because Habibullah couldn't afford a maid. It was a year before the family agreed to their engagement, and another year before they were married. A fashionable, carefree yet demanding Jamila moved in above Moama Qandi's garage, sharing the two small rooms with her mother-in-law. Habibullah promised that he'd cook and clean, making sure she'd be happy. To everyone's surprise, he fulfilled his promise, much to the displeasure of his own mother, who'd wanted a traditional, submissive bride for her son, one who would master the art of housekeeping. Jamila failed to live up to—or down to—that standard. But Habibullah, who had earlier refused to marry a cousin, wanted a companion, not a cook. He told his mother to mind her own business.

Though Habibullah had officially disentangled himself from politics, he had never lost his passion for change. He managed to conceal his sharp tongue—his "red tongue," his friends used to call it—inside his mouth for years. But once in a while, he would indulge in angry outbursts against the authorities. Time was against him. The inner rivalries of Afghanistan's communist parties were contaminating everyone. In addition to imprisoning Parcham members, the government was also hunting down sympathizers or associates of other Maoist or Islamist parties. Accusations were made against anyone whom the government feared or disliked. Days before his arrest, my father had said that the country was being managed by a "group of imbeciles." His view was quite simple: like a premature child, Afghanistan's leftist revolution had come at the wrong time, and it was created only to further the political ambitions of a few self-serving leaders. "It's his fault," my mother said. "If only he had kept his mouth shut." But it was too late. Habibullah had spoken, and someone had reported him.

It has been six days since my father was taken. I have seen him only once, at the detention centre three days ago, but the echo of his voice, ordering me not to cry, is still in my ears, and I have kept my promise to him. My mother has knocked on every door she can think of, seeking help. But so far, no one has come to our rescue. Among others, she visited the city's mayor. He told my mother that Dr. Pazira was too quick to criticize "national leaders"—a communist reference to the authorities. "On top of this," the mayor said, "your husband's refusal to join the Communist Party and support the people's revolution is proof of his anti-government, anti-progressive character. He'll be judged accordingly." A frightened Jamila returned home in tears. She was afraid that, as well as being accused of supporting the old regime, Habibullah would also be branded a Shoulee. How this could be possible when the Shoulees were against the old regime, no one dared to ask. But Jamila knew that, if he was labelled a Shoulee, her husband's life would be ruined forever.

That fear, along with this afternoon's latest information, has left my mother desperate. Mohammad, our neighbour's son, showed up again to talk to her. He said that government agents might come to search the house. For fear they might find something that could be used against my father, Jamila has decided to burn every magazine, newspaper, book, album—every bit of loose paper belonging to my father.

In utter anguish she sits on the bathroom floor, legs crossed, in front of the wood stove. Each morning our bath water is heated in the tank above the stove. The tiny door of the chimney is open, and my mother is relentlessly feeding the beast of fire. She's warming our water not with logs of birch and oak but with books, albums and papers. The cherry-red glow of the fire highlights the lines of tiredness beneath her eyes. I've never seen her so exhausted or lost. She began by throwing several books into the chimney, but they wouldn't burn fast enough. Now she is greasing their covers with diesel oil, tearing out the pages and dropping them into the mouth of fire, slamming the chimney door shut to direct the smoke and smell upwards. When she opens the door again, the flames run like red water over the white pages, darkening their words.

Book-burning is a quiet ritual. The only sounds are of the papers crackling and of my mother's sighs. I offer to help. "Tear out some pages," she says, placing in front of me a stack of magazines and medical journals. After the cover, there is usually a portrait of Zahir Shah, followed by that of his wife, Queen Soraya. Some have a portrait of Daoud Khan, with his bald head and double chin. Almost all publications were forced to include their pictures. These portraits are glossy and in full colour, their protruding eyes fixed on an unknown spot. I tear other pages first, keeping the pictures to the last. When my mother throws them into the fire, the glossy pages curl up as they burn.

Jamila picks up my father's beautiful collection of stamps, neatly arranged in small clear plastic pockets. He always shows them so proudly to his friends or to any visitor to the house. At first, my mother takes out only those stamps that feature the exiled king and the dead president. Soon she decides to throw them all into the fire. The smell of burning plastic goes up our noses. Hussein-dod repeatedly takes away the tray beneath the stove as it fills up with ash, replacing it with a clean one. When we are done, my mother and I wash our chimney-hot faces, as if what we have been doing is an ordinary household chore.

"These are bad times," says Uncle Hatiq, "and one has to take 'necessary measures.'" He has come to visit after dark, hoping no one will see him. "Do we know if they are watching our home?" he asks. "We don't know," my mother tells him, but Aushur and Hussein-dod are taking turns each night guarding the house. "People know that the doctor is in prison and I'm alone with three children," she says. "I'm worried about thieves, not just the secret police." There are no more parties, no more picnics, even among our family friends. They are all worried they'll end up like my father. Uncle Sultani and Aunt Breshna are the only people who still visit us during the day.

Marches are ever more frequent. The secret police organize them in support of the regime. People attend out of fear, as we do; my mother doesn't want to cause more problems for my father. She holds my hand tightly as we stand waiting in the city square for the revolutionaries to give their talks. The main speakers are two young, attractive men—new chickens in the farm, the locals call them. Dastager Hozheber has curly brown hair and a well-kept beard. Khalil Mouj is shorter, with darker skin and straight black hair. They talk about revolutionary values. Mouj shows lots of emotion when he speaks about Kampuchea, which is his favourite topic. People have nicknamed him Mr. Kampuchea, but he probably doesn't know. He says the Afghan Communist Party doesn't need old, conservative people with traditional mentalities. "We are going to create a thousand progressive minds," he shouts into the microphone.

There is also a woman who always sings a song called "Mother," and speaks about women's oppression. She has bushy black hair, yellowish teeth and an annoying voice. Despite that, she could be attractive, but pinkish patches on her face make her more scary than appealing. They say her mother died when she was young and her stepmother treated her badly. The marks on her face are burns she suffered under her stepmother's tyranny. The stepmother forced her into marriage to a bad man, but she ran away from his home. People call her Miss Oppressed. At one of the marches, Mr. Kampuchea announces that as part of his nationalist duties—which include embracing those who have suffered—he will marry Miss Oppressed. Their public engagement stirs more rounds of applause, but little sympathy for either.

Uncle Sultani calls their union a marriage between desperation and the desperation-seeker. "So this is what human dignity has come to," he says. "Now people are to marry for their country, not for love. It's an insult to her. What are our children supposed to learn from this?" Aunt Breshna says Miss Oppressed "got out of the rain to sit below the drainpipe," meaning she's gone from bad to worse. "She deserves more respect than that. How can she stand being put on public display, her integrity as a woman shredded to bits by this stupid guy?" My mother says she finds everything appalling—the marches, the speeches, the couple's engagement and the treatment she gets from men when she visits their offices seeking help for my father.

* * *

Cast in a different mould from the rest of my father's friends, Uncle Sultani has a brave soul. He's just returned from the mayor's office after lobbying for my father in his own way. "I told him that they've imprisoned an innocent man and that it is shameful not only for them, but for the rest of the doctors working in the hospital." Informing the mayor that he had just quit his job and would wait at home in case they wanted to arrest him too, Uncle Sultani walked out without pausing for a reply.

His decision to quit on principle and his abrupt visit to the mayor's office were prompted by his discovery of the man responsible for my father's arrest. "The traitor is one of our vaccinators," says Uncle Sultani with anger. "I always had my doubts about him, but today my suspicion was confirmed when I heard him speak to a policeman. I gave the bastard a beating." My mother puts her hand over her mouth. "At first I walked away, then I felt the urge to settle unfinished business with him," Uncle Sultani says, pacing around the room. I've never seen him so furious. We are so used to him laughing and making others laugh that I would not have imagined he was capable of such anger. "I lifted him by his collar against the wall and shook him a few times." The vaccinator pleaded with Uncle Sultani: he'd mentioned to the authorities that my father had spoken carelessly on a few occasions—he had not meant any harm. "I walked into the office of the hospital director and told him that I had insulted a traitor, and that I was resigning immediately," concludes Uncle Sultani. My mother is in shock. "We're going to leave for Kabul as soon as possible," says Aunt Breshna. "There is no use staying in this chaotic place."

* * *

We are eating our two black hens—the grandmothers, we called them. A fox was chased away from our yard several nights ago after stealing a baby chick; Hussein-dod and Aushur both suggested that if we didn't eat the chickens, the fox would. But this is not just an ordinary dinner. The two hens and a duck were also sacrificed to celebrate my father's release. It is our first dinner together after nearly five months. He arrived home unexpectedly this afternoon, at first looking a little out of place, overwhelmed with emotion. He kept running his hand over my head and my brother's, holding my baby sister in his arm.

He never will show us the marks of torture on his back, but he speaks about his solitary confinement to his uncle Moama Qandi, who is visiting us from Kabul. For the past four months, my mother and Habibullah's lawyer in Baghlan and our families in Kabul have been working simultaneously for his freedom. As it turns out, the secret police had no evidence of any sort against him, just a bogus claim that he was an enemy of the revolution. But it seemed irrelevant. He'd clearly offended someone in a position of authority. Who was to blame? Was it my father's fault? "I got carried away," he tells his uncle. "I thought the monarchy was over."

It's an early spring morning. It hasn't rained, but Baghlan's humidity makes it feel as if everything has been sprinkled with warm water. Within the last eight months, more or less all of the old gang of doctors have returned to Kabul. We are leaving too. A truckload of furniture, a minivan and our orange Passat are packed and ready for departure. Hussein-dod is checking the house for the last time. Aushur is taking my father's sign down from above the door. He has barely spoken

83

a word today. Mrs. Dot, the cute hen that still lays eggs every day, another grey hen, one rooster and the brown mother and her chicks are also going with us. This is their first trip to Kabul, and they look more anxious than sad, staring uncomfortably from inside their cages on the roof of the truck. The rest of their tribe, the turkey and the ducks have been given away. All of our neighbours have come out to say goodbye. Why did the vaccinator report my father? Did some people resent our parties or our wealth or my father's popularity? My parents are not interested in looking back, they say. They wish to leave the past behind, like the ashes of the burned books.

At midday, we stop at a restaurant at the Salang Pass for lunch. Freezing water twists around the rocky bed of a stream. We sit by the foaming river, eating watermelons. My sister's red slipper falls off her foot and is swept away by the water. The slipper, racing off into the distance, is a token of remembrance. This is our last trip across the Salang Pass.

My mother's friends from Baghlan School have given her several photographs as souvenirs of her time there. Unlike most of my father's colleagues, my mother's co-workers were locals. In one picture, they all stand in front of a tree in a yard full of snow. In another, one of them is leaning against the trunk; two others are laughing. In yet another, they are throwing snowballs at each other. Everyone has short hair, except for my mother. One of her friends, dressed in jeans, has dark sunglasses. "She'll be leaving soon," says my mother. "Her husband is in the United States. He was studying there when the communist coup took place and his family told him not to return. She is going to join him."

The truck driver pours water for the chickens. "This one is dead," he says, holding Mrs. Dot by her feet, her head hanging down. He hurls her over the river, and she lands on a rock on the edge of the water. She's reached the end of her journey, says the driver with a smirk, washing his hands in the river.

The smell of fresh paint is strong in the house. My father built the house for us, but we lived there for only a couple of years before he was posted to work in Baghlan. While we were away, one of my mother's relatives looked after our property; now my mother's brothers and sisters have prepared the place for our return. After unloading the cars, we go to my maternal grandmother's for dinner. It is like having a party again, without the doctor uncles and their "tray of colourful drinks"—our name for the cocktails served at Baghlan parties—without Aushur or Hussein-dod, but with lots of food and affection.

Within three days of our arrival, all the Baghlan chickens die. My brother cries a lot when the dead rooster is taken away. It was his bird. To calm him down, my uncle has to bring him another one. "Maybe the chickens couldn't adapt to the climate in Kabul," says my father. Maybe they didn't like to be away from their home.

A few days after our return, my father's mother, Sobera, is brought to us on a stretcher. Jamila has prepared a room for her. Habibullah's entire clan uncles, aunts and cousins—come with her. We've been closer to my mother's family; most of my father's relatives, including his mother, are strangers to us.

Sobera is very ill and needs a full-time nurse. She sits on her bed, combing her fine silver hair. She used to have thick braids that reached down her back under the cover of her half-white see-through scarf, my father tells us. She calls me closer to her as I stand by her bed. Her voice is weak. One of her nieces comes in with clean clothes. She helps remove Sobera's cream dress. There is a long, pink line across her chest, where her left breast used to be. I close my eyes, but the sight of it is so powerful that I can still see the crooked line. I open my eyes. She smiles faintly. Her niece is buttoning the dress in the front, over her missing breast.

Only in her mid-fifties, Sobera has been struggling with breast cancer for several years now. She's been to India for treatment, but it has done little to ease her pain. She's been living with her younger son, Asadullah. They've grown tired of looking after her, he told my father. So she's going to live with us now.

Sobera tells my mother that she's felt like a refugee all her life, living in other people's homes. But she takes a stoic approach to her homelessness. "Homeowners have only one house, but homeless people have a thousand." She's seldom been happy in life. She was just thirteen years old when her father gave her in marriage to my grandfather. "I barely knew anything about life," she says. "I was afraid of my husband. When he came into the room, I used to hide. He had a white beard and was tall. When he came close to me, I used to run away from him." Sobera only vaguely remembers her wedding. "I was happy to have a set of new clothes," she says, "but I didn't want to leave my home." Eventually, she got used to having her husband around, learned how to cook and clean, to look after him as well as the two children she gave birth to in her teens. "For many women life starts with marriage; for me it ended with marriage," she says.

About six months before the communist coup of April 27, almost two years ago, my father decided to take his mother on a pilgrimage to Mecca. She'd already been suffering from cancer for five years. Habibullah had offered to take her to India again for further treatment, but she said her only wish was to perform the hajj. She wanted to die and be buried in Mecca. In a caravan of eleven cars, my father set off on the journey with her. Other members of our family were upset, because it was going to be a hard trip. But she was afraid of flying, so they travelled first to Iran, then to Kuwait, finally reaching Saudi Arabia. All of our friends in Kabul waited for news of her death—after all, that was what she wanted.

"When we arrived at the *kabah*, the very centre of the pilgrimage," she tells me now, "I lost consciousness for several seconds at the sight of the place." The *kabah*, Khonae Khoda ("God's House" in Dari), is the black, square construct where millions of people gather every year for the Muslim pilgrimage. Originally built by the Prophet Ibraham, it is one of the holiest Islamic sites. A visit to the *kabah* once in a lifetime—for those who can afford it—is one of the required rituals in the five pillars of Islam. Having suffered so much in life, Sobera wanted to find her peace there, near "God's house." "But when I looked at the crowd, the mass of people moving in circles," she says, "I prayed to God to let me live a little longer. I didn't want to die there. How would they have carried my body in such chaos? Where would I have been buried?"

She completed her pilgrimage. "For a little time, all the pain stopped," she says. "I'd found peace, and my mind was very clear." From there, my father took her to Iraq—to Najaf and Kerbala, two places considered holy by the Shia. "I sat at the Imam Hussein's mosque, listening to a man chanting a prayer in the middle of the night under the golden chandeliers. His voice was like music from *behesht* [heaven], and it was at this moment that I realized I could forgive everyone—including my father, who'd unjustly married me off at a young age, and my poor husband, who tried to be as gentle with me as he could. He never complained or raised his voice."

They returned by the same road forty-eight days after their departure. To the astonishment of everyone in the family, Sobera came home glowing with life and serenity. She even brought gifts of dates and prayer beads. She praised my father. This trip was the happiest time of her life, she said. My father was pleased that he'd gained her blessing, which he claimed was worth more than the pilgrimage itself. Back home at Baghlan, at one of the parties, Uncle Hatiq teased my father, saying now that he was a hajji—a title of respect conferred upon one who makes the pilgrimage to Mecca—he should try to be a good Muslim and stop drinking. Other uncles laughed, saying he was too young—he still had time to go on the hajj again, and could become a good Muslim after that.

It was widely believed in Afghanistan that those who went on the hajj were cleansed of all their previous sins. It was understood that the soul was purified by touching the *kabah*, that all sins were erased from the "book of records." The hajj was seen as a spiritual rebirth, a chance to start a new life. Sobera hoped it would be that for my father, and asked him to give up drinking. My mother had always wanted this. But my father was a stubborn man and didn't give in easily. He was not a heavy drinker, but he enjoyed an occasional glass of Johnnie Walker, arguing that it didn't contradict his belief in God. Drinking in the company of friends, he said, didn't make him a better or worse person. My mother objected. "It clouds your mind, leaving you confused," she'd say. "Your judgment is impaired and your decisions are affected." My father replied, in a burst of love and affection, "I've married you, so my mind is always clear." Like the suit and tie, miniskirts, short hair and cigarettes, drinking was a sign of modernity, liberty, and it was socially accepted among city dwellers.

—

SOBERA HAS LAIN IN BED in our house for two weeks. Most of the time she sleeps. Her scar doesn't look so frightening to me any more—it's just odd. Our home is often packed with visiting relatives. My father has begun work in a Mother and Child Clinic, and my mother goes to school to teach in the early morning. Our maid, Mother Fatema as we call her, has moved into a room at the corner of the yard with her husband and two sons. She does all the housework and looks after my baby sister, Mejgan, whom she calls "my daughter." My parents spend time in my grandmother's room in the evenings.

Late in the night my parents are still in Sobera's room with one of her nieces. The lights are on, but it's all very quiet. My mother walks out of the room, resigned and sad. My father's cousin follows her into the hallway, asking for a white cotton fabric—for the chin, she murmurs softly. "In the movies, dead people look as if they're asleep, in perfect beautiful shape," says my mother. "But in real life, the skin loosens, the mouth and eyes stay wide open and the hands and feet lie crooked. That's why we need to tie her chin, straighten her body and close her eyes."

"The soul left her body peacefully and calmly," says my mother softly. "God bless!"

Nearly two months have passed since they took Sobera's body away, wrapped in white cotton, inside a wooden box. She'd brought the cotton from Mecca in preparation for her death. My parents have had several Quranic recitations in the house as a blessing for her soul to rest in peace. All the family and guests have gone. Only we and Mother Fatema are left in the house now.

In September, Radio Afghanistan announces that President Taraki has gone abroad for medical treatment and that his deputy and right-hand man, Hafizullah Amin, is now in charge. The euphemism is familiar. Medical treatment abroad means that Taraki's term as president is over. There is more fighting within the Khalq Party, concludes my father: "Taraki got rid of Karmal, now Amin has got rid of Taraki, and another dog will replace Amin. In little over a year, the country has seen three presidents installed or removed, not chosen by Afghans but by the Kremlin." My mother cautions Habibullah about talking politics. It's been only five months since his release, and thousands of Afghans are still being imprisoned on political charges every day.

We've bought a television, a novelty not everyone can afford. My father says it was Daoud Khan who built the television station, but the communist government has taken credit for opening it, and it's now run by the revolutionaries. Mother Fatema's husband, Hassanali, is afraid of it. Before we had the television, he used to come by to say he'd locked the house door. Now, he waves from behind the window outside, with his face turned away. I tell him it is just an electronic box. But he says he's scared that the people inside the box will do something to harm him. They cannot get out of the box, I say. But he doesn't seem to listen.

"Are you afraid of storms?" asks Uncle Wahid, one of my mother's brothers.

"No, I fear God," Hassanali replies.

"But television is not God, so why would you fear it?" we ask.

"I'm not afraid of storms or natural things because God wishes them to exist. But this box is created by man, not God. He has warned in the scriptures that man should not create anything in his own image. This box is exactly that. It's blasphemous for me to see it."

Uncle Wahid, who visits us almost every day, is in awe of this man's logic. "Can't we make him understand that we create objects with a God-given intellect and ability?" But it's no use.

At six in the morning, Hassanali goes to work, where he grinds tobacco all day long in a stone mill in a single dark room with no windows. When he returns before the sunset, he smells of tobacco, the fine dust falling off his clothes and face. When he washes his face, yellowish green water runs over the ground. His thick eyebrows and eyelashes begin to appear. They have a bathroom, but Mother Fatema doesn't let

Clockwise from top left:
Jamıla, Uncle Wahid,
Nelofer, Hassib and Mejgan,
1980.

him go inside until he's put his clothes away, and washed his hands and face.

"Your lungs are all destroyed," Uncle Wahid tells him. "Why don't you do something else? How many years have you been doing this?"

And Hassanali answers, smiling gently, "My brother, for a long time."

"It's probably too late for your lungs," says my uncle.

"It probably is," Hassanali says, shaking his head.

Hassanali can tell when it is going to rain or snow by looking at the moon and the stars. His wife says he has incredible spiritual power. He is a man of conviction. He fasts for thirty days in Ramadan, breaking his fast every sunset with yogurt, a slice of bread, green tea and water. That is his diet for the entire month. As soon as he's back from the tobacco mill, he brings logs for the stove and starts the fire. Yet despite his discipline and resolution, he cannot persuade his son Hywaz—who's my brother's age—not to watch television. Hywaz sits for hours in front of the set with my brother and me. Late at night, his father appears at the living-room window with an angry face. He calls to Hywaz to come home. Hywaz shrugs his shoulders, eyes glued to the screen, saying "later" underneath his breath. His father never comes inside the room for fear of seeing the people in the box. Mother Fatema is neutral in all this. Every so often, to keep the peace, she comes in to bring Hywaz home. When that happens, Hywaz walks out of the room staring over his shoulder at the screen—like a drug addict taking a last long puff, except that the opium he's addicted to is considered by his father to be far more corrupting than the drug he grinds every day in the tobacco mill.

* * *

There is a ring around the moon. Hassanali predicts a big change. He explains it to my father as we stand in the cold December night, gazing at the clear sky. "Once in a while, the halo around the full moon appears," he says. "If there are two stars on either side, brighter than the rest, it means a good change. But the stars are not there tonight." For centuries, human beings have relied on these natural elements for survival. "In our village in Bamiyan," Hassanali says, "when we had a night like this, we knew that it was going to be a tough year ahead."

"Financially? A poor harvest?" asks my father.

"Yes, but also in other ways."

"What does this mean here in the city?"

"A change in the climate, a sinister event, bad news."

Exactly thirteen days after Hassanali's warning, an ominous sound invades our relative tranquility. It's cloudy, so we cannot see anything, but the unending noise of planes moving over our heads is impossible to ignore. The Soviets are coming in, says Uncle Wahid. And, like the ghostly emptiness at the Soviet border we saw twenty months ago, no human beings can be seen.

My mother has bought piles of pastel green striped fabric for new curtains. The woman who's sewing them is sitting cross-legged on the carpet in the living room and the clatter of the sewing machine competes with the planes and helicopters transporting the Soviet forces into Afghanistan.

The curtains are soon finished, but the planes are still landing. For three days and three nights we hear the aircraft. By the third day, the sky is clearer and we can see the helicopters for the first time. It is the beginning of a decade-long occupation. The communist government had been claiming there were only 1,600 Soviet "advisors" in the country. Later we learned that 7,500 combat troops had already arrived in the guise of advisors. During the last three days of December 1979, the large-scale operation brought thousands of Soviet soldiers and tanks to Afghanistan.

Back in July 1977, with Moscow's help, the Parcham and Khalq parties had been reunited as the People's Democratic Party of Afghanistan (just as they had been twelve years before at its founding). Hafizullah Amin had been assigned to a key position within the military, where several Soviet-trained Afghans were already in place as army commanders. The Kremlin believed Amin to be more ruthless than Karmal and a more effective instrument of Soviet control. Soviet logic allowed Amin to rise within the PDPA to a high position of authority and trust. It was at Amin's orders that the PDPA members in the military launched an attack on Daoud Khan's presidential palace on April 27, 1978—the day of the communist coup. Many times, on Afghan television, we watched a grainy newsreel film of Amin on a tank, going to release PDPA members from prison on the day of the coup.

Moscow was silent when, in September 1979, Amin removed Taraki from office and had him suffocated to death in prison. But the next month, General Ivan Pawlowski, the master planner behind the 1968 Soviet attack on Czechoslovakia, came to Kabul to examine the state of the Afghan government and army. Then, on December 2, General Victor Paputin arrived in Kabul to meet with Amin. On December 24, the first units of the Soviet 105th Air Force entered Bagram Airbase, north of the capital. Amin didn't object to the increasing Soviet presence in his country. He felt that, since he had command of the Afghan army, the Soviets would always support him. Despite his military connections, Amin didn't have the same long personal association with the Soviet Union as Karmal or Taraki.

As the Russian tanks were moving through the Salang Pass, and while their helicopters were landing at Kabul Airport, the grasp of the Soviet 40th Army grew tighter around the snow-covered land. Amin was resting in his presidential palace at Dar-ul-Aman, secure in the belief that the Soviets were there to protect him from what he believed to be a Parchami coup. But one of the Soviet officers—Paputin or Bayerneve or someone else—was preparing to carry out the Kremlin's orders: to relieve Amin of his life as well as of his command. The details of Amin's death remain unknown to this day.

To announce Amin's death Babrak Karmal delivered a radio address to the nation; in the afternoon of the following day, he arrived in Kabul in a Soviet armoured vehicle. He accused Amin—who'd once studied at Columbia University in New York—of being a CIA agent.[7] He claimed that "anti-progressive elements" had been weeded out of the Communist Party and that with the help of "our friends" to the north—the Soviet army—Afghanistan had been "freed from the bonds of Western imperialism." He spoke of the "people's revolution" and its mandate to deliver freedom and democracy to the nation.

The son of a high-ranking military officer, Karmal was Moscow's new favourite man. One of the founding members of the Parcham Party, he had been expelled in his second year from the faculty of law at Kabul University. He never finished his studies, only appearing at the university to organize anti-monarchy protests. After months of exile in Moscow, he'd returned as yet another communist ruler. We heard Karmal speak on the radio and watched him on TV. He looked pompous and unpleasant. "He's the one who brought the Soviets in," said my uncle.

But could he really have been responsible? A decade later, dying in Moscow of cancer, he would deny that he had anything to do with the Soviet invasion. So why on earth did the Soviet army invade Afghanistan on that cold winter's day, when the so-called communist revolution was already dead? The credibility of the leftist parties was tarnished, thousands of disenchanted Afghan refugees were crossing the Afghan-Pakistan border, and more than a hundred thousand Afghan civilians had been killed or had died in prison since the communist coup less than two years earlier.

Russian journalist Artyom Borovik suggests that Soviet President Leonid Brezhnev invaded Afghanistan because he was "infuriated by blatant insolence on the part of Amin."[8] Both the KGB and the Kremlin were suspicious of Amin, but more so of the White House. "Moscow was convinced that after Washington lost Iran, the United States was planning to turn Afghanistan into its anti-Soviet outpost in Central Asia," Borovik writes. The Islamic Revolution had provoked fears in Moscow that Iran would politically influence those Soviet republics with large Muslim populations. Some Russians regarded the dispatch of Soviet troops to Afghanistan as a "last crusade" to the East. Whatever the political and military reasons, the arrival of Soviet troops brought only chaos and disaster.

Our new curtains are hanging in our home, and the winter has already been marked by cold and snow. We have circled the Soviet arrival in our calendar, like the ring Hassanali showed us around the moon. It was a bad sign. There are no other stars, other than the fake gold star that shines on the new red Afghan flag. The Shia tradition of concealment of one's faith, once practised only by some adherents of the sect, is now becoming a nationwide tradition, as people feel more and more intimidated by the government and its brutal intelligence service, the KhAD.

It's hardly dark before Uncle Wahid and I ask Hassanali if he can see any good change in the sky. Without even lifting up his head to look, he replies strongly in the negative.

My father arrives home. Behind him is a shadowy character who resembles someone from the past. "It's Aushur," says my father. Seven months ago we said goodbye to him. He looks the same, with his bead-decorated hat, though his chickenpox marks are more visible. We are happy to see him. We tell him how our Baghlan chickens died when we arrived in Kabul. Over the dinner table, he talks more to my father. "It's a good thing you guys left," he says. "It's been madness since then."

My father asks about everyone in Baghlan.

"Mofatish moved out," he says. "The guys who used to give speeches, they were either executed or chased out." He pauses and then, with a smile of satisfaction, says the locals killed Khalil Mouj.

"Mr. Kampuchea?" my father asks.

"Yes, he was shot dead, but the next day locals took his body out of the grave and hung him upside down from a tree in the graveyard."

"Why would they do that?" my mother wants to know.

"To punish him for all the bad things he'd done to others," replies Aushur coldly. "Not only once, but three times, his family buried him, and each time someone at night would dig up his body and hang him up by his feet. Finally, one night, his family took his body down and in the dark buried him somewhere unknown. He will never have a tombstone. His children will never find his grave." Aushur doesn't look disturbed or sad when talking about this. "He deserved it," he says with a smile.

My mother is frightened by such cruelty.

Aushur says he left because there was nothing else to do. "I didn't want to join the local bands who were involved in killing revolutionaries and taking over government offices." My father tells him that he's done the right thing to come to Kabul. Aushur wants to get a job. "I want to save up some money to get married," he says. "My mother is old; I don't even know if she's alive. She was bedridden when I left several years ago. I've not been in touch with my brothers."

Life has changed in Kabul. We don't have the same kind of parties and don't need too many people to do the housework. Mother Fatema and her husband have everything under control. My father doesn't need Aushur to work for him, but finds him a job at one of the hospitals. Aushur stays at our home because he doesn't have anywhere else to go. He watches TV with us. It's the first time he's seen television, and he likes it. But a couple of months after his arrival, he's drafted into the army. He comes back only a few times during his weeks of training. One evening, over dinner, he tells my mother that his division is posted outside Kabul and he will be away for a month or so. My father asks him where and for how long. He is not sure, he says, but he doesn't want us to worry about him. He says good night to us in a sombre mood.

"Are you okay?" asks Uncle Wahid, who has come to like Aushur.

"I'm afraid," he says quietly. "They are sending us to the front line. I don't want to go, but I've got no choice."

Several weeks have gone by, and we haven't seen or heard from Aushur. My mother asks my father to check with military headquarters. "I will soon," says my father, who's overwhelmed with work. Aushur has asked my mother to find him a wife— someone he could meet. "In my village, my mother would've found me a nice woman," Aushur told my mother. Jamila has found a few young girls she wants to introduce to him.

Hassanali sprinkles the garden with water. The gardener was in earlier, checking the flowers and trees. "You'll have lots of nuts this year," he said, checking the buds of the almond tree near the water pump. When my father arrives home after work, I want to tell him what the gardener said about the almonds. But as soon as he sees my mother, he says, "Aushur is dead."

Aushur is dead. It means we won't see him again. My mother sits in the corner of the veranda. "Did you go to his military post?" she asks.

"I was in the clinic when an officer came to see me. He asked whether I knew someone by the name of Aushur from Badakhshan. He'd told fellow soldiers that we were like his family. Then he told me that he was dead and asked if I could go with him to identify the body." My father went to the mortician. "I pulled back the cover, and there he was, the *jawan-marg* [very young dead]. I recognized his face, though it was bruised; his chickenpox marks were very visible. He'd taken a bullet in his skull." The army told my father that the division in which Aushur was posted had been ambushed; only a few of the soldiers had survived.

My father asked the officer to give Aushur a proper funeral and a tombstone for his grave. "They gave me his hat," says my father, searching his pocket. That is all that is left of him—that and his tombstone.

4

THE NIGHT CHOIRS OF KABUL

Hurrah for revolution and more cannon-shot!
A beggar upon horseback lashes a beggar on foot.
Hurrah for revolution and cannon come again!
The beggars have changed places, but the lash goes on.

W.B. Yeats

IT'S PAST MIDNIGHT and everyone is asleep. There is a call in the distance—but it's hard to distinguish the words. Like the dim bluish light that seeps from the corner of the curtain, the sound, too, filters through my window. It is moving, growing closer, and I can now make sense of the words. "Allahu Akbar!" God is great. I walk to the balcony. My father is already there, taking in the experience. "Allahu Akbar!" Now we can hear it clearly. We climb to the roof, where we discover that the entire neighbourhood is awake and that several families, standing on their roofs, are already chanting, "Allahu Akbar." We join in. "Allahu Akbar!"—all around us is the echo of one clear voice.

Neighbours warn each other not to turn on any lights. This is an affair of the dark—anonymous, traceless. For hours, we stand in harmony with the cool late February night breeze, shouting simultaneous Allahu Akbars. There is no doubt that God is great, but what is so powerful about this phrase that it draws us to an unconscious desire to repeat it over and over again like music? We use the cover of darkness to pour our hearts out with these two words, and with it our vexation. What is most potent? Is it the collectivity of the call, enabling the echo of one's own voice to reach so far? Or is it the sense of relief it provides, the feeling that we are doing something to show our discontent? Gradually the sound grows softer, ending as our neighbours say good night in the early morning. We return to bed.

The next day we are tired but, as if concealing our night's secret from the light of day, we don't talk about Allahu Akbars, until Uncle Wahid arrives with the news. In a silent rejection, all Kabul shopkeepers decided to keep their stores closed yesterday, February 22, 1980; they designated the night as the time to voice that day's protest. An anonymous nightly letter had been spread all over Kabul, asking people to cry Allahu Akbar after dark, says Uncle Wahid. For the following two days, Kabul shops remain shut, and for the third night in a row we are standing on the roof, joining in this religious symphony. Until dawn we chant, "God is great." We are all so caught up in this rotation of rhythm and order that no one complains about the lack of sleep. I rub my eyes from tiredness and fill my lungs to find my strongest voice. Three nights of Allahu Akbar is our meek response to the nights of planes moving over the Kabul sky, the aircraft that brought the Soviet army here at the end of December. This is our welcome, Afghan-style, to the Soviet invasion.

Like a storm, the night choirs of Kabul took the government by surprise. The city, with its two million people, was screaming with anger. The call had started in Chindawal, in old Kabul, but soon spread everywhere. Two days of protests in the streets followed the Allahu Akbar nights. The government sent in the army to maintain control. In the Shari Now district, not far from our home, Afghan armed guards confronted a group of protesters. At midday, my mother's youngest brother, Uncle Haider—a high-school student— arrived at our home, breathless, his striped shirt soaked in mud. "They were shooting people down," he told my mother. "I ran away."

The same day, Soheqa's nineteen-year-old son was killed. Soheqa, who lived on the next street, came to see my father. I'd never seen his son, but remembered hearing his music when, late at night, the haunting sound of a flute would reach our balcony. People in Kabul say that only those passionately in love play the flute with such power. "He wore his clean white *perhan-tombon* clothes," said Soheqa. "By the afternoon, we had laid him in the dust of his grave with blood dripping from his clothes. The bullet had hit his heart." They interred him at the same spot where he used to sit and play his flute—atop the Kolola

Pushta hill. "His mother wanted to get him a coffin," said Soheqa. "I didn't let her. He is a martyr and should be buried just as he left the world."

During the two days of protests, people set fire to the police stations in some districts and attacked a newly established Soviet Cultural Centre. In response, the Afghan and Soviet armies killed more than two thousand protesters on the streets in one day, including a group of women who were marching silently in Shari Now.[9] It was becoming awkward for the government to explain this situation to the Kremlin, which was counting on Karmal to play the role of strongman at a time when Afghanistan was in chaos and Moscow was facing international indignation over its invasion of the country. The Karmal government was claiming that the "great Soviet nation" had extended its friendship to help the Afghan people fight terrorism. Time and again, Karmal and other PDPA officials, in their televised speeches, stated that the Red Army was in Afghanistan at "the invitation of the Afghan people," that they were only here until the "anti-progressive, imperialistic" militias were uprooted. "The Russians will be leaving soon, in a month or so," Karmal told his economic advisor, Dr. Siddiquallah Farhang, according to Farhang's own account. The Soviets were here to protect our freedom and democracy, and we were expected to be grateful for the "sacrifices" made by them on our behalf.

But we knew we hadn't invited the Soviets to invade— only Karmal and his government, whose survival depended on the Soviet military, had done that. "Afghans," said Karmal, "have a long and proud tradition of honouring their guests," alluding to the 120,000 Soviet soldiers and hundreds of Soviet advisors now inside our borders. For a government that was announcing on the evening television news that it was in full control of the country, the people's public rejection of these unwanted "guests" was deeply embarrassing.

In Chindawal, and in other parts of the city, the troops were sent in. "The tanks were smashing houses, soldiers arresting people inside their homes, pulling respected, elderly men by their collars as if they were removing insects," reported my father's friend. Simultaneous protests and nights of Allahu Akbars took place in Kandahar, followed by harsh military reaction. The communist government was desperate to quash any uprising—especially of a religious kind. Ever since the Islamic Revolution in Iran a year before, there had been no tolerance for any religious movement in Afghanistan. Immediately after Imam Khomeini's triumphant arrival in Tehran, Shia Hazaras in the central Afghan province of Bamiyan turned against the communist government. Their uprising was crushed, as was a rebellion in the northwestern city of Herat—near the Iranian border—where several Soviet advisors and their families were killed. A few months later, the PDPA killed a prominent Sunni leader in Kabul, along with ninety-six members of his family. And now, the PDPA was suppressing this new uprising.

On the fourth night, I follow my father to the balcony to find out if it's going to be another night of Allahu Akbars. But the only sounds are from the engines of two military Jeeps parked in the middle of the road, their antennas extending high above our wall. I sneak back to bed, only to wake up a couple of hours later to the sound of people talking outside my bedroom. Several uniformed Afghan soldiers with rifles stand in the hallway, along with two intelligence officers in civilian clothes. Other than their stern faces, I notice their dirty military boots. Two soldiers walk into my room, opening the closet, searching underneath my bed. My father walks behind them as they search. There's been talk of money and jewellery having gone missing from homes after these nightly searches. My father hopes that, if they know they are being watched, they may feel too embarrassed to take anything. They search hurriedly, throwing things on the floor, leaving the closets and cupboard doors open.

We cannot ask why they are in our home. The military in communist Afghanistan doesn't require a search warrant. The government claims that anti-government agents are hiding among civilians. Of course it is the Afghan civilians themselves who are anti-government. My father says the searches are also an intimidation technique to show us that the army is in charge. Although they may succeed in instilling fear in us, they don't seem to realize that they are also cultivating hatred.

While the soldiers move between rooms, the two intelligence officers stand in the hallway, watching. One leans against a large poster of Gogush, a renowned Iranian female singer in the time of Reza Shah. They notice the poster, and one of them throws his gum at it. It hits Gogush's forehead. His friend throws a pin—it hits Gogush's nose and disappears in the crimson carpet. They decide to challenge each other, each trying to hit her lips with pieces of paper, used tissues and even the cap of a pen. They miss. Finally, one of them punches his fist into Gogush's mouth. The beautiful smile at the corner of her mouth survives the hit, but the poster rips and the security man laughs with satisfaction.

My fists are clenched in anger. I like Gogush's songs and chose this poster from many because of her smile. I stare at the rigid faces of these two moustached men, one of whom is going bald. My dislike for them has turned into contempt. My first thought is to find something heavy, hide behind the door and hit them as they leave. I think of the story Sikander, my father's relative, told us about his aunt Mariam. When the Afghan and Soviet soldiers went to search Aunt Mariam's home, she poured a large pot of boiling oil over their heads from above the door as they were leaving. The burned men were rushed back to their units for treatment; later she pleaded ignorance to the officials who came to question her. They left her alone, but she's been elevated to heroine status by the locals in her hometown of Charikar. Sikander said that Aunt Mariam is growing poppies in her garden to drug the Soviets who have established a base near her farm. Furious at my help-lessness and inability to punish the men who search our house, I stand mutely and watch them go. The mud from their boots, drying on our carpet, has left a dark, humiliating mark.

Karmal was desperate to win Afghans' confidence and Moscow's praise. A few weeks after his arrival in Kabul, around mid-January 1980, he announced that all detainees from the Puli Charkhi prison would be released.

On a cold snowy morning, Zarghona-jan, a teacher and one of my mother's friends, came to our home so that my parents could drive her to Puli Charkhi, where Karmal's show of clemency was taking place. Her husband, a third-year economics student at Kabul University, had been arrested the previous year, just nine months after their wedding. She had returned to live with her parents after being called "the black luck bride" too many times by her mother-in-law, who blamed her for his arrest. Zarghona-jan was not rich, but she had sold all her wedding jewellery and gifts to bribe officials to find out her husband's whereabouts. She'd even escaped a near rape by an officer who had promised to help her. Finally, she had managed to locate her husband in the west wing of the notorious prison.

With Karmal's announcement, Zarghona-jan hoped that her husband would be released. She showed up at our house dressed in a smart crimson suit, with her hair and makeup perfect. She was anxious to reach Puli Charkhi—about an hour's drive from Kabul—wanting to be there on time. She'd even brought her husband's jacket for the cold. She told my mother that as soon as he was out, they'd leave the country.

At noon, my mother returned home alone with a sheet of gloom on her face. "Zarghona-jan waited and waited, but there was no sign of him," my mother said. "At one point, she even thought someone else was her husband." As the line of prisoners walking out of the gate came to an end, she sat on the ground, spreading his jacket over her legs, holding her head. My mother tried to help her get up. "She kept whispering, 'I can't see any more,'" said my mother.

Altogether, some two thousand prisoners were released. Families of the freed men cheered, but there was no consolation for the thousands of disappointed relatives also gathered at the grey fortress. They left even more infuriated at Karmal and his government, who had claimed all inmates would be freed.

Where were the rest? When Zarghona-jan inquired, she was told that, if her husband was not among those released, he was dead. She tried to explain that just before the announcement she had been told he was alive and so she was bringing him clean clothes and money. "You have to write to the Revolutionary Council," an officer told her. Babrak

Karmal was the head of the Revolutionary Council. No one who sent him a letter ever received a reply.

A few months later, Zarghona-jan comes to say goodbye, quietly. She's leaving the country. There's no hope for her any more, she tells my mother. Her husband has disappeared, and she does not have the money and patience to start her search all over again.

Karmal's propaganda campaign backfires when, in early April 1980, Kabul high-school students march in the streets, protesting against the Democratic Republic and the Soviet invasion. On April 29—the week of the second anniversary of the communist coup—students at Kabul University join the high-schoolers' protests. Once again, Soviet tanks fire live rounds and the Afghan army struggles to stop the protesters. For several weeks, the demonstrations continue. Finally, using the 1980 summer Olympic Games as an excuse, the government announces a month of holiday for all schools and universities. In addition, Kabul TV—which ordinarily shows only evening programming—broadcasts the Games all day long, a vain attempt by the government to provide a distraction. Meanwhile, each night, government agents continue their house searches, sending more and more people to Puli Charkhi's torture cells.

A woman in second-hand clothes with a dark brown patterned scarf over her head appears at our door. Behind her is a tall, dark young man in military uniform. "My brother is ill," she says. "Could the doctor see him?"

Her brother, Ismahil, is a military guard at the Puli Charkhi prison. For the past week he's been suffering from a strange problem. He is melancholy and depressed, he shakes and sweats when trying to speak, and his sister claims he has not been able to sleep for the past thirty hours—since he returned home on sick leave. My father offers what he can in terms of advice and medicine, but is concerned about Ismahil's ambiguous condition long after he's left.

Two days later, the sister knocks at the door again—this time looking even more distraught. Her brother's condition has worsened, and she hopes to take my father to visit him at their home. In situations like this, my mother feels concerned about my father's safety. "You don't know them," she says. "How can you trust them?" But my father thrives on being needed, so he takes his black briefcase of medical equipment and puts on his silk *chapan,* a long Afghan coat. "They come as patients, and as a doctor my job is to help them if I can," he replies.

Each time my father goes on visits like this, my mother sits by the window, keeping one eye on the clock and the other on the door. We know that some people lie about the distance they want my father to go. They say their home is "on the next street." It often turns out that they are somewhere over the fields, far away from any road, more than forty-five minutes from our home. But my father doesn't seem to care. He speaks nostalgically of the time when he worked in the northern province of Foryab and would travel for two hours on horseback to visit patients. My mother argues that back then the country was at peace. The occupation has changed everything.

It is two hours before my father is back. He sits in the hallway, staring at the wall for several minutes. "The soldier died," he says. "He was twenty, and had joined the army less than six months ago." No one knows for sure why he died, but the soldier had spoken to my father, shaking and sweating, suffering from the pain of describing what he had been through. His sister told my father that they'd taken him to the hospital, but he'd refused to talk. He hadn't said much at home either. Ismahil died of a mysterious illness that no one was prepared to deal with. And with good reason. Night after night, he told my father, he was on duty when they were executing prisoners. "He said the night he fell ill he had to watch prisoners being buried alive. The inmates were ordered to dig a large grave, put their shovels away and stand by the edge of the hole they'd just finished digging. A guard was ordered to shoot them from a distance. But after just a few shots, a commander stopped him, saying it was a waste of bullets. Two bulldozers pushed all the bodies—dead, wounded and alive—into the grave, covering them with earth." My father is holding his head as he relates the soldier's last words to him. "He kept repeating—over and over—'I saw the ground moving for a long time after the bulldozers were gone.' I tried to comfort him, but it was too late." I've never seen my father cry before. "The poor guy, he couldn't believe in that degree of human cruelty. Nothing in life could have prepared him for that."

Ismahil had joined the army to help his family make ends meet, the sister told my father. The family survived; Ismahil did not. "The burden of the pain was greater than his innocent soul could bear. Perhaps he's found his peace now. But how can you tell a family to be happy that their young son is no longer being tormented?"

My father's brother, Asadullah, dressed in grey trousers and a checkered jacket with a red star pinned just under his left collar, is visiting late one Friday afternoon. For the past hour, he hasn't stopped talking about the greatness of the Afghan communist government. Several neighbours are waiting in the hallway to ask my father's medical advice. My father goes back and forth between the neighbours and his brother, his anger increasing all the time. "Since when have you become such a staunch supporter of these murderers?" my father finally asks.

Uncle Asad's face turns red. "I warn you not to speak like that about the leader," he says.

The two brothers have always respected each other and cared for each other's families. This is the first time I have seen them having a row. Uncle Asad, who quit school after grade two, has become a very successful car mechanic. He built a beautiful three-storey house for his family—four sons and a daughter. His wife works as a secretary in the ministry of finance. Uncle Asad tells my father that he's recently joined the Communist Party and started to work in a factory. Now, he announces, he's on a mission to spread the "true values of the people's revolution." The brothers speak louder, exchanging harsher words. My mother stays out of it.

I wait in the hallway to see what is going to happen. Uncle Asad leaves the room, fuming. My father follows him out into the hallway, shouting. "As you leave, kiss that door," he roars. "Don't ever return."

Uncle Asad is already at the door. "From this day on," he says, "I assume my brother is dead."

"From this day onward, I assume I never had a brother," my father shouts back.

Uncle Asad slams the door behind him. My father returns to the living room. Uncle Asad's half-drunk cup of tea sits on the table, his half-eaten biscuit beside it.

* * *

We return to school after our long summer holiday. On my way home one day, I see four Soviet soldiers searching houses. *Shurawi, Shurawi* ("Soviets, Soviets"), says a classmate. We stand and watch them as they go inside a house. Some kids gather near the door, trying to see inside. But I leave. I've never seen a real Russian before. It's an insignificant event—I already know I hate them. They have come to occupy and rule our country and steal our goods.

A few of my father's friends have joined us for lunch. One of their wives—originally from Czechoslovakia—tells us about the Soviet occupation of her country. Since the Soviets' arrival, Czechs have had to line up for a kilo of potatoes, and months go by before they can obtain a meat ration, she says. She points at our lunch table. "You're lucky to have such fine food. If the Soviets succeed, all your products will be shipped to Russia, and you'll have to wait in line, like people in Czechoslovakia, to buy these oranges—if you can still find them."

Mother Fatema complains that she's working twice as hard nowadays to keep the house clean. "Mother of Nelofer," as she calls my mother, "I dust the living room and the guest room, all the shelves and windowsills every day." The dust falls courtesy of the Soviet tanks and BMP armoured vehicles that thunder down our street. When we heard the roar of an unusual engine for the first time, and felt the slight vibration, we didn't know what it was. I peeked over the wall and saw a long line of tanks, like a chain, thrashing along the road. Kids in the neighbourhood stood to watch. Now, holding to the edge of the wall, I watch until the last tank disappears from sight. Usually, one or two Soviet soldiers sit on top of each vehicle, and we stare at each other like aliens. Neither they nor I ever smile.

We believe the Soviets must hate us, just as we despise them. They act as if they are afraid of us; we behave as if we resent their existence. Trust is not something we can speak of these days. It's hard enough to trust Afghans, let alone Soviets. Once the last tank has gone, the dust from their tracks settles on the surface of the wall, on the leaves of our almond, pear and fig trees, over the roses, on the grapevines and on my hair and face. On the pond, a thin skin forms on the surface of the water. It is this fine, soft, almost greasy dust that is driving Mother Fatema crazy. With each layer, the barrier grows between the Soviets, their Afghan allies and the rest of us.

On the way to school, we sometimes have to wait to cross the road until the tanks have gone by. We stand and watch, pulling our white scarves over our noses as our black school uniforms turn grey. The old paved road begins to crumble under the weight. If the tanks are muddy, they have just returned from a battlefield. When we see the Soviet soldiers looking dirty and lost, we know they have been defeated. When they look clean and a little nervous, they are heading to the front line. The tanks go slowly after they've returned from a battle; they move faster when they're heading to one. Sometimes the soldiers are wounded, with bandages around their heads, faces or arms. They look tired, confused. Even their gauze bandages look grey or brown; some still have blood on them. They sit on top of their tanks, where the afternoon sun exposes their disturbed faces and their wounds. We almost feel sorry for them. They are all very young. Still, it is hard to feel sympathy for an occupying force—especially the Red Army, the "army of bastards." We don't know where this description came from, but someone used it and now it is widely believed that all Red Army soldiers are orphans or illegitimate children raised by the military. They are brutal because they have no family; they have no compassion because their only loyalty is to the communist state. We also call them "Lenin's illegitimate sons."

We fear the Red Army. They have no mercy, says Uncle Wahid. They were brought in along with special units to replace Central Asian Soviet troops. It became apparent that the soldiers from Central Asia, who were sent to Afghanistan in the first months of occupation, were less willing to fight Afghans. "The resistance infiltrated the Tajik and Uzbek Soviet soldiers," Uncle Wahid says, "telling them that they were like Afghans but deprived of their ancestral culture because of the Soviet occupation of their lands years earlier." On one occasion, says Uncle Wahid, the mujahidin—who have emerged as the resistance to the Soviet occupation— announced that they wouldn't kill Tajik and Uzbek soldiers. "You're our Muslim brothers," they told them. After that, Central Asian Soviets who surrendered were given an amnesty. They defected as fast as the Afghan army. So they were soon called back to the Soviet Union.

—

IT HAS BEEN ALMOST THREE YEARS since the Soviet invasion; Karmal's propaganda machine still claims the Soviets will soon be returning home. But their presence is everywhere: on the roads, in the markets, on television, in the schools. At our school they are distributing red-and-navy-blue dresses, and we are given a lecture about being grateful for these wonderful gifts from the Soviet Union. Two students—members of the youth communist group—speak on everyone's behalf, expressing our "gratitude." Then the deputy principal reads our names from a list. A Russian lady—with short brownish hair, pink lipstick and bright blue eye shadow—smiles as she hands each one of us a dress. Another Russian woman, standing next to her, watches us from the corners of her eyes. Their Jeep, with two soldiers in it, is parked in the schoolyard.

As soon as the deputy principal and the Russian women are gone, we examine the dresses. They are identical—large, thick fabric, buttoned blouse and sleeves. We think the Soviets are out of date when it comes to fashion. By now we have seen enough Russian movies to know what poor taste they have. In most of these films, women are overweight, working on farms or in the military, dressed in old clothes. In Western catalogues, women are slim and have beautiful hair, and they wear suits, skirts and colourful dresses. My mother often uses these catalogues to have her clothes made. In school, we brag about following European styles. But would we admire Western Europe if their soldiers were the ones walking on our streets? Would we still follow their fashions if their planes were dropping bombs, killing an entire village, if their tanks destroyed homes and their rifles shot Afghans dead? I doubt it. We hate Russian music, Russian fashion, the Russian language and these Russian gifts because they represent our occupiers.

After school, we talk about the dresses and find the whole ceremony humiliating.

"We should have told them we have enough clothes to wear and don't need these," says Noriya.

"And our clothes are much nicer than theirs," says Dyana.

"I'm not going to take this home," says Farhatnaz.

Both Farhatnaz and Noriya talk openly about their hatred of the Soviets. Dyana is more cautious and reminds me to be careful too. But the four of us share the same sentiments. As we leave school for home, we see flames about a hundred metres away. A few students have decided to say thanks to Mother Russia by setting the red-and-blue dresses on fire. We don't know who they are, but several others walk close to the blaze and throw their dresses onto the pile. We look back, making sure the school guard is not watching us. We too throw our dresses on the fire, and cross the street—fast.

In addition to the gifts and speeches, there are also decrees introduced by the government to show that they care about us. Dr. Anahita Ratebzad—one of the earliest members of the PDPA and Karmal's closest ally within the Party—promotes female education. With her well-styled hair, now turning grey, Ratebzad delivers long speeches in girls' schools and on television about women's conditions in the country. She argues that the communist decrees recognize women's equal rights, and she is correct: all government speeches and decrees emphasize the role of women in society. What Ratebzad and her supporters fail to understand is that we regard them all as Soviet agents who want us to become just like them. Each time Ratebzad talks about women's rights, we are appalled. "What a hypocrite!" Farhatnaz says.

Farhatnaz's brother is in prison for "anti-government activities." He was arrested in Kabul in 1978, around the same time my father was jailed in Baghlan. But he was not as lucky as my father. His wife gave birth to their first child two months after his imprisonment. Now the child is almost four years old, and has never seen her father. He doesn't even know he has a daughter.

Since the day of her brother's arrest, Farhatnaz has worn a black head scarf as a sign of her resistance to the government.

"Ratebzad doesn't have a brother in prison, an elderly sick father and two martyrs in her family already from the war," says Farhatnaz. "What does she understand about being a woman?"

Ratebzad claims that all women in Afghanistan are oppressed by religion and tradition. What she doesn't realize is that it's her own government that is oppressing women— its iron fist pressed against our throats, all the time.

"The equality she talks about sounds good in speeches," says Dyana.

My father knows Ratebzad from her days at university and says she is an intelligent woman. So how can she talk about women's suffering yet ignore their ever-growing tragedy?

Norbebi-jan is a dear friend of my mother. She is twenty-four, tall, with long brownish hair, green eyes and a soft voice. She teaches math and biology where my mother also works. Her fiancé, a law student at Kabul University, has been missing for the past three years. He was rounded up by government agents, taken to the KhAD headquarters in downtown Kabul for questioning, and has since disappeared. Norbebi-jan remembers seeing him that morning; he walked her to school and headed towards the university. Their wedding was scheduled for Wednesday—six days later. The invitations had gone out more than a month before and everything was ready, but the groom was never seen again.

According to a friend who was with Norbebi-jan's fiancé at the time, two soldiers and one man in civilian clothes were waiting for him at the university entrance. After examining his ID, they asked him to go with them to a Jeep that was standing a few metres away. He gave his friend his car keys to take the car home. What was going on in his mind at the time? What did those men tell him? Everyone hoped he'd be released in time for his wedding, but they had to cancel the arrangements. They searched everywhere for the missing man—the KhAD, the Puli Charkhi prison, the local police station. "Three full years," sighs Norbebi-jan, "and not a word. But I still believe in my heart that he's alive."

She has shown my mother her wedding dress—hanging under a dark grey plastic cover in her closet. "The net for her hair and face, the shiny white shoes, her untouched makeup set and his unworn suit all sit in the same closet," says my mother. "It's a closet of doom. I couldn't bring myself to look at everything. I don't know how she manages to do that."

Norbebi-jan is suspicious that her fiancé's arrest may have been provoked by rivals. "His best friend asked me to marry him six months later," says Norbebi-jan. "I asked him if he knew something I didn't. He was embarrassed and said he pitied me and wanted to help. I told him if he wanted to help, he should just get lost." Norbebi-jan belongs to a very wealthy, well-respected family. Many relatives, including their own cousins, envy them. It's not inconceivable that someone reported him for all the wrong reasons. These days it is easy to get people arrested if one has connections with the KhAD.

Many teachers from the school, and some of her family members, want Norbebi-jan to get married, and she has lots of suitors. When my mother met her for the first time, she was thinking of introducing Norbebi-jan to Uncle Wahid. But she told my mother that she felt like a married woman with a missing husband. A year after his disappearance, her fiancé's family told Norbebi-jan she was entitled to marry someone else if she wanted. "I cried many nights," says Norbebi-jan. "I told them that even if they've given up, I won't."

Thousands of other women have already given up hope of finding their husbands or fiancés. A few have had to deal with tragedies greater than imprisonment. Farhatnaz's cousin from Logar was taken to Puli Charkhi to see her husband. "They told her they were going to release some prisoners and she was needed to identify her husband," says Farhatnaz. "Once inside the prison, she saw her husband behind a glass. They told her that he had to answer some questions before he was let go. Then they tried to rape her in front of her husband to get him to confess and give information." The woman had screamed, punching the soldier and biting his hands. Shouting so loud and struggling so hard, she had fainted. When she recovered consciousness, she was in the military hospital. "We had to bring her from the hospital," says Farhatnaz. "She's still not well and screams in her sleep." There is no news of her husband.

Hashimi's wife was told that her husband, one of my father's friends, was dead. The family had a funeral, and she returned to her parents a widow. Soon she remarried, this time to a member of the Communist Party, the head of the municipality in the Shari Now district. He was a handsome man with newfound wealth and some popularity in the Party. She was seven months pregnant with the child of her second husband when the first one turned up alive, released from prison.

Hashimi, a short, bald man with observant eyes and a narrow nose, was in charge of an underground resistance movement when they imprisoned him. "I was supposed to serve life, then it was reduced to fifteen years, and before I knew, one day they opened the door of the cell and ordered us to walk behind the guards," he tells my father. "Even when we were led out the main gate, I couldn't believe I was free. I kept thinking this was a game, especially since I didn't see anyone from my family."

When he returned home he discovered his wife was no longer there. Hashimi is in his mid-thirties and is well educated. Like my father, his family comes from Chindawal. Hashimi managed to have a decent life. But this tragedy, he says, is too much for him. "I've not seen the bastard," he says of his wife's second husband. "He is the one who brought the false news of my death to the family. How could she do this? And now she's pregnant with his child. What can I do?"

It's not safe for Hashimi to stay in Kabul, so he has to leave the country. He says he'll certainly return, if only to take his revenge. "God willing, I'll kill him, with these two hands." He holds his open hands in front of his face.

My mother tells him he should try to forget this misfortune. "It's not worth it to taint your good, capable hands with someone's blood."

"My dear sister, no one will ever understand the burning fire inside me," he says to my mother. "Do you think I want to be a murderer? Of course not. But it hurts so much. . . ."

My father tries to tell him he should pay attention to his health and be careful.

"I don't care," he says. "I'll die—but not before killing him." His head is bowed, his eyes to the ground. He's guilty of a crime he hasn't committed yet. "I wish I was dead," are his last words before leaving our house.

War has its rituals. Every night, shortly before ten, my father closes the living-room windows and pulls the curtains. It's time to listen to the BBC Persian Service. But for us to hear the broadcast, our poor shortwave radio must first lose its leather cover and then nearly perform an acrobatic dance in my father's hands, being moved from side to side to catch the elusive signal so we can hear ten minutes of the news. The announcer's voice is often mixed with music from other stations, and sometimes it disappears. But the real problem is the danger of being caught listening to or discussing the news, since listening to the BBC is banned.

We feel the ominous presence of KhAD agents all the time. In addition to "anti-government elements," they are now also looking for weapons. When we hear that there's been an uprising in one of the provinces, we know the manhunt has restarted. At these times, it's doubly dangerous to tune in to a Western radio station.

The daily Afghan television broadcast begins at six in the evening with a children's show, followed by songs, then two newscasts at seven and eight in the Dari and Pushtu languages with commentaries at the end of each. Watching the news, we are supposed to believe that life is flourishing under the communist government, that the Soviets are welcomed, that all resistance has been crushed. They always say that the *baqoyohie* (remnants) of anti-government militias have been defeated by the brave Afghan army and their Soviet supporters. If this nonsense were true, then obviously by now there wouldn't be any opposition left. The trick is that the more the state-controlled media count government victories, the more defeats the government has suffered. There is an Afghan expression that says the higher the beating of the drum, the emptier it is.

They broadcast lengthy speeches by Karmal and other PDPA members that sometimes last over an hour. I watch them all. But Uncle Wahid pleads with me to turn the TV off as soon as he notices Karmal or the other usual suspects on the screen. "They repeat this rubbish every day in order to convince themselves," he says.

I watch other programs on Afghan television. There is a once-a-week youth quiz show—sometimes hilariously if unintentionally funny—that tests people's knowledge of Afghanistan, the Bolshevik Revolution and communism. The host poses a question: Who was the leader of the 1917 Revolution? The answer comes back: Lenin. The host gives only half a mark. "You should've said the full name," he explains. "It's Comrade Vladimir I. Lenin." Who said the following: "Religion is the opium of the masses"? The answer: Karl Marx. The audience applauds wildly. But what, I wonder, would Marx have said about Afghanistan, which produces both religion and opium? Religion for the Afghan masses and opium for the Soviets.

We watch Indian movies on TV religiously every Friday night. The next day we talk about them in school. We used to go to movie theatres to watch Iranian, Turkish, Indian and Western films. Now all Western films are banned. There have also been bomb explosions in cinemas. I watch all the films that are broadcast on Afghan television. Most are produced in the communist bloc. But nothing can compete with Russian black-and-white movies of the Second World War. I'm glued to the screen when they show these. The Soviet army liberates Poland, captures Czechoslovakia in twenty-four hours and cuts across Hungary in a week. That famous scene of Soviet officers carrying captured Nazi banners into Red Square and contemptuously throwing them into a pile before Lenin's tomb—the final symbol of victory for the Soviet Union—is engraved in my memory.

The Soviet soldiers in these films are brave, disciplined, organized, inspiring characters; if anything could impress me about the Soviets, this is it. Despite my hatred for the Red Army, I find these films fascinating; they are about justice and heroism. Afghans say that a person of dignity will always praise the courage of his enemy as well as that of his friends.

As the years go by, however, I have learned that history is not like the movies. The army that freed Eastern Europe in 1945 was brutal and rapacious and corrupt as well as brave. I would not have imagined, watching those films, that a wartime Soviet soldier would rape women. The Soviets, it turns out, didn't trust even members of the Polish, Czech or German communist parties. The Soviets who had been German prisoners of war since 1941 faced reprisals for having been weak enough to be taken alive by the enemy. Only in the Soviet Union, I have realized, could they punish people for surviving.

For Stalin, the Second World War was a military game— a play of intrigue and rivalry through which he wanted to expand his sphere of influence. His plan to deceive the Western Allies—constantly and falsely reassuring Churchill and Roosevelt that Russian troops were not moving towards Berlin—was an example of Soviet-style diplomacy. When I read Antony Beevor's *The Fall of Berlin 1945,* I saw many parallels with Afghanistan. For Stalin, human life, dignity and morality had little relevance.

It is as if Stalin lived on inside Leonid Brezhnev and the other Soviet dictators. And the Soviet Union gave Afghanistan a Stalin—a modern version, modified to fit the Afghan screen—called Babrak Karmal.

My parents return from a wedding. It is still early in the evening. Uncle Wahid is helping me finish my math assignment.

"How pathetic these *sozmonie*s [party members] are with their suits and ties, their drinking and dancing," says my father under his breath.

"How was the wedding?" Uncle Wahid asks.

My mother shakes her head, with a meaningful smile.

"They are a bunch of idiots," my father says angrily. "They get drunk at someone's wedding party and grab women on the dance floor. It is disgraceful."

We want to know more. Halfway through the wedding reception, my father tells us, a group of drunken men took over the dance floor and harassed the women. It became so embarrassing for the groom's family—relatives of these young men—that they denied they knew the drunks. When someone tried to send these unwanted guests home, one of them—probably a guard or a member of the KhAD—began shooting in the air. At that, other guests decided to leave.

"As we were saying goodbye, the two families were already into a shouting match, blaming each other for the behaviour of their relatives," says my father. He is in a strangely philosophical, resolute mood. "If this is what progress means, I don't want to be part of it—so this is it!" And he walks to the dining room, where he keeps his alcoholic drinks. One by one, he removes the whisky and wine bottles from the little cart where they stand and throws them in the rubbish bin. "From this moment on," he says, "not one drop of alcohol will touch my lips."

My mother is surprised, if only my father could have been persuaded a few years ago, my poor grandmother, Sobera, would have seen her last wish come true before her death. Uncle Wahid quietly asks whether my father is serious about this. Jamila has no doubt. She knows that when Habibullah says "quit," he means it. After their engagement, when

Habibullah decided to stop smoking, none of his friends could believe it, because he used to smoke two packs a day. But he stopped at once and never touched a cigarette again.

In 1983, members of the Iranian communist Tudeh Party face persecution by the Islamists in Iran. They find a sanctuary in Kabul and become cultural advisors to Afghan television and radio as well as to most of the magazines and newspapers. They are the kind of progressives that the Afghan government and its Soviet friends would like us to become. It's a bit late, however. The Iranians might have had more influence on us if they hadn't supported and justified the Soviet occupation of Afghanistan so enthusiastically. They suffered at the hands of the radical Iranian clergy and then blamed Islam for all their problems. I find it odd that we—the Iranians and Afghans— share a common language, history and heritage, but hate each other's friends and admire each other's enemies. They idolize the Soviets; we demonize them. They despise religion; we admire it as the foundation of our resistance to the occupation. Is it easier to live under the tyranny of one's own leaders or to suffer the brutal treatment of an occupying force? We cannot, of course, discuss this. The word "debate" has been erased from our vocabulary.

5

TOKEN OF SHAME

It's better that I see rather than remember,
Because my tears have not put out the fire.
Each grave in this cemetery is a martyr;
So which should I cover with flowers?

Qahar Ausi, 1989

IT BEGINS AS FUN—exciting, even exhilarating. I
don't know who starts it, but someone throws a stone at a military vehicle on the Taymanie road. Without thinking, Dyana
and I and two other grade seven classmates also pick up
stones to hurl at a government bus. It's shortly before five in

the afternoon, the time when government-provided buses, Jeeps and minivans drive employees home. My stone misses; Homera's hits the back end of the bus with a clang. We search the side of the paved road for more stones. More military and government vehicles are coming.

The Taymanie road, which leads to Shari Now, is a narrow street with shops, bakeries, public bathhouses and pharmacies just a metre or so apart. It's one of the main bus routes to downtown Kabul and one of the busiest streets in the city. Our junior high school, Tajwarsultana, is just around the corner, in a wide alleyway off the main road.

When Dyana and I arrived at school earlier, Shakela, one of our classmates, said students in other schools were protesting and we should wait for a signal to walk out of class in support. The signal came at the break, around three. By then, the school gate, a well-guarded single entrance, was locked. We refused to return to class and at first gathered around the concrete water tank in the centre of the schoolyard. The deputy principals began to hit us, as usual, with their wooden "discipline" sticks. We moved like cattle, shifting from one side of the yard to the other to avoid the sticks. Finally our teacher arrived, pleading with us, telling us she would be in trouble if we didn't go back into the classroom. We felt sorry for her so we gathered in front of the door, but still refused to go inside. She was nervous, pacing up and down inside the tiny room, between our benches and desks, holding her roll book against her chest. Then the bell rang, announcing the end of the school day. The principal, hoping to avoid further confrontation, saw an early end of study as the solution to the escalating problem. However, it hasn't worked out as she planned. We evacuated the school premises, but instead of heading home we are now roaming around in search of stones.

We throw our stones at the moving cars, watching the terrified faces of those inside as they try to put the windows up to avoid being hit. The power of a tiny stone is much greater than it might appear. After only ten minutes, the road is dressed in broken glass and drivers are trapped in a traffic jam.

The unpaved roadside is hardened by the rain and too much traffic, but we discover a construction site around the corner. We take turns filling our school satchels and arms with large pieces of concrete and stones. Like an army, orderly and organized, students line up on both sides of the main road. We no longer throw the stones hastily; we take our time and aim. Shakela hits a man in the passenger seat of a military vehicle. He leans forward in pain, a stream of blood running down his face. We cheer Shakela. Dyana has left, worried her father will find out. But the rest of us are caught up in the pleasure of watching the strong officers, soldiers and government workers transformed into chickens, fearful of being hurt. Some even run from the cars, but we throw our stones anyway.

At first, a few shopkeepers stood by their doors watching. Now they have gone inside. I've lost track of time, carried away by the drama and enthusiasm of the day of protest. I'm not sure what we are protesting, but anything against the Soviet occupation and their puppet communist regime is a good cause.

A couple of girls from grade eight are shouting from a distance. I've seen them around but don't know their names. "Don't hit taxis, don't hit civilian cars—just the military." A taxi driver has been hit, and he has turned onto one of the side roads because he is bleeding. A man is running to the Tawifiq Pharmacy, where we are standing, to get a first-aid kit for the driver. Then someone calls, "Soviets, Soviets."

And there they are—three vehicles in a row. We wait for them eagerly with our stones. It feels good to see their white faces turning red from fear. A few more cars go by, and then a Soviet tank approaches, followed by two other cars. We aim again. This time Shakela hits a soldier who is standing in the back of one of the cars. We hear a gunshot. A Soviet soldier in the car behind is shooting into the air. Everyone is targeting him with stones. All of a sudden, he turns his rifle towards us and shoots. The sound of a bullet whizzing by is so unexpected that we all throw ourselves to the ground. The Tawifiq Pharmacy's large window bursts into shards.

By the time we get back on our feet, fear has replaced the joy of throwing stones. Shakela throws her stone to the side of the road and waves goodbye. I walk home fast. The street is covered with glass and stones.

In class, we talk about yesterday's adventure. Shakela says that a student and a shopkeeper were hurt in the shootout. We were too scared to look around at the time. The teacher arrives, accompanied by a deputy principal, who wants to know if anyone can identify yesterday's "troublemakers." "I saw most of you idiots myself," she says. "If I ever see any of you throwing stones again, you'll be in serious trouble."

Dyana didn't come to school today. She prefers to stay out of trouble, mainly because she's afraid of her father. He is a member of the Communist Party and a very harsh man. She hates him, and fears him too.

Because of yesterday's misbehaviour, we get a shorter break. Someone passes me a piece of paper, which says we should continue yesterday's protest by refusing to return to class. Excited at the idea, I pass the note on to Shakela and several other classmates. Our five-minute break is up, but we are not returning to class.

Instead of the deputy principals with their sticks, the principal shows up, in her forest-green uniform and uncombed dyed hair. She stands on the balcony in front of the grade eight classrooms. She says "bad elements" are trying to take advantage of our innocence. "These anti-government elements will be punished for their crimes—but if you fall into their trap, you'll also be punished." The more she shouts, the less interested we are in her words. Shakela whispers into my ear, "We are old enough to know. She's insulting us. I'm out here because of my brother, who's been imprisoned by her stupid government." Shakela is right. We are out here for reasons beyond our principal's comprehension. She is just a little puppet, like the rest of the high-ranking officials.

Her speech does little to encourage us or force us back to class. We stand and chat long after the principal has returned to her office. Three of us—Shakela, Noriya and I—plan to stay and write some slogans on the wall to show what we think of the government. Shakela is the tallest in the class. She has long skinny legs that look like sticks when she wears jeans. Noriya is shorter, friendly, and has a boy's haircut that suits her face. As soon as the bell rings at 5:30, the three of us go into the classroom. Shakela and I stand on the desks with colourful chalks while Noriya guards the door. "Death to Babrak Karmal," we write. "Death to the Soviet army." "Sultan Ali Kishtmand is a donkey." (Kishtmand is Karmal's deputy.) "Write 'Down with the Communist Party,'" whispers Noriya. Shakela is already on it. "Fight against Soviet invaders."

I cannot wait to return to school tomorrow. We plan to have more protests.

* * *

In the evening, Uncle Wahid comes in to help with my lessons. I tell him enthusiastically about the stone-throwing and slogan-writing. A university undergraduate, he tells me that students at Kabul University and most high schools are protesting the new conscription. Three months ago, in January 1984, the government announced that all men between eighteen and forty must join the army; then in February, it raised the conscription term from two to three years. It's a desperate attempt to make up for the soldiers who have been killed or who have deserted. With the start of the new school year in March, students have decided to object.

Now I understand why we are protesting. "Should we have written different slogans?" I ask. "No," he says fiercely. "You are too young to do these things." I regret telling him. Eleven years old is not young—not, at least, for a generation growing up under occupation. I tell Uncle Wahid that it is the grade eights who are organizing the protest—they are the seniors in our school, and we follow their lead.

On the third day of protest, we refuse to go to class and the principal calls in the police. A girl we all hate because she is a member of the communist youth group—we call her "Monkey"—arrives with a list of people who must go to the principal's office. Shakela and I are on the list. We sit in the principal's office, chewing our nails from both anxiety and boredom. The door opens and a squad of police officers with white hats, night sticks and long black military boots walk in. The principal, who hasn't even bothered speaking to us, greets them with a big ugly smile: "Here they are."

For the next hour, the officers call us individually into the document room, next to the principal's office. Two officers stand guard at the door. The rest have gone into the yard to force the students into the classroom. "Who told you to join the protest?" the officers ask. "Was it your father, someone at home or school? If you tell us, you're free to go." No one told me, I say. "So, you're not willing to co-operate." One of the officers gets up, calling the guard in. "Take her to the van."

There are two other people inside the van. Shakela has handcuffs on. "I tried to run," she says. Soon there are nine of us, sitting on blue glossy seats in the back of a van that looks like a container, with two small windows.

At the main police intelligence office, we are taken in for separate and more thorough questioning. At first, the man in civilian clothes is friendly and fatherly. Gradually, he gets annoyed. "What do your parents say when they see Mr. Karmal speaking on television?" Nothing. We listen to his speeches. I say my father knew Karmal when he was a student, and Kishtmand was my father's classmate in high school. "Why did you join the protest?" Silence. "Who is your leader?" Silence. "She's the leader herself," laughs the officer in the military clothes with a red star on his cap. Silence. They eventually lose patience, and the fatherly one turns nasty. He slaps me very hard, holding my hands back against the wooden bars of the chair where I have been instructed to sit. "Now you'll tell me," he yells. I won't tell you anything, I say to myself. He slaps me again. I lose my patience. "Hit me as hard as you want, kill me if you wish," I shout my heart out. He stands back. Without thinking, I reach for the collar of my school uniform, pulling it open. "Shoot me," I say, offering my chest, lifting my neck up—I've seen prisoners do this in the movies. They are taken aback. I feel stronger. "Shoot me, what are you waiting for?" Silence.

By the time we are sent back to school, everyone has gone home, including the principal. Shakela has been beaten too. We go by the water tank, wash our faces with cold water, curse at the principal and then walk home. The revolution inside me feels just as it did when I visited my father in the prison in Baghlan. I want to have the power to burn the school, destroy the police office and slap the principal just as I was slapped—three times on each cheek.

The next day, we are ordered to stand in straight lines in front of the school's main office. The principal speaks again, threatening us if we disobey her orders. A few students break away from the line. The pushing begins spontaneously. In the midst of the chaos, I reach for the principal's skirt and pull it down. As soon as she gets her balance back, she runs inside the building. I nearly made the principal fall over, I tell Dyana. I've got my revenge. Soon the same group of officers is back with their night sticks. Everyone is forced into the classroom; anyone who doesn't go in is handcuffed and dragged to the van.

In the late afternoon, the girl we call "Monkey" shows up at the classroom door. She's come for me. Our science teacher is a kind woman who, like us, abhors the government. Most of her family have already fled to the United States. "I can't let her go—we are in the middle of studies," she says.

"But the deputy principal wants to talk to her."

The science teacher picks up the book, asks me to stand up and read page forty. "She has to study—come back after class."

The girl leaves. The teacher tells me to sit back in my place and carries on with her lecture. The girl returns with a slip of paper, which she hands to the teacher. It is for me. I've been suspended from school for disobedience and rude behaviour towards the principal.

"What are you going to do?" asks Dyana.

For the first two days, I pretend that I'm going to school as usual. But my parents find out the truth. "What have you done?" asks my father. I tell him that I pulled down the principal's skirt. When he wants to know more, I hesitate, but then I remember his prison face and I tell him about the protest, the stone-throwing and the police station. He is furious. "Who asked you to do these silly things?" he screams in anger. "It's good that they suspended you from school to teach you a lesson. Now you'll have no education, no future."

His words hurt, more than the slaps of the officer. I feel betrayed by my own hero. You give me books to read, I manage to say to my father, fighting the impulse to cry. It's your fault. You wanted me to be like you, and now you blame me. You've no right. I burst into tears and walk out of the room.

Now I'm my father's nightmare, but more so my mother's; she says she thought she had only one rebel to deal with.

I'm back in school after a week. My father has made some phone calls, promising the principal that I'll not only apologize to her, but behave. I will do anything, I plead with my father, but please don't ask me to apologize to that woman. "Because of your future, I've had to talk to people I loathe, asking their forgiveness for you," says my father. "And you're telling me you won't even pretend to say you're sorry?"

I have spent a whole day of class moving between absolute fury and utter remorse before finally working up the courage to go to the administration. The principal is on the stairway. "I was expecting you," she says harshly. I walk up to her, stand on the step above her, equal to her height, and utter the single sentence in haste: "I'm sorry." She smiles with satisfaction. I walk down, defeated, destroyed. My only consolation, I tell

Dyana, is that I stood above her on the stairs—placing myself, at least physically, on a par with her.

I apologized to the principal, I inform my father, but I want to leave that school. "Transferring in the middle of grade seven is not a good idea," he says. "Maybe you can leave next school year."

I would have loved to go to Lycée Malalai. The school is named after a woman who became a national symbol of resistance. She is not featured in our history books, nor is there any information about her life in other school texts. She appears only in poems and speeches. But like many other girls my age, I know her name and that she sacrificed herself for our nation's independence.

The historic Afghan victory at Maiwand was a major British defeat. In his account of the battle, the Afghan historian Mir Gholam Mohammad Ghobar relates how on July 20, 1880, Ayoub Khan's army reached Maiwand, near Kandahar, to fight a British invading force that had camped out in the desert under the command of Brigadier-General G.R.S. Burrows.[10] In Ghobar's account, Ayoub Khan is the ultimate Afghan hero. Yet he appears to have had little interest in fighting the British occupation in the first place. In fact, he had even offered—or so it is said—to befriend the British government and be rewarded for it—not unlike the Afghan presidents who, a century later, give their allegiance to the Soviet Union rather than to their own people. The British authorities declined Ayoub Khan's offer. A week later, according to the official British account, a jihad was declared against the British troops. And on the hazy morning of July 27, 1880, the Afghan army fired its first shells. The British returned fire. "Afghan men were crumbling down on the flat ground, like leaves falling off a tree," says Ghobar.

An obscure sixty-year-old Pushtu-language book by Abdul Raouf Binava relates that in the hot desert, "the Afghan army was near defeat from exhaustion and thirst and the Afghan flag had fallen from the hand of its bearer who had been wounded. At this very moment, a young Afghan woman arrived and lifted the Pushtun national flag and shouted these lines:

> . . . Young love, if you don't fall in the battle of Maiwand,
> By God, someone is saving you as a token of shame.[11]

The girl was Malalai. A cloud of dust rose into the air from the galloping horses of Afghan fighters, says the British report. Amid artillery fire, abandoned horses, and a battlefield scattered with dead and wounded men, the British, says Ghobar, could no longer withstand the Afghan attacks. A chilling passage in the British account of the fighting includes the evidence of an infantry officer, Captain Mainwaring, who describes how "the *ghazis* [Afghans honoured for killing an "infidel"] were actually in the ranks of the [British] Grenadiers, pulling the men out and hacking them down with their swords."[12] By early afternoon, the British army's artillery fire was slackening, the confidence of its troops shaken and the number of dead and wounded rapidly increasing. The onslaught that followed reduced a mighty invading army into a humiliated squad of exhausted and wounded men. At the end of the day, only twenty-five Englishmen, dressed in Afghan clothes, managed to reach Kandahar. About 3,500 British soldiers and Afghans were killed in the Battle of Maiwand, including Malalai.

For her heroism, the resistance movement has come to regard her as a symbol of the traditional, honourable Afghan woman, who joined her brethren in battle against the infidels—the foreign enemy. But as the narrative of her existence and meaning changes from one group to another, the real Malalai turns into a ghost, a myth. These days, we are taught more about Joan of Arc than about Malalai. How strange that we in Afghanistan—in much of the Muslim world—know so little about our own heroes and heroines. In the West, they write painstakingly researched history books and analyses about their historical characters, but we indulge in myths and songs, rewriting our history, ignorant of the real lives of those who inspire us.

So little is known of Malalai that her exact age during the Battle of Maiwand is uncertain. Binava claims she was twelve; another source says she was seventeen. There are a few Afghan books that make brief mention of Malalai, but many don't. Dr. Siddiquallah Farhang's three-volume *Afghanistan in the Past Five Centuries*—one of the most distinguished works of Afghan history—doesn't make the slightest reference to her. Ghobar mentions a group of women who fought in the battle of Maiwand, stating that the story of Malalai started there. That's it. He leaves out the story of the veil. It is a Western writer, Louis Dupree, who says that "at the battle of Maiwand a legendary Pushtun heroine, Malalai, used her veil as a standard, and encouraged the warriors by shouting a couplet (*landay*) in Pashto [sic]." Binava claims, "as long as Pushtuns are alive and our country exists, her name will be written in gold in Pushtun history."

But where is the scholarly research that would turn Malalai into a real woman? As usual, the colonial power—the British—wrote the definitive account of this engagement, even though they were defeated. There is an intriguing sentence—a single, extraordinary line—in the British account of Maiwand. Buried way at the back of my copy of the old 734-page report, its red cover long ago stained by colonial tea and bleached by Indian suns, it says that among the *ghazis* of Maiwand there were "twelve women who were admitted as *ghazis* and were allowed to remove their 'purdahs' (veils) on condition that they followed the *ghazis* into action, and took water, etc, etc, to the wounded." In the British account, these women have no identity and little purpose save to nurse the wounded, "etc, etc." But in just one "etc" there is a wealth of meaning. Twelve Afghan women fought in a war against the British more than a hundred years ago—and we have heard of only one name, Malalai.

My mother, Jamila, who graduated from Lycée Malalai in 1965, knows very little about the school's namesake. But she has many gripping stories about her days at the school. Her school stories are of a different Afghanistan, one that reminds me of our early days in Baghlan. "Lycée Malalai was once one of the best schools in the country. Luxury cars lined up at the school entrance to take young, fashionable girls home. It was the chosen school of the elite, and the royalty."

When Jamila was growing up in the 1950s, the link between high society and Lycée Malalai elevated its profile. But it was its connection to France—a country praised by many Afghans for its so-called high culture—that raised the school's reputation. "We learned French as a second language, taught by French teachers. Madame Fouler spent hours teaching us how to pronounce the French *r* and how to distinguish the sounds of *o* and *e*. Madame Roland picked a group of graduates each year to go to France for higher education." Along with Afghan history, mathematics and science, students were taught how to bake a soufflé, cut and sew a décolleté dress, converse in French and discuss Baudelaire in Dari. French teachers or Afghans educated in France made sure that the next generation of Afghan women attending the school were accustomed to high European standards. But there was also discipline—with perhaps a touch of socio-religious morality. "We had to wear a uniform—black skirt and blouse and a white narrow scarf. No one was allowed to wear makeup or leave her hair loose if it was more than shoulder-length," says my mother. Failure to study or obey orders was punished with a verbal reminder, a written note or an occasional slap on the face. All this went well with the monarchy, which, of course, wanted a modern but totally obedient society. This was Lycée Malalai at the height of its glory.

I take pride in a photo of my mother's graduation—the black-and-white shot of a young Jamila receiving her high-school diploma. Dressed in her school uniform, she shakes the hand of Princess Mariam, the king's daughter. Both women are dressed in short skirts and collared blouses, with their hair carefully arranged in a neat pile over their heads; in other words, they are two "modern-looking" women marking an achievement—and a significant one, given that only one percent of Afghanistan's ten million women were given any education. Malalai might have been shocked at or might have disapproved of their appearance. These women have little in common with her.

It was only later that I discovered that Lycée Malalai was the first school for girls, established in 1921 by the Afghan reformer-king, Amanullah Khan. It was originally called

Esmat—a Dari word meaning "chastity"—then changed to Malalai. For the king and his successors, Lycée Malalai marked the victory of modernity over a traditional and conservative society—which is strange since Malalai herself represents the traditional loyalties of rural Afghanistan. And for my generation, for my friends and me, Malalai has come to mean resistance to foreign occupation. The very name "Malalai"—a Pushtu word meaning "beautiful"—has captured our imagination.

No one—except my dear friend Dyana—knows that I secretly carry a black scarf with me. I carry it to protect me, to bring me luck. It comes from the grave of a *shaheed* (martyr), which is now a holy place. Mother Fatema has been going there to pray that she will find her lost daughter—her name, too, is Fatema who has been missing for almost a decade now. I've heard the story of her disappearance several times. "Fatema would've been fourteen that month," her mother says. "You were in Baghlan at the time. We woke up one morning to discover that both my sister, who was staying with us, and Fatema were not in their beds. After an hour of searching, we realized that they had run away. I don't know why." The family searched everywhere. "Her father even went to Sare-pol in Bamiyan—our village of origin—but couldn't find them." As the years went by, they gave up the search, but Mother Fatema has never given up hope. "I know God will help bring her home to me, safe and sound."

I don't have Mother Fatema's deep religious conviction; I don't even know how to pray. But I still went to see this grave, for the word *"shaheed,"* and the mystery surrounding this martyr, interested me. As we walked past neighbours' houses and along a row of oak trees, Mother Fatema told me the story. A man in the neighbourhood, on his way home one evening, noticed a lantern in the distance. He assumed it was someone in the field. But on repeated evenings, he saw the same light. When he walked towards it, the light disappeared. Struck by fear, he called upon his neighbours to help him solve the mystery. Several of them took turns on subsequent nights watching the light. Some suggested it marked hidden treasure; others argued it was a holy site. A few skeptics said it could be government secret agents.

Finally, a group of men and women decided to find out the truth, and set out, carrying lanterns and candles. Minutes before the curfew, which begins at 10:00 P.M., they discovered a grave at the spot where they had seen the light. By morning, someone was saying that a martyr had been buried there—a victim of the 1980 Allahu Akbar nights of anti-Soviet protests. The word spread that after four years a martyr had been found, and the lone grave—lying at the foot of a thin birch tree—has become a shrine that locals visit to offer prayers. Every day now, women flock to the site, carrying candles, sweets and dishes of rose petals. Others take scarves to wrap around the tree or nails and thread to affix to it. There are so many people with unfulfilled wishes. The martyr has no name—he is simply called the *shaheed.*

When Mother Fatema and I arrived, a group of women had encircled the grave. I imitated Mother Fatema in her ritual. Following her steps, I was touching the tree in a ceremonial manner when a knot opened in a piece of material tied there and a scarf fell into my hand. Mother Fatema, wiping away a tear, smiled in approval. "Keep the scarf," she said. The opening of a knot is seen as a good sign. "It means that any wish you have will come true," she said.

All the way home, I was troubled. What if I failed to make the right wish? It was as if I suddenly had a genie-in-waiting to command, but didn't know what to ask for. I even felt guilty. I didn't pray at the grave, I told Mother Fatema. "What's in your heart is what counts," she said.

The black scarf grows more valuable as I think about its power and its resemblance to the scarf of Malalai—this martyr's gift becomes even more precious. Perhaps it can bring me Malalai's courage. A seed of anger, planted at the time of my father's imprisonment, is inside me. Touching the black scarf, and thinking about Malalai, stirs this anger even more.

—

I AM NOW IN HIGH SCHOOL—where I will attend grades nine to twelve. These days, we are often ordered to line up in pairs in front of our classrooms. Like unarmed soldiers mistrusted by those who require our services, we are bused or marched to a political rally where we are supposed to show our support for a government that we hate. The teachers, deputy principals and members of the communist youth group watch us like hawks.

The first time we were taken to a rally, we were happy to leave the classroom for a stroll around the city. We thought being in high school would award us certain freedoms. At the rally, when we were told to chant a slogan, we shouted the opposite. "Long live the Communist Party" became "Short life to the Communist Party." When told to cry "Down with America," we screamed, "Down with Russia." It was fun until we were reported to the school authorities. We were told that being in high school meant we were adults, that our actions would not easily be forgiven, that we would be punished and there would be consequences for our families.

Supposedly, we live in a free society. We are told we are free as long as we obey orders. Now we don't want to attend these staged rallies any more. Instead, we discuss escape routes. It's become a cat-and-mouse game—except we don't know who's the cat and who's the mouse. When we saw buses arriving inside the schoolyard, we hid inside the bathroom until the buses left. Now a teacher waits for the last person to leave the bathroom to make sure no one is left behind. We escaped through the windows to hide behind the trees. Now several teachers search the schoolyard to find the deserters. Once, a few of our classmates managed to climb up the school's back wall and jump down to the street. Nadiya broke her leg; another student twisted her ankle. We stayed home on days that were marked in the calendar as "important" dates, the anniversaries of the Saur Revolution, Lenin's birthday, Babrak Karmal's arrival in Kabul and many more. At first we could simply present a note from our parents saying we were sick. But the school became suspicious, and it no longer accepts sick-leave notes.

On the "important, historic-event days," as our principal calls them, we are forced to abandon our studies and join a march or go to the school conference room to listen to speeches in unutterable boredom, or watch films about Soviet industry. My mother's generation went a long way in educating themselves; now some families stop their daughters from attending school. They say their daughters no longer receive a proper education. My mother complains that the quality of education has been badly compromised by these marches. "If members of the communist youth group cannot read or write, we still have to give them good marks," she says. "The hard-working students who deserve a good grade are downgraded or fail because they don't support the government." Boys are not learning more than we are, but they want to stay in school as long as possible—they are safe from the military draft only while they are still at school.

Amanullah Khan may have had a dream about Afghan women's education when he established a school for girls, but girls' schools are now little more than showcases for the communist government, which has adopted heroines such as Malalai as national symbols of Afghan progress, but has done little to help the women. "Progress" and "progressive elements" are the clichés of the day, and Malalai fits nicely into this paradigm. In the speeches of government officials, Malalai is now the ideal Afghan feminist who broke away from traditional culture to become an example of a "free Afghan woman." She is being resurrected to serve as an icon of a struggling, underclass woman who marched on the path of liberation by discarding her veil and sacrificing her life in a battle not just against tradition, but against Western imperialism. For us, this interpretation of Malalai is a grotesque distortion, a betrayal. There is no difference between those who came to claim her hometown of Maiwand—the British—and those who march on my roads, the Soviets.

After school, Dyana and I go for walks. We buy cookies from our favourite shop. They are freshly baked and crumble in our hands. We hear so many sad stories—in school, at home, even at wedding parties—that we search for something different. Poetry reading is our escape. She chooses the poems; I read them aloud. They are often love poems, with some in praise of nature. It's not just the hardship and sadness of life we want to forget; we need to break away from our feeling of helplessness.

* * *

In the Afghan political drama, another curtain falls—this time bringing Karmal down at the hands of those who installed him six years ago. In May 1986, the news reports say Karmal has gone abroad for medical treatment. On the streets of Kabul, more Soviet tanks and soldiers move in, stopping the few Karmal supporters who wish to protest his sudden departure. Dr. Mohammad Najibullah, the former head of KhAD, is picked to champion the new Soviet policy in Afghanistan. He is trusted to win the support of the people—including the opposition. The cost of war has become unbearable for Moscow. We receive the news with indifference. "They are all the same," says Uncle Wahid. "The heads change, but the ruling body remains the same."

It is a hot June day and the last three classes of the day have been cancelled; all students in grades nine through twelve are hauled into the conference room. "Another film about Lenin's life?" asks one girl from the back of the line. "God help us!" replies someone else. As soon as we see the deputy principal, everyone is quiet. We walk into the conference room, which has been cleaned and sprinkled with fresh water to cool the air. The stage is dark, with two school desks and a few chairs, a podium and a microphone. "Oh God!" says Dyana, appalled. "More speeches." She rolls her eyes with boredom. I'll ask a question, I tell her. "Why bother?" she asks. "One of these days, you'll get yourself in trouble." I know Dyana is fearful for me when I do things like that. She is too kind to say so, but I'm sure she thinks I'm stupid. I loathe the cronies who run our school, our principal, the deputy, several teachers and some students—"bubble gums" we call them, because they stick to people with power.

The principal is away on a trip to Moscow, someone says. The bushy-haired old deputy principal climbs up to the stage with her high-heeled shoes: click, click, click. Someone keeps pace by clucking her tongue. The deputy turns with venom and stares at us from behind her thick spectacles. There is silence. The door of the conference room opens. Following the head of the youth communist group are two unarmed soldiers and a couple of suspicious-looking Afghan guards in civilian clothes. As the soldiers pass, our heads turn to follow every step of their military boots. One of the soldiers is so good-looking we can't take our eyes off him.

As the guests take their seats on stage, the deputy welcomes them. "Today," she shouts into the microphone, "we are lucky to have two friends from the Red Army, who have come to talk to us about their experiences in Afghanistan." With the words "Red Army," an alarm bell rings in my head; an automatic correcting machine comes into operation. "Not 'friends,' 'enemies,'" I whisper to Dyana. "Hush," she says.

The first soldier is introduced. Standing behind the podium, he starts by saying "*Salam*" (peace), the Afghan greeting. With the help of a translator, he talks about his mission in Afghanistan. He is not bad-looking: clean-shaven, in a well-pressed military uniform.

The deputy introduces the second soldier, and there is absolute silence—every girl sinks into the uncomfortable wooden seats, dreaming of something impossible. He is called Misha, says the deputy principal. He's been in Afghanistan for six months, and is here today to tell us about life in the army. We all drool, our mouths half-open, our eyes fixed on the soldier. In the thirteen years of my life, I've never felt my heart beat as fast or as loud.

Misha is not only handsome, he is charismatic. He wears

a mischievous smile, and exudes self-confidence, charm and warmth—a devastating combination in an awfully attractive young man. We are not listening to him; we are all just watching him. The deputy principal asks if we have any questions. Obviously, everyone has a question for Misha. How long have you been in Kabul? What do you think of our climate? How long will you be staying in Afghanistan? How long have you been a soldier? He is Russian, and not any ordinary Russian but a soldier with the Red Army. We should have asked how many innocent people he's killed so far. What the hell are they—he and the Red Army—doing in our land? Do they know how much we hate them? But who has the guts to think these thoughts, let alone raise them?

Minutes before the bell rings, Misha and his company depart. Two teachers stand by the door to make sure no one leaves the conference room until the bell announces the end of the school day.

I'm glad I resisted talking to Misha or asking him a stupid question. It's good, after all, to walk away with some integrity. "Even if you lost your heart," Dyana teases me. "So what do you do when you find yourself attracted to an enemy? Do you betray your country and people or your own emotions?" I have already decided, I tell her. The enemy is the enemy. No compromise.

Throughout the mid-term exams, we rave about Misha while cursing his country. It's a relief to know I'm not the only one with a love-hate dilemma. Farhatnaz, who has one missing brother and two already killed in the war, has an even harder time justifying her interest in Misha. "It's shameful for me to find him attractive," she says. "I can never forgive myself for such a thought." Forgiven or not, we know she has fallen for him, even though she's trying to convince us otherwise.

"I'm sure the mujahidin are heartthrobs, even better than Misha, because they are Afghan and they are Muslim, and they are resisting the occupation."

Noriya, quite taken with the soldier herself, admits that if the Soviets hadn't bombed her family village in Logar, killing the cattle as well as the people, she could have pardoned this one good-looking man.

The tragedy is that before we could see a human face, we were shown jets, helicopters, tanks and machine guns. Instead of genuine smiles, we were given fear, death and destruction.

6

Scud versus stinger

Don't ask where our garden is, what happened to our nest
Don't ask where the musicians are, what happened to
    the chants
Don't ask why our loved ones have left
Don't ask what has become of our nightly songs
Don't ask about the caravan of travellers
Don't ask where the morning birds have gone
Now it's the kingdom of crows.

Qahar Ausi, 1989

"Ashura marks not the end, but a beginning," says Ali Shariati, one of the founding fathers of the Iranian Islamic Revolution. Ashura is the tenth day of the Arabic month of Muharram—the day that Imam Hussein became a martyr. Sitting in our living room, gathered around the tape recorder from which Shariati's call for vigilance echoes, we listen attentively. Shariati argues that Hussein's death is the beginning of a struggle for his followers. So instead of just mourning his death, Shias should follow his example and resist injustice. "The battle is not over," he screams. "It's just started. But are you, my brother, my sister, my mother, are you ready for it?" he asks. These words move us to tears. Even my father and Uncle Wahid sob involuntarily.

I cannot begin to imagine the extent of Shariati's influence on Iranians when he was delivering his sermons. An Iranian sociologist, Shariati is dead, but the power of his voice and argument lives on. Just days before the Islamic Revolution in Iran, an anonymous killer poisoned Shariati in his hotel room in Paris, near the Sorbonne University. But he has re-emerged as a symbol of religious awakening in Afghanistan. Shias and Sunnis alike circulate in secret his books and tapes, smuggled in from Iran. Throughout Muharram, Uncle Wahid brings us various audiotapes of religious sermons, but Shariati remains a favourite. For about two weeks during Muharram, in place of music, we listen to Quranic recitations. We don't buy new clothes or attend wedding parties; instead, we wear black, and on Ashura we prepare a special meal of sweet rice and distribute it to relatives and neighbours. The observations surrounding Muharram are part of Shia history, but my father says that, in occupied Afghanistan, remembering the seventh-century massacre is becoming more relevant. "It's the times we live in that make this tragic event in history more poignant." It certainly has become significant for my family over the past five years. I don't recall honouring Muharram in such an elaborate way before. Everywhere in the city, more than ever, Ashura is celebrated by both Shias and Sunnis.

However, this year—1986—for the first time since the communist coup, the government of Dr. Najibullah has introduced a new policy of religious freedom. Everyone is suspicious of such announcements, but our neighbours have decided to take advantage. They have transformed the small mosque across from our house into a *takyee khona* for Muharram ceremonies. The white walls are covered with black fabric, and the inside is decorated with religious poetry written on green strips. A group of boys, my brother among them, are organized to wear black clothes and green headbands with the word "Allah" on them. In the afternoon, they play a Quranic recitation tape, which is broadcast over the loudspeaker from the mosque's roof. Then there are the communal prayers, which my father has been going to with my brother. In the evening, they are going on a bus to join other *takyee*s.

My mother never goes to *takyee*s. But Mother Fatema does. I walk with her to the Takyee Husseinya, one of the largest in our district. Flocks of women, most dressed in black, make their way to the upper balcony. The man who's giving the sermon takes his seat at the centre. He speaks for at least forty minutes, with a passion that makes men and women cry. It's here that I begin to understand the meaning and power of the *takyee*s. A single man, humbly dressed in a brown abaya—an Arab-style coat—talking about an event in distant history, can move a large crowd to tears. The words of this man are more influential than any drug.

On the day of Ashura, Dr. Najibullah wakes up to realize the power of religion. If the forces of discontent are let loose, they will overthrow his government. Kabul is a bomb, ready to explode. Never before have the Kabulis been so publicly religious. Muharram has become an expression of popular fury with the communist government and its rhetoric and harsh policies. My brother, Hassib, returns home disappointed. Their buses were stopped on the main roads and ordered to go back immediately to their local mosques. Religious interaction, it seems, has been stopped before it can transform itself into rioting. "The government got scared of our power and organization," says my brother.

At age eleven, Hassib has already learned how to recite the Quran from memory and debate religious matters. My father has never learned to recite the Quran like that. But this is a different time, a different generation. Traditionally, young boys were sent to mosques to learn a few verses of the Holy Book, some lines of poetry, and to read classical works of literature like Hafiz and Sa'adi. My father's generation grew up with a modern education. Now that the country is occupied by the Soviets and our religion and culture are in danger, families insist on sending their children to mosques during the winter holidays. Both my brother and my sister, Mejgan, who is eight years old, along with Mother Fatema's two sons, have been learning recitation of the Quran in the mosque near our home. The new educational system is based on the Soviet model and doesn't include religious studies. My sister is studying under the new system; she's also studying the Russian language, something the old generation—as we are called—rebelled against. For us, they've introduced a new subject called "politics" as part of the Russianization of our studies. "Politics" is Marxist-Leninist ideology. The tall woman who teaches politics earned a degree in Moscow. Her husband is the head of a local communist committee. A military Jeep brings her to school. She has no smile or time for questions, just gives notes and expects everyone to understand. Memorizing *The Communist Manifesto*—the "Communist A, B, C," as it is called—is torture. But if we don't know it, we'll automatically fail politics. Some students, even the smart ones, are trying to find ways to cheat.

Dr. Najibullah now claims he'll change everything for the good. All his predecessors said the same thing. His long televised speeches start with the phrase "in the name of God" and refer to Afghanistan as a "Muslim nation"; he's announced that there will be funding for new mosques. Even the word "Democratic" is dropped from the name "Democratic Republic of Afghanistan"—not that it ever meant anything. But it's all just a show—in my father's words, another act of the same play. Najibullah assumes that by adopting a religious outlook, he'll be exonerated from all the crimes he and his party have committed. As the head of the KhAD under Karmal, he was responsible for the torture, imprisonment and murder of thousands of innocent Afghans.

Najibullah should heed the words of Abu-Muslim Khorasoni. Abu-Muslim was an influential and popular resistance leader in eighth-century Arabia. His last words before he was executed were addressed to the man who'd decreed his death, Abu-Mansour, the Abassid caliph. "You—father of all sinners! Remember that the people won't forget." Najibullah hopes that people have forgotten, but knows he is not safe. Brezhnev is dead, as are the two who succeeded him, Yuri Andropov and Konstantin Chernenko. Some say Najibullah was chosen by the Kremlin to replace Karmal, but Najibullah fears—given the changes in the Soviet Communist Party under the leadership of Mikhail Gorbachev—he may not have the same support from Moscow. "At the end of the day," says Uncle Wahid, "Najibullah's going to have to negotiate with Afghans." As part of this negotiation, in December 1986, just six months after becoming president, he has issued a National Reconciliation offer to the mujahidin: if they give up their guns, they'll be pardoned by the government and can join the Afghan army. "Some bandits and road robbers have accepted this offer," Uncle Wahid says. "They turn their old, rusted guns in to the government in return for a military uniform and a new Kalashnikov. Then, in the name of defending their district on the government's behalf, they continue their crimes more efficiently. The true mujahidin will never compromise."

Najibullah's offer of pardon has done little to end the war; it has, in fact, brought it even closer than before. It is now mid-May of 1987, a year since his takeover, and we've got a new phenomenon: nightly rocket fire. A couple of weeks ago, I woke up to the sound of a rocket so close it felt as if it was right over my head. I sprang from my bed and ran to the hallway. It was eleven at night. I looked at the clock as soon as my father—rushing from his room at the sound of my screams—reached the hallway with a light. The boom of the detonation had all the Paziras staring at each other in the hallway. At the second roar of sound, my father walked onto the balcony.

There was nothing to see. The sky was clear. The stars shone brightly and there was a quarter moon, its reflection captured in the water of our pond. Not even a murmur of wind or the croaking of a frog could be heard. It was as if the rockets were a dream. But the next evening the rockets came again at the same time. Now we know that the mujahidin are telling us the communist government can't protect us. More deaths may prove this political point. We used to see these rockets on our television screen, the government loudly boasting that they had captured them in an arms raid. The camera zooming in on a coding—marks, numbers and letters—on the weapon, the reporter telling us that these rockets were made in China and the United States. "The United States has given the mujahidin a new rocket called a Stinger," says Uncle Wahid.

In school, we can tell the kind of rocket from its sound. We know the short-range variety because they make a soft, squeaky noise. The common one that can be launched from the shoulder is called an Oawan. There is the regular long-range missile, its roar longer and louder. And then there are the Stingers. They are the surface-to-air missiles that are aimed at the airport, not too far from our home. We hear them go by—a terrifying sound, their volume and tone changing from a low pitch to the sound of an electric saw as it grows closer. But they never hit the target, at least not in Kabul. There are rumours about their effectiveness in other parts of Afghanistan, where Stingers are credited with shooting down a hundred Soviet aircraft in just two months. People say that Stingers will eventually destroy the government in Kabul.

The head of our Muslim youth group says the Stingers have destroyed three Soviet MiG-24 helicopter gunships at the Jalalabad Airport. I have recently joined this underground organization, which is countering the activities of the communist youth group. The mujahidin have always been my heroes; it is exciting to be so closely associated with the resistance now. It all happened like magic. I was spending time in the public library in early summer when one day an elderly bespectacled man with uncombed white hair, looking more like a mad scientist than a librarian, handed me a slim book with a pale blue cover: *Neyobat* (Prayers) *in Dari,* by Ali

Shariati. I was fascinated. I liked the book, I told the librarian. The next day, we started to talk about geography, the cosmos and the distance between moon and earth. I was impressed with his knowledge. Then he asked if I knew much about art, painting and drawing. "You see that flower?" He pointed at a painting. "You may think that rose is pink. But it's not. There are many shades in that one colour. Would you like to know more about shades and colours? If you come around two P.M. the day after tomorrow, you can meet many students in my studio. They are like you, young, interested, concerned. They discuss art; you can meet them."

His studio, of course, is a meeting place for the resistance movement. The members come in with portfolios and brushes. The basement room is lit by a single lamp and two candles. In one corner is a large unfinished painting of the Kabul sky above the Balahissar—a centuries-old fortress on a hilltop from which the entire city can be seen. It was the base for British troops in the last century, and now the Soviets occupy it. Perhaps the Soviets don't know that the Balahissar was also the site of a British defeat.

That first day, I looked at the painting for a while. No introductions were made. Those who came in sat down on boxes, on piles of blankets, on old chairs. They talked about how many copies of books had been distributed in the city. Books and tapes were exchanged. The librarian made notes. I'd never seen so many of Shariati's books in one place before. There was information about the mujahidin's success in battle, and a stack of leaflets about the importance of resistance. The librarian asked if I would be interested in sharing Shariati's books with someone else. I said I would; it was my entry into the organization.

* * *

I distribute books, but am not allowed to say where I get them. Shariati's books are regarded as more dangerous than guns. In the meetings, everyone says that if government agents find you with a gun, they'll take you to prison—if they discover you have a copy of Shariati's book, you'll be executed immediately.

I also have a gun. But the gun is not for distribution—it is for self-protection. It took me six months to study guerrilla methods and to learn how to use a gun. I'm worried my parents will find out about the gun, so on a damp spring morning I dig a hole in the mint garden where our baby wolf used to sleep and hide the gun there.

I've been thinking about telling Dyana. Although I have no doubt that she'll approve of what I'm doing, I'm still cautious. I've alluded a few times to Shariati's books, but she hasn't shown much interest. One afternoon during the exams, when she came over to study for history, I showed her a large volume—a catalogue of pictures and names of young martyrs. The book was produced by the Harakat Islamic Party in memory of those who had sacrificed their lives resisting the Soviet occupation. Dyana pitied the young martyrs, turning the pages rapidly, as if in fear. She never asked how and why I had the book. She probably suspects something, but doesn't want to know more. Perhaps it is safer that way.

Najibullah admits that about eighty percent of the countryside and forty percent of Afghan cities are outside the government's control. But he doesn't talk about the "military circle" that's been built around Kabul. In the basement, one of the resistance members says that her cousin is in the military and has brought new information about the infrastructure of a three-layered security belt that's been constructed with the help of Soviet engineers. It's a combination of landmines, heavy artillery and special guards. It's supposed to protect the capital from any outside attack. "They don't want to lose the capital," says the librarian with a cunning smile. "But those who are afraid of losing have already lost." He takes a philosophical approach to everything, including the resistance.

The winter of 1988 is one of the coldest in years. There's a heavy snowfall, and people are dying from hunger and frost. The majority have little to eat and nothing to heat their homes. People wait for hours in below-zero temperatures to buy gas, wood, oil, flour, bread and sugar. Many have frozen to death while waiting in line, mostly elderly men, women and children. By now, most of the electricity poles have been destroyed in the course of the fighting. For a while, generators, public and private, provided some power, but the war is now depriving the city of fuel to run them. Our homes have become cold and dark; to go anywhere, we have to walk for kilometres on icy pavements.

Forces loyal to Ahmad Shah Masoud, one of the mujahidin commanders, have blocked the Salang Pass, the main highway to the Soviet border. All convoys carrying food and supplies are stopped, robbed or destroyed before they reach Kabul. There is heavy fighting outside the city, we hear, and the government is running out of men, supplies and time. Kabul is on the brink of starvation. It is not a question of poverty. Even people with money cannot buy the most basic necessities—not even on the black market.

My father's relative Sikander lives in the countryside. He used to visit us several times a year with food from his farm. In summer he would arrive with fresh berries and grapes, and just before the coming of the first snow in Kabul he would bring baskets of dried fruit. But for several years now he has arrived only with stories of the mujahidin victories and the difficulties of surviving a war. No longer able to collect the fruit from his farm, he has become a carpenter and handyman. He's always concerned about getting home before dark. If he is delayed in Kabul, he spends the night at our home.

In the midst of winter, Sikander arrives to tell us that long convoys are stacked one behind the other on the highway near his hometown of Shamoli. The Shamoli plain is about an hour and a half's drive north of Kabul. For years now, the mujahidin have controlled this prosperous countryside by night while government forces held it by day. It was an absurd situation, coping with two opposing armies at the same time. One of his sons joined a mujahidin unit; the other became a soldier in the army. Sikander shrugs his shoulders, saying one has to survive. But now the government is losing its grip, and his hometown is becoming mujahidin country. "The mujahidin told us we could take anything we wanted from that convoy," says Sikander. "But they said we couldn't take anything to Kabul." He says there are trucks on the road with food rotting inside, with flour, milk and rice running over the ground in streams. There are lots of fridges lying beside the trucks, he says. The food is all gone or damaged, but the fridges are still there. Who needs a fridge at a time when there is no electricity and the land is frozen?

For years, the government provided subsidies. Fresh meat, packaged chicken, canned goods, eggs, cereals, flour, oil, clothing and accessories, household appliances and other supplies, medicine and even cars came from the Soviet Union and the Eastern bloc countries. Suddenly it has all stopped— there are no more eggs, frozen meat, bottled oil or sugar in the government-run collectives or even in the free markets. Government employees have a monthly ration coupon. They wait in line for food, but now there is nothing to buy with the coupons. Once the coupons were so scarce they were sold on the black market for twice their price. Now the tiny blue square papers, with numbers and dates marked in dark black ink, pile up as each month goes by. At first, there were a few less kilograms of flour, no sugar and only half a bottle of oil instead of a full one. Then there was oil only once a month, no sugar or soap the next, and little flour. Now there are longer lineups, and people are told the warehouses are empty. And if anything does arrive, the distribution point turns into a mini war zone. There is talk that the Soviet army is withdrawing from Afghanistan, but it's hard to believe that this mighty army will ever leave our tiny country alone. "The Soviets have brought SCUD missiles to counter the American Stingers," says Uncle Wahid. "No way will they leave now."

It's a sad spring sunset. I have just returned from Radio Afghanistan, where twice a week I read poetry for a couple of programs and host a youth show. Last week Qahar Ausi, a poet I know, showed me an unbound copy of his first book. "I've managed to get this only copy out today," he said. I sat and read a few poems from the cheap-paper pages. One of them mentions a martyr's grave where poppies grow:

> Someone is singing from the bed of red flowers,
> A lover recounting his past passion.
> What has happened, friends?
> The solitude of this house of flowers has been shattered,
> A broken wing is mourning its lost feathers and its flight
>   through the universe.

I'd never seen Ausi so happy; at last his book had been published. "I'm going to take this to my mother tonight," he said, holding the loose pages with both hands. "Next week, exactly at this time, I'll present you with a signed copy." He smiled involuntarily. When I saw him at the radio station today, the battered look in his eyes said it all. The government banned his book as it was being printed. More resolute than ever, he says he's not going to give up. Ausi's poems are about resistance, about love, about bravery; they cast shame upon hypocrisy and lies. That's why the communist government doesn't want the book published. The popular Afghan singer Farhad Darya, his close friend, turns Ausi's poems into songs, which often end up banned as well.

As I sit by the pond at home, Ausi's description of the sunset as the "blooded skirt of sky" comes to mind. I look over and see a man with a long Iranian-style *abuyee* over his shoulders, a well-trimmed beard that has a few threads of silver, spectacles and a *tasbeha* (prayer beads) in his right hand, walking into our home behind my father. I don't recognize him. "I'm your uncle, you fool!" he says with a smile. It's only his voice that I recognize—it is still the same tune. My father, too, has a big smile as he announces that his brother has returned from Iran for a visit.

It's been more than seven years since we last saw Uncle Asad—since the day of his row with my father. My father said several times that he still felt hurt about his brother's choice of the Communist Party, that Asad had betrayed the entire family by supporting a government my father considered oppressive and corrupt. Now, it seems, time has changed their attitude towards each other.

"Do you always dress like this?" asks Uncle Asad, after examining me from head to toe. I'm wearing a red dress that falls just below my knees, with full sleeves. I don't understand why he's asking such a ridiculous question. "*Istaghfour-Allah*

Nelofer in Kabul, weeks before fleeing Afghanistan, spring of 1989.

[God forgive us]," he says, putting his head down. "You should know that it's not *mohram* [lawful] even for your father to see your bare legs, your hair; it is all *haram* [forbidden] in Islam." Instantly angry, I feel like saying that the red colour of my dress should please him, given his communist days. But my mother calls me into the hallway. "Don't say a word," she says. I tell my mother he has no right to insult me like this. "He is your uncle; he is older than you. You don't have to agree with him. Just tolerate him for now. He'll be leaving soon."

I decide not to return to the living room, where my transformed uncle is having tea with my father. I remember vividly his last cup of tea here, and his half-eaten biscuit. His loud voice carries into the hallway, much as it did that other day. But another extreme has replaced his earlier communist fever. Now he is full of praise for the Iranian ayatollahs and the Islamic government. He brags about his four sons and four daughters, who are learning the Quran, suggesting to my father that he should advise me on matters of Islamic law and codes of behaviour. His family is in Tehran, and he himself is in Kabul for a short visit only, he says to my mother. Taking advantage of Najibullah's National Reconciliation policy, Uncle Asad has come to sell his house and leave for good, he says. My father prefers this version of his brother to the earlier communist one.

A few days later, at the wedding ceremony of my mother's cousin, Uncle Asad sits like an executioner on Judgment Day, eyebrows raised, hands crossed, watching and complaining. He obviously doesn't approve even of my long dress. My head is not covered. Men and women are sitting together. There is a live band playing love songs. "It's provocative," he says. "Everything, everything. You'll burn in hellfire."

The wedding is being held in a hotel called 555. These days people are frightened to attend weddings in hotels. Bombs go off in crowded places, inside buses, in schools and hotels. There is no security. Despite it all, we try to enjoy the party. But Uncle Asad, the doomsday messenger, wants to crucify us for laughing, for listening to music and for living. "You're not going to dance," he asserts authoritatively. I will do whatever I want, I tell him. He watches me with angry eyes, asking my father to discipline me. My father, who's embarrassed by his brother's comments, says he prefers not to interfere in my personal matters. I don't care so much about dancing, but I'm hoping my attitude appalls Uncle Asad, who accuses my father of being weak. "God will punish you," he says. There is no argument between the brothers this time, but by the end of the party, Uncle Asad has been told to stay out of our lives.

*　*　*

One afternoon in early May 1989, I am following my father and the gardener as they walk around the yard. Pleased with his grafting of two coloured roses, the gardener is proposing to do the same with the two eglantine bushes that go over the wall. One is pink, the other silky white. As the conversation about roses and grafting is going on, someone enters the house. We look towards the door. A young boy dressed in a military outfit, holding a school bag, is in the yard. It takes us a few seconds to recognize my brother. My father seems shocked by the sight of his son in military clothes. By the time Hassib walks into the hallway, my mother is in tears. "What is going on?" My brother has a big smile on his face; he tries to calm my mother. "This is from school," he says. "We have military training now."

My father is pacing the hallway. All talk of gardening and roses is forgotten. Hassib shrugs his shoulders and goes to the living room, saying that the military training is a temporary thing. Those who were drafted into the army used to receive three to six months of training before being sent into battle. They needed the training to learn how to load and operate a gun and follow orders. Now, however, the government is so desperate for soldiers that it has introduced a military training program for boys in grades ten to twelve while they are still pre–conscription age. It means that all boys will be ready to go to the front line as soon as they are drafted into the army. It is part of the government's emergency program to fight an enemy that is gaining territory day by day. So, for a period of several weeks, my brother and the rest of his classmates will live and behave like soldiers, receiving military training instead of going to regular classes. While they have not been given guns to carry, they are supposed to learn how to use them.

Two nights later, Habibullah raises the subject he has been avoiding for years—fleeing the country. "I've been talking to some friends and contacts in the army about Hassib," he says in a sombre voice. One of his old friends, now a high-ranking military officer, has offered to take my brother as his personal security guard. But there are no guarantees that he'll be safe. "I don't want my son to be corrupted by the poisonous power of the military."

I didn't know until now how much my father hates the military. As a young man, he spent a year in the army himself, arguing with his officers, refusing to follow orders. "Being in the army is being stupid," says Habibullah. "Once in the military, you've got to follow orders; you cannot speak your mind, criticize or protest. I refused to serve as a mindless being under the orders of impotent commanders in peacetime. If Hassib is my son, he will follow in my footsteps." And that is the conclusion. My father still wants to stay and serve his people—his patients, those who need him most. But he has agreed to let my brother leave the country. It is a major breakthrough for my mother.

Uncle Wahid is also preparing to leave the country. In his late twenties, Wahid is among the last of what are called the American-style trained engineers. He graduated from Kabul University in the mid-1980s, and then like all young men he was obliged—even before he could get work—to serve in the army. After two years of what he described as "daily fighting death," he was released from his duties as a foot soldier. Not long ago he got married, anticipating a normal life. Now he is required to return to the front line because of the government's "national emergency."

Uncle Wahid, like the rest of us, lives each day in the hope that tomorrow will be better, even if prospects don't seem encouraging at all. Uncle Wahid is like an older brother to us: he supervises our studies, shares some of our hobbies, plays chess with us and reads us poetry. But these days he appears distracted and melancholy. He and his wife, Samera, who is three months pregnant, are being forced to say good-bye to everyone and everything dear for what he calls an "unseen future."

Samera was a third-year university student, but she has quit school so she can help Wahid hide from the conscription searches. The government cannot afford to search the entire city at once to capture all the deserting soldiers, or the men who are trying to avoid military service. On different days, different districts are targets. Depending on which area is being inspected, Samera slips back and forth between her family, my grandmother and us, finding a suitable hideout for Wahid. Most women now have this same preoccupation, hiding their sons, brothers and husbands. Samera often arrives in the area

Nelofer and Samera on the Kabul University campus.

first to make sure it's safe, then Uncle Wahid shows up shortly afterwards.

Several days ago, Wahid was hiding in our home. Mother Fatema's younger son, Joma, returned from school saying there were lots of soldiers on the street, searching houses. It was too late for Wahid to leave, so we began looking for a spot to hide him. Underneath the bed, in the basement, inside the closet, behind the curtains, in a kitchen cabinet—each of these places was too obvious. There is an armoire in the living room. The bottom part is like a cabinet with sliding doors; it's about a metre and a half wide and a metre tall. I suggested that Uncle Wahid try to hide inside it. But it seemed impossible to fit a six-foot-tall man into such a confined space. Joma was asked to watch the soldiers and report as they drew closer. By the time a scared Joma arrived in the hallway to say the soldiers were approaching, they had already entered the house. My mother and Samera went outside to keep them busy. It was too late. We couldn't even leave the room. I watched my tall uncle suddenly shrink and fold himself up and enter the bottom cabinet. I quickly put a sheet over him and closed the doors, leaving a slight opening for him to breathe. The soldiers walked in, looked behind the curtains, opened the armoire—the top level—and pushed a few clothes to the side. Then they went to the next room. My mother almost fainted. Our hearts were beating fast, but not as hard as my uncle's. Once the soldiers left, it took us more than half an hour to pry Wahid out of the cabinet. We still can't believe he managed to fit inside. Fear works in mysterious ways.

On May 30, Uncle Wahid, Samera and my brother, Hassib, each pack a small bag and depart in the evening, leaving a trail of sadness and tears behind. It was decided several days ago that it would be best for them to go to Pakistan. Saying goodbye to them reminds us of Uncle Haider, my mother's youngest brother, who fled to Iran some five years ago. Just out of high school, Haider was a newly inducted soldier, but he soon deserted. We haven't seen him since the evening he said goodbye. Most of us, especially those who were quite young at the time, have to think hard to remember what Haider looked like. But my grandmother says she has counted every day of those five long years, and now she has one more date to keep track of.

June 1 is a bright, sunny day. Eighteen hours have passed since Hassib's departure with Uncle Wahid and Samera. My mother misses her son, and I am beginning to feel his absence too. I tell Dyana about it as soon as I see her at the corner of the street. It was supposed to be a secret, but I find it too hard to remain quiet. They are already gone; it doesn't matter now if people know. The government tries to stop people from fleeing the country. But once they cross the border, only their families remember them. Still, Dyana cautions me not to mention this to anyone else.

That night, I am anxious to get home to comfort my mother. As I walk inside the house, I see my aunt Najmeya, one of my mother's younger sisters, standing by the water pump. She tries to smile. But I hear my grandmother's voice. Something is wrong. My grandmother, who has gone blind after failed eye surgery, visits us only on rare occasions, such as my birthday, and during the month of Ramadan. Aunt Najmeya, who looks after my grandmother, always accompanies her. I hurry into the living room and kiss my grandmother's hand and face in the traditional way. Then I see my father, lying down with a sheet pulled half over him, and one of my uncles sitting near him. "What is going on?" I ask. "Nothing," comes the reply. "Your father was not feeling well and came home early," says my grandmother. "They brought me here to be with you for a few days, if that's all right!" She's being deliberately casual. I rush to my father's side. He looks faint, but otherwise seems fine.

My mother comes in with a glass of juice for my father, her eyes sunk deep into dark circles, her lips dry. I follow her into the hallway. "What is really going on, Mom?" I ask. She can hold back no longer. Her voice is shaking. She tells me that this morning Wahid, Samera and Hassib were caught on their way to Pakistan and taken to a police station. Distraught at the news of their capture, my father left the office to come home. Then he became weak and unwell. They sent for my grandmother, knowing that she must also be having a hard time. "We thought it was best if we were all together," my mother says. "We don't know where they are being held," says Aunt Najmeya, coming into the hallway.

Dinner is served, but we have no appetite. My father is asleep after taking a tablet of *mosaken*, a painkiller. I walk on the balcony, dreaming that the phone may ring and we'll have good news. It is a pleasant evening. A fresh northern wind is blowing. But I can hear my father throwing up, which makes me feel sick myself. I stay outside, trying to breathe. Aunt Najmeya's scream, calling my name, forces me back into the room. "Your father is throwing up blood," she says, terrified. I rush to help him keep the towel to his lips. My mother is holding his head. He sits back, shaking and covered in sweat.

It is too late to get him to the hospital—the curfew will begin in five minutes. The streets are virtually empty by this time of the evening, but there are so many wounded arriving at the hospital these days that the emergency rooms are overwhelmed.

Unless you have a mutilated face, broken bones or a shattered body, no one cares—unless, of course, someone pulls rank.

The clock strikes ten, the hour of the curfew. There is a knock at the door. It is Samera and Hassib; they have been released. We are overjoyed to see them, but by now my father is nearly unconscious. Still, we have no choice but to wait until dawn. Crowding into a single room, we sit by candle-light, helplessly staring at each other.

Occasionally, I hear Samera crying quietly by my grand-mother's side. "No matter how we pleaded," she says, sobbing, "they wouldn't let Wahid go." At the time of their arrest, they were each taken in for questioning. Hassib was beaten when he denied that they were fleeing the country. Samera wasn't physically hurt. Neither of them has seen Uncle Wahid since their interrogation. "What are they going to do to him?" Samera keeps asking.

At midnight, the rockets start again. Curled up like a child by my father's bedside, an exhausted Hassib has fallen into a deep sleep. My mother is awake, eyes wide open—though without their usual warmth. The candle is dying softly. It is the longest and darkest night I've ever sat through in the sixteen years of my life.

At dawn, we sip black tea. My mother is going to take my father to the hospital while I try to find out where Uncle Wahid is and what's happened to him. Hassib and Samera must stay home. My grandmother will handle the relatives and friends who will arrive with questions about my father's health and my uncle's disappearance.

By the afternoon, my father has been hospitalized and the news of his illness is spreading fast. He is in the emergency room. No one is allowed to visit him. My mother has just returned from the hospital to see if there is news of Wahid. I have spoken to a couple of friends who have contacts with the KhAD; they will try to find out his whereabouts and call us. Aunt Najmeya warns that the lines are all tapped; we cannot forget that we live in a police state. I reassure her that we use coded expressions on the phone that no one else will understand. Another night of anguish awaits us.

It has been four days since my father was admitted to the hospital. I went to see him yesterday. Although the heavy bleeding has stopped, he is not doing well. One of his friends, Dr. Qatra, whom I call uncle, told me as he walked me out of the building that unless we find a large quantity of blood for my father—and soon—it will be difficult to help him. Dr. Qatra thinks my father has an ulcer, but is waiting for test results.

Most of my father's medical friends and colleagues have gone abroad. Not many specialists and doctors are left, just a few friends who've been able to help. As result, my father has been given decent care and proper medicine. But blood is in short supply. "We've given him what we could find here and have requested three extra pints from the Aliabad Hospital," said Dr. Qatra. "But he still needs a bit more than that to survive."

Six days after his capture, we finally learn Uncle Wahid's whereabouts. One of my friends, Mir, discovers that he is being held in the Shari Now local intelligence office—not too far from our home. Mir has told me that, with the help of his cousin, he's certain he will be able to get him out soon.

Mir is a few years older than I am, but a hundred years ahead of most of us when it comes to survival. He's a university student majoring in economics, but he rarely attends class. No one knows who he bribes and how. He's a soldier somewhere, or so his military haircut would suggest. But he has taken on other duties that are rather unusual. He brings illegal visitors to Kabul, including foreign reporters, for a tour of the city, making sure they get back safely before anyone in the government finds out about them. Mainly, Mir helps his father in their family business of running a shoe store—that is probably his real work. He is short but always smartly dressed; he has a cute smile and is recognizable immediately by his cologne. We share a passionate hatred of the communist government, its corrupt administration and bankrupt policies—at least, I think we do.

Samera has gone to her brother's home for a few days. Our house has become a reception room for the friends who come to find out about my father. My mother spends her days at the hospital, by my father's side. Hassib hides because he's abandoned school and we don't want anyone to know about his failed escape attempt.

Despite the difficulties of handling visitors, hiding a fugitive, caring for a sick man and trying to find a detainee, the rest of us have to show up at school and work. If we were to miss a few days, our absence would be reported to the authorities. We have to pretend that everything is normal. Just as the war is normal. The pretense of normality is so pervasive that turmoil, physical and mental agony and family rows pass as something quite routine, just as cheating, lying, betrayal, bribery and deception have become normal. By day, we fake smiles. At night, we try not to cry. All the while, the Katyushas and Stingers go on flying. And now we can hear the response of the government—the howl of the Russian-made SCUD missiles. They have been used for the past several years, but recently they've been launched from nearby bases, and we can actually hear them being fired into the night sky.

Uncle Latief has found someone who may be able to get Uncle Wahid home in return for a hundred thousand afghanis. Everyone in the family is in favour of paying the bribe. I'm anxious to give my friend Mir a chance. I want to be the one to bring Uncle Wahid home. He's the older brother I don't have, a good friend and teacher. He puts up with my inadequacies in math and science and encourages my interest in poetry and music. But Uncle Latief, otherwise a very quiet and shy man, insists we go ahead with his plan.

A week passes. My father is still in the hospital and Uncle Wahid is still being detained. We learn that the man who originally promised that he would bring Wahid home within eighteen hours of receiving money now says that after we pay him it may be twenty-four hours or even more. We don't feel we can trust him any more. My grandmother finally announces that we should put the man on hold; instead, I have two days to see if Mir can help. Mir is on the case, calling me every few hours. "They know we're trying to get him out, so they keep moving him from one location to another," he says.

As the family-imposed deadline looms, I'm beginning to doubt Mir myself. He has asked me to meet him at ten in the morning at the university, outside his classroom. Minutes before ten, the professor opens the door. Leaning against a marble pillar, I watch all the students leaving. I peek inside the lecture hall, where the professor is alone, cleaning the board. Disappointed, I go outside—and there is Mir, with his usual smile, waving as he walks towards me. "Go home," he says, as he checks his watch. "By the time you get there, Uncle Wahid should be with your family." I'm stunned.

It turns out Uncle Wahid was taken to the military base in Gharga, outside Kabul. Mir brushes the dust from his black trousers as he tells me the story. "He was a soldier there, but he was closely watched by others; he wasn't allowed to make any calls or talk to anyone. Yesterday my cousin phoned his commander, who said he'd release him. We went there at six this morning to make sure, and Uncle Wahid was still there. It seems they had no intention of letting him go. But once we got there, the commander couldn't say no to my cousin—in fact, he lied and said he had been planning to send Wahid home today," Mir says. Mir and his cousin had a cup of tea at the main office while waiting for Uncle Wahid, who didn't know he was going to be released. They took Wahid away and drove him into the city. "He was in military clothes and had no money or anything," says Mir. "So we put him in a cab at Dehe Afghanan and sent him to your home." The only thing Mir paid for was the cab.

I arrive home and find Uncle Wahid surrounded by my family. I receive many kisses from everyone—I'm the hero of the day. But it is Mir's cousin who should be credited. At the insistence of my uncle and the family, I arrange to see Mir and his cousin in order to present him with a small gift and thank him. They are in the middle of something important, Mir says on the phone. However, they agree to meet me at the corner of a street midway between our houses.

Mir's cousin is an influential army commander by day, with an intelligence job, but by night he works with mujahidin groups. In both circles he is called the man who came back from the dead. His friends saw him blown up by a bomb on top of the steel remains of a destroyed building, Mir has told me. For hours the military doctors extracted pieces of metal from his body—he was left with a noticeable scar on the side of his face. He also had seventeen bullets removed from his body, and walks with a limp.

Mir is waiting for me at the end of Taymanie Road. His cousin is in a blue Volkswagen. There he is, the hero, in flesh and blood. The man who risks his own life to help others looks like a fashion model. With bright eyes, dark curly hair and dark skin, Mir's cousin is young and elegant— completely unlike the military muscleman I'd imagined. I discover that he is in his mid-twenties, recently married with a ten-month-old daughter. "But he lives such a danger-ous life," I say in awe. What drives him to be who he is? I don't dare ask. Instead, I just say "Salam" and thank him for his help. "No problem," he replies. "But you should get your uncle out of here soon." I tell him that we are hoping to do that, but it isn't easy. I don't mention that my brother is hid-ing at home and my father is hospitalized. I thank them again and return home.

In the middle of recording our radio show, there is a power cut. We sit and wait. I'm anxious to finish the show so I can visit Habibullah in the hospital. The assistant producer, a young university graduate, asks what is wrong with my father and I mention that we're desperate to find him some blood. "Have you tried the military hospital?" asks a voice from the corner. I look up to see a clean-shaven man in a suit and tie sitting at the far end of the row of seats in the edit room. I'm sure I've been introduced to him, shaken his hand. But I can't remember his name or what he does. I've never thought of the military hospital. He tells me there is a real chance I can buy blood there. Hearing his deep voice, I remember that a few weeks ago the old anchorman who used to read Pushtu poems left the country and this man came in to take his place. I don't know anyone there, I tell him.

The power comes back on and we rush in to record. The words "military hospital" are echoing in my head as I begin to read a poem by an Azerbaijanian woman named Jaula.

Life is a stage in our performance;
We sing our songs and leave the stage.
The stage remains behind.
Cherish the song, that the people will remember.

With my eyes closed, I'm giving these lines all my emotion and energy. Military hospital, I am thinking. Where is it? How can I find out? I open my eyes to utter darkness. The technician opens the studio door with a flashlight in his hand. Another power cut. As I walk into the edit room, the Pushtu anchor says that he is a doctor at the military hospital and will try to help. This is incredible. We wait for another thirty minutes to see if the power will come back on. The producer finally decides to replay last week's show, so we can all leave.

The doctor is no conversationalist, but he is precise and direct. He softly offers to take me to the hospital now. Without hesitation, I walk with him out of the studio.

Dark clouds have gathered. "We must take a taxi," the doctor says. Such an adventure I couldn't risk on my own—it's too dangerous for a lone woman to get in a cab. There are too many kidnappings and robberies in taxis. Sitting next to the doctor, I wonder which of the two men I can trust: the driver, an elderly fellow with an old hat over his grey hair, wearing a traditional sky-blue shalwar kameez, or the young, mysterious military doctor in his navy striped suit. The military hospital is a closed society, where doctors are required to be members of the Communist Party. More than that, they must be trusted by the communist government. Would the young doctor still help if he knew why my father had fallen ill?

I offer to pay for the taxi. He won't let me, saying he had to come to the hospital anyway. He leads me into a hallway crowded with wounded soldiers, some with bandages around their skulls, others with hands or legs in casts, several with their eyes covered. It looks like a scene from a black-and-white Russian war movie. Everything is black and white— even the patients in their striped pyjamas. We walk through a long corridor with large windows and stop in a waiting area. "I'll be right back," he says.

I've only just sat down when he returns. He tells me it will cost five thousand afghanis for 500 cc's of blood and another fifteen hundred afghanis for the man in charge of the lab. That's fine, I tell him. I have the money. As I reach for my bag, he says that if I don't have enough he can help and I can pay him back the next time we are in the studio. I carry at least nine to ten thousand afghanis with me these days. That's a lot of money for a girl of my age, but Mir told me it was a good idea.

We walk into a large hospital room, where he introduces me to a couple of people. "Miss Pazira," he says, "a colleague from Radio Afghanistan. Her father is in the Ibn Sina Hospital and is in need of blood." One of the men goes to the next room and comes back with a red plastic bag in his hand. "Type B," he says. I never thought I'd feel happy at the sight of blood. "You're lucky," the man says. "We have only a couple of bags of type B left." He wraps the blood bag in a plastic sack with some ice around it. I count the money. They give me a receipt for five thousand afghanis, a slip of paper attached to the bag. The fifteen hundred afghanis is obviously his bribe. They show me to the hallway. Along the corridor, I see the doctor and thank him. "Hope your father feels better soon," he says. In absolute disbelief—I actually have blood for my father—I walk into the street.

Outside there is lightning and thunder. I walk fast to the bus stop, holding the bag like a baby to my bosom. I'm terrified of dropping it and spilling its contents over the ground. How can I protect it on the bus? As I struggle onto the vehicle, I try to hold the bag up high, but it keeps slipping. A woman pushes my hand. I call her an idiot and she pushes me again. Fortunately, it's now my stop. It's pouring rain. I hold the blood bag close to my chest and run. The rain and wind slap me on the face as if I'm being punished for a crime I haven't committed.

I arrive at the entrance to the hospital. The lightning shivers across Sher Darwaza (Lion's Gate) Mountain, which stands behind the two-storey white building where my father lies. The rain is pelting down savagely.

Inside, I hand the blood bag to Dr. Qatra. Here, I say, is 500 cc's of blood for my father. Water is dripping from my hair. He takes the bag, wipes off the water, opens the bag and checks it. "I'll have this given to him immediately," he says, rushing from the room. I look around. There are freshly sliced apples and pears under a net next to my father's bed. My mother must have just left. The only sounds are the rain and the drip-drip of the type-B blood down the plastic tube into my father's arm. I look at my dad, sleeping peacefully in his bed with his head to one side. I don't want to wake him. I touch the bar of the bed with my wet, stiff fingers—I'm soaked. I walk out. My blue mascara has run into my eyes. I can cry now. But I remember my father's voice in that prison so long ago: "You mustn't cry."

7

SHADOWS ON THE WALL

Everyone has quit this land, departed from those they
love,
Everyone has packed up their hearts and travelled away.
The thought of "foreign lands" has destroyed this
country.
From the province of mourning, everyone has left for
decaying places.
Why should they stay?
One lost a loved one, another's family is already gone.
The country of light and spirit is in ruins;
Only tears and sighs remain.

Qahar Ausi, 1990

THE SKY OVER KABUL is lit with fire, the orange
flames spread over a carpet of darkness. I can see the thin
red trails of bullets. In the middle of the night, we have all
gathered in the hallway as the impact of heavy explosions
shakes the house, rattling our doors and windows. At the

sound of each explosion, our voices become louder. "*Ya Khoda! Ya Allah!*"—Oh God! Oh God!—we cry. This is not the routine bombardment. The explosions turn into one long continuous roar, and our windows start to crack. Something falls off a shelf in the guest room, breaking into pieces. No one dares to find out what it could be. "It's probably not safe to stay in the hallway," my father says.

There is another exchange of fire. Backs bent, knees weak, heads tucked down between our shoulders, teeth clenched in fear, we move one by one towards the basement. My blind grandmother has to be helped down the stairs and nearly misses her step. Aunt Najmeya catches her just in time. In the basement, we sit on the floor, with our backs against the stone wall. As the explosions get closer, we sink lower to the ground. But underneath us is concrete and stone. We cannot push down into it to hide.

I'm holding a copy of the Quran, which I grabbed from the shelf in my room as the explosions pounded the house. With my arms wrapped around me, I hold the book tightly. Neither have I learned to read the Quran—which is in Arabic—nor have I much knowledge of its content, but I still feel protected by it. I bow my head and press my face against the soft fabric that covers the heavy volume.

My grandmother is reciting her prayers—out loud—asking God for forgiveness. My aunt needs to go to the bathroom, but is too scared to leave the room. My father offers to walk her upstairs. At first she refuses, then she agrees. Trembling with fear, she takes a few steps. Another explosion and she is back in her place against the wall. My father encourages her to get up again: "It's okay," he says.

Just two weeks out of the hospital, he seems stronger than the rest of us, at least in spirit. After helping my aunt and then my mother reach the bathroom, he returns to the basement with a lantern. My ten-year-old sister, half-asleep, half-terrified, hugs my grandmother as each explosion erupts with more power. Samera and I are nailed to the ground by fear. My mother, sitting next to me, presses both hands over her heart. Her blood pressure is rising. My father risks walking up the stairs again with the lantern as we all call to him, "Don't go, please." He returns with a couple of apples, a small knife and some water. While the explosions bang heavily against the walls, Habibullah, sitting on the bottom step of the staircase, slices the apples. "Apples strengthen the heart," says my grandmother. We stare at each other as we chew pieces of apple, sipping water. The fire, the rockets and the gunshots get louder still.

"We are going to die tonight." Samera repeats these words in anguish. She's right; if the fire and explosions continue like this, we will die. As the fear of dying takes hold, the desire to live grows stronger. If we can only survive this monstrous night, we may be able to join my brother and uncle in Pakistan. It has been fifteen days since they fled the country. We could follow and be reunited with them, if only we may live.

More Katyusha rocket fire. Not seeing the explosions makes their vibration all the more terrifying. None of us has energy left to talk, cry or even whisper. We have done all our talking, apologies, regrets, goodbyes. We have said all our prayers. My father is leaning against the wall, resting his head on his left hand. The lantern has run out.

Sullenly we watch morning break. The gunfire is sporadic now, but the air in the basement is thick and filthy with the smell of burned rubber, smoke and cordite.

Who lived through this night? I meet Dyana and another friend at the corner of the street. Dyana looks as tired and listless as I feel. "We didn't sleep at all," she says, sighing in despair.

"It was near the airport; the Stingers and God knows what other explosives burned down an entire arms depot," says our friend with a sense of satisfaction.

Does this mean that the mujahidin are close to taking over the city? We hope so. As if cut out of cardboard, we move, speak and work, even smile—little fake people who have not yet come back to life. Perhaps it is the hope that we'll see the end of this brutal government soon that enables us to carry on. This is a new phase in the war, and in a sad way we welcome it, though we are not yet used to it.

No matter what may happen to us, we are happy about one thing: Hassib and Uncle Wahid finally made it to Pakistan. It had been an epic task to get them out. After meeting Mir's cousin, who'd originally helped bring Uncle Wahid home, I had been encouraged to ask Mir for further assistance to get Wahid out of the country. A week later, Mir found a smuggler. There were some moments of hesitation when Mir told us that Wahid and Hassib could leave as soon as they wanted, but Samera—Wahid's wife—couldn't go with them. How could Wahid leave behind his young, pregnant wife? Would she be able to join him any time soon? Should he wait and find someone who could take the two of them together? My mother didn't want Hassib to go without his uncle. He was too young—just turned fourteen, perhaps a bit naive. But every day was proving to be more difficult than the one before. Hassib and Wahid were hiding in our home. From sunrise to curfew they stayed put, fearing that they might be seen or discovered. My father was still in the hospital.

One evening, after dinner, after the doors were locked and the windows shut, we all sat by candlelight to make a decision. Wahid and Hassib were in immediate danger. They had to go. Samera agreed to join them later in Pakistan. Some of her cousins were planning to leave too, and perhaps she could go with them. That evening, for the first time in months, the power came on. It felt like a celebration, though we had nothing to celebrate. We had had to live so much in the dark that we'd adopted its colour and mood.

A few days later, the smuggler picked up Wahid and Hassib in the early hours of the morning. "No tears, no cries," ordered my grandmother. "Just wish them well." Like dried-up trees, we stood in a row by the door, saying goodbye.

For several days afterwards, our hearts beat faster every time we heard a knock on the door. In a few days, Mir came by with a note and a set of keys. "The smuggler gave me your house keys," he said. "Hassib must have taken them by mistake." They weren't the house keys, but Hassib's bicycle keys. It was our secret code. When we received them, it meant they both had made it safely to Pakistan. The note was from Wahid, handwritten in haste. "We have arrived safe and sound, though with some problems on the road. Don't worry about us. We'll be in touch soon." We breathed a collective sigh of relief. But with it came sadness and tears.

—

AROUND THE DINNER TABLE tonight the mood is different. There is a sense of resolution and unexpected calm. Uncle Latief, his wife and their baby daughter are visiting.

"Now that we know Wahid and Hassib have arrived safely in Pakistan, you should return home," says my uncle to my grandmother and aunt, who live with him.

"The doctor is still not well," says Aunt Najmeya, referring to my father.

My grandmother is adamant. "We're going to stay here for a few more days," she says. Uncle Latief and his family must leave before tea is served in order to reach home before the curfew. After we see them to the door, my mother suddenly turns to me. "We are going to go to Pakistan," she announces, with as much excitement as her tiredness permits. "We" turns out to mean my parents, Mejgan, Samera and me. My grandmother and aunt will stay in our house until they hear news of our safe arrival in Pakistan. No one must know about this until after our departure, not even our other aunts and uncles. "The sooner we leave, the better," says my mother.

My father has remained silent throughout this conversation. "What do you think?" I ask him.

"Whatever you decide," he says as he leaves the table.

Once a ferocious tiger, firm and resolute in his decision not to abandon Afghanistan, he is now a sheep, obedient, without an opinion. Does war makes us give in? Does too much pain make cowards of us all?

My father is still on sick leave. He spent twenty-one days at the Ibn Sina Hospital and was sent home to recover for two months. He looks pale and is physically weak. But he is also unusually sad. He misses my brother a great deal.

"Will the decision to leave the country affect him badly?" I ask my mother.

"He is not excited about it," she says. "But he's resigned to the fact that it's better to join Hassib—especially after last night."

While my father has agreed to leave Afghanistan, he will do nothing to organize our escape. He is not well, of course, says my mother, unconvinced. But I understand my father. This is his last stand. He has claimed for years that he would be the last to leave, the captain who would stay aboard ship until all was lost. Planning our departure would demean everything he had stood for. He wants to walk out with dignity.

My mother considers it beneath her to deal with the grubby details of our departure. Although she can fight to persuade my father we should go, she is not capable of finding a smuggler and negotiating a price to take us out of the country. That would be too much to expect of a lady who decides on a menu and the number of guests, but will not shop, cook or clean. "It is left to you to see this through," she tells me. "Your father trusts you, and besides there is no one else."

At sixteen, I feel more like sixty these days. I am physically exhausted, mentally preoccupied with so much responsibility, emotionally overwhelmed. Boys my age are sent to the front line and return dead or injured. Girls carry the burden of an entire household.

"You're hardly an exception," Dyana reminds me. "And you're lucky—at least you have managed to persuade your father. You're going away from all this war and misery." Dyana and I have a lot in common, but she is indifferent towards the mujahidin and the resistance to the government. She is not as passionate about Afghanistan's independence as I am. She doesn't understand the depth of my attachment to my country. She supports me in anything I do, she tells me. It's just that politics doesn't interest her. She didn't grow up visiting her father in prison, reading from his library and following his discussions with friends. She would be indifferent towards her father's suffering because she dislikes him. Or that's what she says. Dyana's father is also a doctor, but he is on the other side of my political line. Her family wishes to leave the country, but her father resists. He is confident that he can send his son to Moscow to save him from military service. For years now, it has been Dyana's father against his entire family, and there is no discussion around their dinner table. "Only his orders and nothing else," my friend says. Her mother is so afraid of his anger that she prefers to cry quietly to her daughters rather than talk to him of her wish to leave. "He wants to sacrifice us all for his party and his job," says Dyana angrily. "This is why I dislike all politics."

Shortly before curfew, we hear a gentle knock at the door. It is Mir, in a wretched state. I ask him to come in. "We have to go somewhere else," he says, pointing at a man who's waiting in the car. It's hard to see much in the dark, but I can make out the expression on Mir's face—worried, nervous. "My brother was arrested some hours ago," he says. "I'll tell you the details later, but if you can go to the university tomorrow morning and find a girl in the school of political affairs . . ." He pauses for a second. "Find her, and tell her to stay away from the university for a few days." Mir looks at me. Of course I can do that, I assure him. He hands me a slip of paper with the girl's name and her class number. "She doesn't know about the arrest. The sooner you get to her, the safer she will be." "I don't need to know any more," I tell Mir. I've no hesitation about helping him. He was an angel in my darkest days. While we are not part of the same organization, we are like a family when it comes to resistance.

Despite his worries about his brother, Mir is helping organize our escape. He has found a couple of smugglers, one of them more reliable than the other, he says. I have to meet him, and our house is not a safe place for such a rendezvous. Now that my father is home, people arrive to visit him all the time— some relatives, colleagues and friends more than once. It could be love, courtesy or a reciprocation of my father's years of service to them. But it's also possible someone may be keeping an eye on him or reporting to the authorities. We have no idea.

Other than a few close family members, no one knows yet about Uncle Wahid and Hassib—or at least, we haven't told them. We are trying to pretend that all is normal and that my father will soon be back at work. My mother cannot miss a day of school lest someone become suspicious. I continue with my daily schedule, and my sister attends her classes. Samera, meanwhile, is spending more time at her brother Ali's house.

I meet the smuggler at Mir's house. I am introduced to a tall, chubby man with broad shoulders, strong hands and a thick dark moustache, who sinks into the sofa when he sits down. I feel uncomfortable, but Mir wants the two of us to talk on our own. I prefer that he stay. I'm afraid this man won't take me seriously. He jokes and laughs. Isn't he too relaxed for a smuggler? Shouldn't he be more concerned? I take Mir aside. "Not to worry," Mir says. "He deals with people like you every day. He may appear rough and scary, but he's trustworthy."

When I go back to the room, the smuggler says, "Let's get down to business." I lock my fingers together to stop them from shaking. He wants to know how many people intend to go to Pakistan, their ages and occupations. I want to know how he's going to get us out. He asks how long it will be before we are ready to leave. I ask him how much it will cost us. He is reasonable. "I don't want any money now," he says. "I want you to make it safely across the border, send a letter to your relatives here to tell them you're happy, then I'll go and collect the money." He agrees that we should leave the money with a third party. He will inform me about a possible date, but we must be ready in the next few days. We have to think of a place other than our house to leave from, and we cannot take much with us—only a few belongings and a little money. Everyone must dress in traditional clothes, the women wearing burqas. Until the day of departure, we must carry on as usual. The list of things I must remember goes on.

As I leave, Mir is standing in the hallway, nodding approvingly. "It will be fine," he says. I ask to see his mother, who has been grieving over her son's arrest. So far, none of their high-ranking government contacts have been able to get him out. Mir's mother is tired, and complains that her sons have taken after their father. "They are adventurous, always taking risks," she says. She has three sons, and tells me she feels the absence of a daughter more now than ever before. She is worried that Mir, too, will get into trouble. "Does he attend his classes?" she asks me. "Is he a good student?" I'm not his classmate, I say, head down. But, I tell her, I'm sure he is a very good student. What can I say to a mother who wants her children to be hard-working students and lead a peaceful, normal life? She doesn't understand that life for our generation is not that simple. She doesn't even know the extent of Mir's brother's supposed crime, and the potential punishment. During the whole conversation, Mir stands by the door with a big, fake smile.

The Soviets used to move freely around Kabul, flocking to our streets, markets and restaurants in the richer districts. Gradually people grew bolder, expressing their hatred in various ways. Soon there were threats, then systematic attacks were carried out, and the Soviets no longer felt safe to roam the city. Whether military personnel or civilians, they now had to plan their visits to the market, and they went in groups, often with armed soldiers who guarded them as they went into the shops.

The resistance group to which Mir's brother belonged had planned to kidnap a Soviet general. They had information that he was going to be shopping in Chicken Street. The general arrived around three in the afternoon with his entourage and his military guards. The kidnappers made sure they outnumbered the soldiers in case of a gun-battle in the market.

Within minutes of the general's arrival, Mir's brother made his move. But they'd failed to notice the general's personal bodyguard, a young man in civilian clothes who was walking a short distance behind him. As they tried to bundle the general into their car, the guard opened fire. A military vehicle packed with soldiers immediately turned onto Chicken Street from a small alleyway. The general struggled to free himself, but was shot dead.

Mir's brother and two friends managed to escape in the car and drove to a safe house. Several of their friends took refuge in the neighbourhood. Soldiers had blocked off the entire area and were searching houses. The kidnappers who were left behind made a call to the safe house. The call was intercepted; a little later, the safe house came under fire. By the end of the day, all nine young men were arrested on murder charges and now face the death penalty. They are mostly university and high-school students, all under twenty-one. The fact that the dead general was Russian makes their crime more serious. In the Soviet Union, an enemy of the state is put to death without trial.

Mir says they are trying to buy some time, bribing whomever they can to postpone the date of the execution. More time means a chance to organize an escape, or to find other ways to get the prisoners off. Mir is certain that it was not a case of assassination, but a kidnapping that went wrong. Was it just bad luck—sloppiness—or were they betrayed? No one knows. I only know what Mir tells me.

His mother knows much less. "Their father tells me he'll be home soon," she says, with hope in her broken voice.

It's early in the morning. I've barely woken up when I hear a knock at the door. It's Samera, wearing a black skirt and a patterned grey blouse that badly needs ironing. Her stockings are wrinkled. She's always been so keen on her appearance, always wearing neatly pressed and smart-looking clothes. But it is her messy hair, swollen eyes and red nose that shock me. When my aunt asks if everything is all right, she bursts into tears. "They've taken Ali," she cries, throwing herself into my grandmother's arms. Another crisis, my God! We all circle around her, anxious to know what is going on.

"One of his students came last night to tell me that Ali and some professors were taken away yesterday afternoon," says Samera. This is hardly surprising. Professors have always been the target of government arrests. But why Ali? And why now? Samera keeps crying. We try to comfort her. "What are they going to do to him?" We tell her that Ali will be fine, that the government will discover a mistake was made and will let him go. After all, it's not as if he's committed any crime. Has he committed a crime? We don't really know. Samera knows little, but suspects a lot.

Samera lost both of her parents to life's misfortunes. Her mother died of cancer when Samera was twelve. While they were still mourning her mother's death, her father—a renowned religious reformer—was arrested by the communist government. He was never seen again. Ali, the eldest, looked after Samera and her three other brothers.

Ali used to take them to the prison where their father was held. "We never saw our father, but we used to take books and clothes for him. Every two weeks, they gave us his dirty clothes to take home to wash and they took the clean ones," Samera says. A year later, the prison guard told them they shouldn't bother to come any more. "We went back several more weeks, just in case. But there were no dirty clothes any more." Later someone told them he was dead, but the family never saw his body, and don't know the circumstances of what had happened.

Nine years later, his children still hope he may be alive—in an Afghan prison, in Siberia. It is widely believed that some political prisoners are sent to northern Russia for forced labour. But no one has ever come back to prove this. What if Ali disappears like his father? That is what Samera fears the most.

A couple of years after their father's disappearance, Samera's second brother fled to Pakistan and then to the United States. For years they considered him missing too, since they hadn't heard from him. But one of their relatives has recently brought a letter and some photos. Dressed in jeans and a blue shirt, he is standing in front of a water fountain, smiling into the camera. Another picture shows him in a grey-blue business suit, shoes well polished, standing in a street with some English signs in the background. Samera keeps these two snapshots with her all the time, staring at them for long hours. Last year, her third brother, who played hockey with the national team, went to India for a game. He told her that if he could, he would not come back. Fifteen days after his departure, he sent a letter and a photo, which Samera now carries too. He also wants to go to the United States.

Her youngest brother, eighteen-year-old Radwan, whom Samera used to mother, is a runaway soldier. He escaped to Pakistan and sent a message, but no pictures. So Samera carries a photo from her wedding that features him. Radwan stands next to his sister, his hair cut military-style. Samera is dressed like a doll in a white fluffy gown, with a hairnet over part of her face, holding a bouquet. Next to her is her husband, Uncle Wahid, in a dark suit.

This is Samera's life. "How much worse can it get?" she asks. All her men—the people she's leaned on for support—are either locked up or living in exile.

I walk around our house, calculating what to take and what to leave—years of my parents' hard work and ambitions.

I was a baby when they bought the land on which their dream home now stands. The first few years of the republic in the early 1970s—the opening of trade with neighbouring countries, peace and security, improved economic times—had given people hope for the future. Landscapers had been consulted, architectural plans drafted and all the necessary materials gathered. My father travelled outside Kabul to find the right type of stone. He was helped by a cousin who'd been working as an engineer in a mining project in northern Afghanistan. Several rare types of stone were brought in from various parts of the country.

Our house was not just a building; it was the dream of two young people, a symbol of their love and commitment to each other. The foundation was laid with much care. Though he was working as a physician, my father personally supervised the building of the house. It was his idea to build it part brick, part stone. The guest room was large, divided from the dining room by a decorated stone wall. The living room had large windows, like a sunroom, facing the garden. The basement was to provide a cool summer retreat. My father's love of flowers and trees transformed the yard and the pond. Grape vines were planted to shade the garden. An almond tree stood next to the water pump, surrounded by roses, petunias, irises and lilies.

In one corner of the yard, there was a room with a small corridor and a kitchen for a maid. My brother was about to be born, and my mother needed help running the household and raising her children. My parents had it all planned: their future, their children's future, the birthday and graduation parties they were going to have. And all went according to plan, until the war. They had thought of everything but war. No one—not even the most informed politician or journalist—could have imagined any such conflict, let alone one that would force us out of our home in little more than a decade.

My father's love of old things, of chandeliers and carpets, had made our house look like an antique shop. My mother sometimes complained that there were too many carpets, too much heavy furniture. Modern houses were lightly decorated; ours was packed with ornaments, with odd chairs and dressers.

For me, the most precious gem was my father's library, which expressed his love for books. My passion for reading was making it grow every year. I had a long love affair with that library, my silent best friend. Each book was a fond memory, each page a witness to my emotional attachment to the written word. It was a world where I felt safe, confident and happy.

—

AS WE MAKE OUR PREPARATIONS to leave, I step into my father's library. The first book I ever read came from these wooden shelves. I can see the book in the right-hand corner, between Jack London's *White Fang* and Edgar Allan Poe's short stories. The book is *Death Row*, by Caryl Chessman, and is the story of an American criminal counting his last days before going to the gas chamber. As death got closer, his attempts to hold on to life became more desperate. I cried when I finished the book—he was dead. I was eight years old, and it took me three months to finish the book. When I was done, my father told me to write a two-page summary, along with the moral lesson I'd learned from the story. I concluded that one must be careful not to commit any crimes, and my father presented me with a gift: another book, *The Story of a Real Man,* by Boris Polevoi. The title is still engraved on the leather cover, as bright as when my father showed it to me for the first time. It is the story of a Russian pilot in the Second World War whose plane is shot down by the Germans. The pilot, Alexei Maresyev, survives the crash, and walks for days in the cold and snow to make it safely back to the Russian lines. But frostbite costs him both his feet. The last third of the book details his struggle to fly again, which he finally does in 1943, when he shoots down seven enemy planes. The words are so powerful that I was totally caught up in his struggle. The first time he flew with his wooden legs, I felt I was flying with him. For years I thought that if the Russian with his wooden legs could fly a plane in time of war, then I could do anything. I would go back to those pages to regain my courage, especially in times of disappointment and depression. Now I'm afraid I may not have the courage to leave all this behind.

After I presented my review of *The Story of a Real Man* to my father, he took me around the entire library. "You have the right to use my books," he said. "From now on, this is your library too—make sure you take care of it." For years, I have. I'm the only person in the family with such a privilege. No one else, not even my mother, is allowed to touch his library, especially since the burning of his books years earlier in Baghlan. I've been buying books of my own as well, adding them to the collection. Now there are some five thousand volumes—all in Dari, mostly translated from other languages. There are several crime novels from a couple of popular Iranian writers, Ghazi Parwez Sayed and Sadegh Hedayat. There is a collection of Greek philosophy, from Pythagoras to Plato and Aristotle. I found Homer's *Odyssey*— incomplete. But the image of a blind poet was more captivating than the story of a traveller. I found Dostoevsky and Gorky, and Lenin, Marx and Mao, next to a life of Buddha. I read Rousseau, Goethe and even Sartre. Among the books, I discovered a few loose pages of Lamartine's work. There is an entire section on Persian poetry, all the classics from Jomi to Sanahi, Rumi and Sahdi.

There are handwritten volumes as well. When we leave, can I not take just a few of the most precious?

Then there are the newspapers and magazines. The papers, week by week, month by month, are the product of an era that my father calls the time of a free parliament and a free press. The papers are rare copies. Not many people would have them, he says. And there are my father's medical books, with coloured drawings of human bodies, which fascinated me each time I sneaked a look at them—especially when I was twelve, and more curious about life than fearful of it.

The first love of my life has been this library and its treasures. How can I abandon them? My mother has always said it is my father's love of his country and my attachment to his books that has stopped us from leaving. The smuggler insists we cannot take even a piece of paper with us, let alone books. Even if we could take a couple, which ones would I choose? I think of Mohammad Hajozee's essay that describes a young woman in a flower shop sorting and separating flowers for two bouquets, one for a wedding, the other for a funeral, having to decide which will end up in the hands of a bride and which will lie over the dark soil of a grave. I understand this. Perhaps it will be easier not to take any at all.

After school these days, my mother sorts out her closet and my father's. Their bedroom looks like a salesman's stall, clothes piled on the floor, legs of trousers wrapped around a blouse, part of a skirt lost underneath. My mother tells Aunt Najmeya to take what she likes out of the pile and give the rest to the poor. But Aunt Najmeya is not interested. "I'll keep something from each of you for the memory," she says. "But don't ask me to touch anything right now."

"You can sell some of the books," she suggests, noticing that I'm having a hard time letting them go. "That way," she says, "you won't have to worry about them." "But I do," I tell her. "If I can't leave them, how can I sell them? It would be like asking a mother to sell her children. I want to store the books. What if I dig a hole in the ground, cover the books properly and bury them in our own yard?" "They'll all rot and decay," my mother warns. Finally, I decide to empty a large cupboard and pack most of the books in there. After a day's work, every moment filled with inexpressible sorrow, I now have a cupboard full of books. I lock the door, thinking that one day we'll return and the books will still be there. But there are lots of books still on the shelves.

My mother would like to sell a few of her possessions. But it's not that simple. A couple of days ago, she heard a man on the street asking to buy old and new furniture and she called him into the house. As he drove away with some of our furniture tied with a rope to his wooden cart, a neighbour walked into the house without knocking. "Please don't tell me the doctor is leaving too," she said to my mother. "What are we going to do if he goes? He is our doctor, the only one left who helps us." My mother had to sit her down and reassure her that we weren't going anywhere, and is afraid she wasn't completely persuasive in her lie. We cannot sell anything else, we conclude. It's too dangerous.

Besides, more and more people sell these days, and fewer and fewer buy. Most of the corner shops in the city have been transformed into pawnshops for furniture. At a time when everyone is on the run, expensive things have lost their value. It is not even worth selling our belongings; perhaps it's better to give them away. At least it makes one feel more moral.

My mother instructs my aunt and grandmother on what to do with clothing and jewellery that were being kept for us, the children, for our future—the one we may no longer have. "I'm not worried about those things," says my mother. "It's our lives that matter most. What the hell are we going to do with all this if we're not alive?" I think my mother is the most courageous of us all.

My father wants to go to his office to bring home his files— he hasn't been at work since Hassib, Uncle Wahid and Samera were captured and he fell ill. Now he wants to clean up his desk. As he leaves the house, I urge him not to take too much, and he promises he'll be very careful.

I find another solution for the books. Two very tall, round iron canisters, used to store flour, stood empty underneath the stairs. The flour has been transferred into smaller containers, more manageable for relatives to divide once we're gone. With my aunt's help, I fill both canisters with books and cover them.

It's early evening. Mir calls to say, in many coded words, that his brother and friends are not going to be executed. They may get a life sentence, but anything is better than an execution order. This is a bit of good news, I tell my aunt.

My father has not come back yet. My grandmother is murmuring softly, praying for him. "God bring him home safe. Help bring all missing loved ones home to their families." We sit in the living room, eyes fixed on the door.

"Give me a glass of water." My father sits on the hallway sofa to untie his shoes. It is dark, close to nine o'clock. "I spent the last five hours in an interrogation session," he says.

He left his office around three, but just metres away from the clinic, two men approached him. "I could tell from their greased moustaches that they were government agents," he says. "They asked me to follow them to their office." My father asked if he could call home to tell us he might be late. "They said it would be only a few questions and wouldn't take too long." Anger and fear are written on the lines on his forehead.

"What were they asking?" inquires Aunt Najmeya.

"The usual nonsense," he replies.

The question is how worried we should be. Was it a random check, or do the authorities know what we're planning? My mother tells me to get in touch with the smuggler. We are running out of time. "What if they had kept your father today? What if they come for him again?" My father's guess is that the government is on another aggressive round of arrests, targetting those with a prison record or with one in the family. In that context, Ali's arrest makes sense. Najibullah is desperate to maintain some degree of rule over a country that has long been out of control. For the past three years, he's been trying to do this and failing. There is talk that the mujahidin have managed to take the city of Jalalabad, that heavy fighting is going on to recapture it. Rumour has it that the Soviets have temporarily withdrawn from Afghanistan.

In the morning, I get confirmation on our date of departure. Samera now says she doesn't want to leave with us. How can she leave her imprisoned brother behind? My grandmother and aunt try to comfort her. They remind her that her husband is waiting for her in Pakistan, that she is going to have a baby soon and that it would be very difficult for her to leave later. I assure Samera that our remaining family and friends will do their best to help Ali. Still, she feels that if she leaves she's betraying her brother.

It is a special night. The power has been on since seven this evening and we actually ate dinner under the electric light and watched the news on TV. Other nights we'd be in bed by eleven, but tonight we are still up. My father is playing cards with my sister, trying not to think about anything else. My mother is sorting my brother's clothes, packing them to be given away once we are gone. The only person asleep is my grandmother. Samera, looking bewildered and lost, is quietly talking to my aunt. I'm packing a diary and a few other things to give to Dyana tomorrow. A lot of it is my writing, un-published, unedited, which at first I wanted to burn. Then I decided to ask Dyana to keep my papers for now. I'll instruct her on what to do with them after we arrive in Pakistan.

There is a knock at the door. "*Ya Khoda!*"—Oh God!— exclaims Samera, standing up. We are all pale. It is nearly an hour and a half past curfew—no one would dare leave home at this time. I peek outside through the pink eglantine that runs over the front wall. I can see the antenna of an intelli-gence vehicle. My mother is murmuring, "God, what are we going to do . . . God help us."

"Calm down," my father tells her.

"I'll get the door," I offer, terrified. My father follows me as I turn the yard light on. "Who is it?" I ask from behind the door.

"Security," answers a stern voice.

My father opens the door. "What can I do to help?" he asks, as if annoyed.

"Are you Dr. Pazira?" asks a man in military uniform.

"Yes," my father replies impatiently.

"We would like to ask you some questions," says the man. I ask them to come in. They refuse.

Two military Jeeps are parked one behind the other, centimetres from our wall. Two agents talk to my father in front of the house. An armed guard stands farther away. The driver of the first vehicle is talking on his radio. I go inside to let the rest know what is happening. My mother is waiting on the terrace. I tell her to turn the terrace light off so I can peek unseen over the wall. There's a guard and driver in the second Jeep. I can see the shadows of the two agents near the door, and the shadow of my father's hand gesturing. I raise my head a little higher. There is another man in the back of the second car. The guard turns the inside light on, searching for something on a piece of paper while talking to the driver, and I realize I know the man in the back. As if waking from a dream, I search my memory. It is Sikander. My God! Sikander, my father's distant cousin, who used to bring us fruit from his farm.

After some thirty minutes, my father closes the door. The vehicles are still there. So they've got poor Sikander, we whisper. We go to the back room to unravel this new mystery. But we don't know much. "They asked me about him," says my father. "How do I know him? Why did he stay at our home, et cetera?" They wouldn't tell my father why they'd detained him—probably for some connection to the mujahidin. My father hopes it is not more serious than that. As the state TV keeps informing us, the government is cracking down on what they call the "remnants" of the anti-government militias—enemies of the people, they call them. People like my father, Ali, Sikander and others. "I told them he was my cousin, a friend and an innocent man," whispers my father. "But I don't have much of a track record to vouch for him." Sikander has been tortured. "They said that during the past few days of interrogation, he mentioned some names, people he knows or who know him." Ours was among them.

"But why would they bring him here?" I wondered.

"The intelligence service's behaviour has no head or tail," Aunt Najmeya says. "Who knows why they do anything?"

We are still in the dining room, whispering, feeling even more confused than before, when we hear the Jeeps driving away. They are gone, at least for now.

"They'll be back," says my father, leaving the room.

"Did they say that?" I ask him.

"In so many words," he replies.

Ever more uncertain about our ability to get away, we carry on according to plan. We have procured several sets of traditional outfits, some belonging to our maid, and a few burqas. Everything has to look well used.

My mother is preoccupied with her precious jewels. Where can she leave them? Should she try to take some with her? Parting from them must be hard, but she assures me it is the least of her worries.

I take two full bags of money—amounting to nearly three million afghanis—to Mir's house. There is more, I tell Mir, putting the bags down on the floor of his living room—I just couldn't bring it all. "Leave everything at home," he says. "I'll come and get it." The money is all of my parents' savings, which they've kept hidden in various places at home. No smart person puts money in the banks. In earlier days, the government confiscated large sums, accusing the owners of being bourgeois. People, capital and land belonged to the state, they claimed, and the state had the right to redistribute such wealth to the masses. Except the masses never really saw any of the money. It was the party members and government cronies who were the real beneficiaries.

My father is now resigned to leaving, not because of the war and the oppression, he says, but because of what is yet to come. Perhaps he understands something we don't. We cannot take any real savings with us on the road, only pocket money—we have to protect ourselves from thieves. But Mir has found a *saraf*—a man involved in a traditional banking system—who will help transfer our capital once we're settled. We hand Mir all our money and get a small piece of paper, handwritten, in return. The slip says we've given so-and-so a sum of afghanis on such-and-such a date and are entitled to collect its equivalent in Pakistani rupees from the following address in Peshawar, Pakistan. "Are there any guarantees that our money will be returned?" I ask. "It is a gamble," Mir says. "But people do it all the time—there's no other way." Necessity! Necessity is the day's new order. We must do what is needed to get out. "You've got to find a place to hide this piece of paper on the journey," adds Mir, "somewhere you won't need to see it until you're in Peshawar, safe and sound."

Rockets are being fired as I arrive home. My mother is clutching her left arm; she is more scared than ever. Now that we are so close to leaving, everything seems more terrifying. Now that there is a glimpse of hope, a chance for survival, life feels more precious. How can we protect this little piece of paper from falling into the wrong hands if we are caught or robbed? "Sew it in the dress you're going to wear," says Samera. She did that on her first escape attempt. They also emptied a toothpaste tube and stuffed some thousand-afghani notes inside. But my grandmother has an even better idea: "Fold the paper into a small piece, roll it up and wrap it in ordinary fabric. Then sew the edges of the fabric and hang it around your neck from a black thread." It will look like a *tawize* (an amulet)—verses copied from the Quran that many people wear for health, protection or good luck.

By evening, Samera has finally decided to come with us. Ali's fiancée and her family have promised to pursue his case and already have some contacts who may be able to help get him released. Samera is comforted by this. Tomorrow afternoon, Mir will come and help me transfer our travelling bags to my mother's aunt's house in the Selo district of West Kabul. It is far from our home, and the last place anyone would suspect us of departing from. My mother's aunt has only been told that we are planning to visit her tomorrow afternoon. The idea is to explain as little as necessary to as few as possible. Our main concern is what we should do if they come for my father again.

Everyone is quiet around the dinner table tonight. There is no power. I look at our shadows cast by candlelight on the wall. There is my grandmother, a full circle with her scarf giving the appearance of a dark halo. My aunt's profile as she reaches for something. My father's jaws move, chewing silently. My mother and Samera face each other; my sister and I are shadowless, I think. Then I spot our images on the curtain, wavy and uneven. How much longer will these shadows cross each other's paths?

8

NASEEMA'S REVENGE

The village is a coffin—loneliness;
All footsteps are of escape, fear, terror, contempt.
Over the lips of walls, the colourless smiles of goodbyes,
Instead of water;
They spread knives for the thirsty branches.
The door of the mosque is broken, its roof in ruins;
Only a tired voice sings inside.
Time has imprisoned cries of "No!" "Why?" and "Never!"
Only the ducks from the upper stream, the sun and I,
Only we know that tomorrow
Will be born from the fetus of this brutalized,
        mournful place.

Qahar Ausi, 1991

THE YELLOW-AND-WHITE TAXI moves swiftly,
passing the last of the old houses in West Kabul. It's 5:30 A.M.
on July 20, 1989, and as we move away from the city I can see
the haze on the horizon, at the far edge of the empty fields.
The man behind the wheel is the smuggler I met two weeks

ago at my friend Mir's house. Mir sits next to him, in a traditional white shalwar kameez, with a checkered scarf hanging around his neck. He looks like a militia leader. Next to Mir is my father, in pale blue traditional clothes, a white crochet hat and a blue vest. He has let his beard grow for this journey so he will fit the image of an Afghan rural patriarch. The rest of us are squeezed into the back of the car—me, my mother, Samera, Mejgan and a woman cloaked in a blue burqa. We too are wearing burqas, but ours are more ragged. Samera's has a patch over the nose area. Mejgan's is too long for her, and the top of the burqa is loose on her small head. It was not made for a ten-year-old girl.

Inside the car we are silent, except for Mir, who makes a few jokes to help us relax. The only female voice in the back is that of the unknown woman, who leans towards the driver as she speaks to him in Pushtu. They laugh at some personal joke. We don't know who she is or why she's in the car. No one has bothered to introduce her. Like a ghost, she moves her burqa-covered face to the right and the left, looking at the road and at us as she talks. The stranger in the car, the heavy voice of the driver, the silence of the road—the fact that not a living soul can be seen—makes us more nervous. Our destination is Pakistan, but we don't know how we will make it there.

"You're pressing the baby," Samera whispers to Mejgan, who's leaning on her, half asleep. Samera is five months pregnant and trying to hide it. "The smugglers don't take pregnant women because they are slow walking," Mir said this morning. It was too late to tell us this—Samera was already prepared to leave. "As long as he doesn't know it at the beginning, it'll be fine," Mir concluded.

It is years since we've travelled outside Kabul. And this trip is different. We have been forced to leave behind our extended family, our friends, our house and all its belongings and the country that is our home. Now that we're driving away from the city, Kabul suddenly seems very dear to us.

Yesterday, my last day in Kabul, the heat and the stillness of the air were overwhelming. I was walking on my shadow under direct sun, the paved road under my feet a grey carpet spread on an endless floor. I walked around for hours, saying goodbye to every stone, to every window of every house I knew. I looked at everything in sadness, as if the trees and streets wanted me to remember them. I wanted them to remember me.

When the clock struck two P.M., I stared at the mirror in my room, touched the brass of my bed, read once more the note attached to the inside of my closet door— something my father wrote when I was eight years old: "Whoever rides the horse of self-confidence, fighting life's battles with the power of will and faith, will always be victorious." These lines always give me courage. Yesterday, I read the note aloud for the last time, every syllable echoing in the room, flat and empty. I kissed my blind grandmother's hand and face. She ran her hand over my head, as she used to do when checking the length of my hair. It was an intimate thing between us. She knew I always liked to have long hair. When I was a child and my mother wanted to cut my hair short, my grandmother took my side. My grandmother partly raised me, and called me her daughter. My winter holidays were largely spent in her home. Regardless of heavy snowfall, cold, war or family problems, she always made the trip to our house for my birthday.

I went walking with Dyana for more than an hour along the roads where we used to buy cookies, the pavement where we loved to walk over autumn leaves, watching them crumble underneath our feet, the places where we read poetry together. We stopped by the Abul-Fazal Shrine in downtown Kabul. In the past year, the shrine had become our place of refuge, peace and hope. The blue tiles on the wall, the green flags, the wooden box where we put our donations, the silver door that had hundreds of locks hanging from it. A woman once told us that if we could pull the locks open it would mean a door to happiness and luck had opened in front of us. From that day on, on each visit we pulled on the locks to see if we could open them. We never could.

We sat in the yard of the shrine watching men and women as they prayed, distributed sweets, or sat like us, motionless, reflecting on life. I felt only sadness, and I saw it on everyone's face. I didn't know if they could see it on mine. I said goodbye to Dyana at the bus station. For the first time in years, we were travelling in opposite directions. She was returning home to Taymanie Road. I was going to West Kabul—to Aunt Shafiqa's house. Several buses came and left, with crowds pushing and pulling to get on. Pretending that the crowd was too large, she said she would wait for the next bus. In the end, we saw it was beginning to get dark and we would have to part. We said goodbye in our usual way: three kisses on the cheeks and a handshake. I watched her get on the bus, holding my diary in one arm. As the bus moved away, I realized that I was not returning home.

The day before our departure, we each had to leave home separately and at different times. We had to be at Aunt Shafiqa's before dark. My father was the last person to arrive. Aunt Shafiqa had prepared an elaborate meal. We sat around an oil lamp—there was no electricity—with little desire to eat or talk. The night air was warm; it was too uncomfortable to sleep. Around three in the morning, the power came back on. With the light, everything came to life and we all got up.

Shafiqa started the electric water pump to get fresh water. Her husband put a pot of water on to make tea, then went to find his electric shaver. Their daughter, Florance, got up to finish the ironing from a few days ago. My mother also ironed her clothes. I checked our cotton sacks. Divided into four bags, there were four thin red-orange blankets, several pieces of fabric (to be made into clothes once we arrived in Pakistan), my father's double-breasted navy suit, his favourite antique tea set, a few candles and matches, a silver teapot packed with emergency medication, and my father's stethoscope and blood pressure monitor. I warned against taking items that might look suspicious if we were searched, but he insisted on these ones. They were part of his identity.

The tea was made, the clothes were ironed, dawn was near. My mother took out the traditional clothes that we had to wear for the journey. "These are Mother Fatema's gifts," she explained.

Months before the drama of departure and desperation started in our house, Mother Fatema had rushed to embrace her missing daughter, Fatema, who had shown up at the door. Was it a miracle bestowed by the martyr's grave, from which I took the black scarf? Fatema looked well and happy. Holding her hand was a four-year-old boy. "This is Abass, my son, mother," she said. She asked if her husband was welcome in the house. Mother Fatema, thrilled to see her daughter alive after a decade, was ready to welcome anyone. A tall, heavyweight man was introduced as her daughter's husband. In his arms he carried a two-year-old boy, who was fast asleep.

"This is my younger son," said Fatema. We all celebrated their happiness.

Fatema and her aunt had escaped to Bamiyan with two brothers who wanted to marry them. Fatema, who'd been barely fourteen at the time, blamed her aunt for encouraging her to run away. "I was young and stupid," she told her mother, and pleaded with her parents to forgive her. "My aunt said that my father would never let me get married to this man. But if we escaped, we could get married and then return home." When Fatema's father asked his daughter why she hadn't even sent a message in ten years, she explained that the two brothers had split, and the other brother had taken all the money. "I felt too embarrassed to return." She never explained what had brought them home now. She kept putting her arms around her mother and brothers, expressing her happiness at being reunited with them.

Five months after her daughter's return, Mother Fatema moved out to be with her family, but she came frequently to visit. As we were preparing to leave, my mother asked her if she knew where one could get some traditional clothes—long dresses and the baggy pants that are worn underneath them. In just two days, Mother Fatema produced these dark-brown, flowery dresses and pants as her gift. My mother never told Mother Fatema we were leaving, but she probably guessed. After all, she had been the nerve centre in the body of our household. She looked after my mother's jewellery, my father's money, our books and clothes. If anything was misplaced, she'd be the first to notice it, as if she were the owner and we were her honoured guests.

As we put on Mother Fatema's gifts in an attempt to transform ourselves from city dwellers into villagers, Florance was giggling. Then came the big test. None of us

Jamila and Mejgan in Kabul before fleeing Afghanistan—and a few weeks later, summer 1989.

had worn a burqa before. When I lifted the face piece, my hair would peep from the sides, and Aunt Shafiqa became worried. She brought a scarf and told me to cover my hair with it before putting on the burqa. "If they see a strand of your blondish hair, the mujahidin may take you for a Soviet and kill you at once," she said. Her elder son had escaped to Iran several years ago to avoid conscription. She sent out clothes and money for him with travellers, so she knew about the dangers of the journey—probably better than the rest of us. At her suggestion, we put Vaseline on our hands, then "washed" them in ash and clay. "It's better if your hands look dirty," she said. Samera and my mother wrapped bandages over their golden bracelets. "There are robbers and bandits on the way."

The clothes and rubber shoes were hard to walk in; the burqa made it even worse. But anyone who wants to escape through the countryside must be fully covered or risk getting caught at government checkpoints.

When Mir knocked on the door at five A.M., we were ready to leave. The smuggler objected to our bags, claiming they could raise suspicion. "I'll take you out of the city today, and we'll send someone for your bags later, I promise," he said. We took one small bag and left the rest with Aunt Shafiqa.

* * *

The car moves at such speed that it's hard to keep an eye on the road. It's the third day of the Eid, the Feast of the Sacrifice. "That's why I could come along," says Mir. "We'll drive you to Meydan Shahr, and then I'll go back." Meydan Shahr is forty minutes southwest of Kabul. What about the rest? "He'll explain," says Mir, referring to the driver. Fear creeps in.

Without notice, the driver turns the car around and stops on the side of the paved road. "From here on, she'll take you," he says, cautiously looking around before telling my father to open the door. As we climb from the car, Mir says goodbye, still smiling. "She'll be your guide for the rest of the way," says the driver, shaking my father's hand.

The mysterious woman leads the way. We walk on the paved road away from the car. "It's better not to look back," says our guide. And so we walk. In less than three kilometres, we reach the first army checkpoint. A man dressed in camouflage with a gun over his shoulder orders us to stop.

We stand still at the side of the road. Across from us, there are two concrete rooms with iron doors. The soldier fixes his beret—a red star shining in its centre—and asks my father where he is taking us. My father, lost for words, mumbles: "To the next village." The soldier laughs loudly. "Ah," he says, "you say this same thing every time you take a family out of the country, don't you, *baba* [father]?" My father stares at him helplessly. Our guide takes the soldier to the side. She talks to him for a few minutes. The soldier goes inside one of the concrete rooms. "I think we are free to go," I say. Mejgan and my mother start to walk. Another soldier who is watching us shouts: "Stop." It's hard to know what's going on. Our guide comes closer. "Don't move," she says. "You can sit on the ground if you're tired. I'm waiting for the soldier who's gone inside to return."

We sit in a circle, facing each other. The woman sits a short distance from us. She pulls her burqa from her face. Until this moment, I was under the impression that she was old, but once the curtain is lifted we see a young woman—about eighteen—with delicate features, thick dark eyebrows, black eyes and pink cheeks. She has a kind, innocent face.

"She's so young," my mother whispers. We all look in the direction of the room, from which one of the soldiers is watching us. "If he asks, tell him we're going to Ibrahim Khel," instructs our guide. "We should say we are originally from there, but we've been to the city for a funeral and are now returning home." Like schoolchildren, we try to memorize these words. "What's your name?" my mother asks. "Naseema," she replies shyly. Then she walks to one of the concrete rooms. We repeat her words, "Ibrahim Khel," "wedding"—"No, funeral," says my mother. "Returning home."

We see Naseema returning with one of the soldiers. "There are no buses today to take you to your village," he says in a loud voice. "It's fine," says Naseema. "We like to walk—it's just after the next village." She shrugs her shoulders. We nod in agreement. "Okay!" says the soldier, "I'll let you go now, but if I see you here another time, I promise I'll send you to prison—especially your father." My father wants to answer back, but Naseema intervenes. "Thank you," she says, leading us away.

It's not until later that we discover Naseema bribed them to let us go.

We walk behind Naseema. Her face is now completely uncovered. The soft breeze blows her burqa to the side. Encouraged, Samera and I uncover our faces too. There is silence all around us. Under the midday sun, not even a fly moves. I watch the road as far as I can, but it disappears into the distance, behind a slope.

All of a sudden, we hear a gunshot. There is nothing to hide behind. The hill, cut in two by the road, is about thirty metres ahead. We don't know which direction the gunshot came from, but it was very close. Naseema pulls her burqa down. We follow her closely. "Continue to walk, slowly," she orders, her voice a little shaky. We move at her pace. Then two gunmen jump at us from behind small bushes, and there is a moment of panic. All of us—except for Naseema—automatically sit on the paved road, right at the centre, sheltering in each other's arms, imitating what we've seen in the movies. As in the films, one imagines the worst. I think they are going to kill us. My mother even starts saying her prayers, out loud.

The gunmen walk closer. Now we can see their military uniforms and boots, and their rifles, held at the ready. Naseema takes a couple of steps towards them. "This is my uncle and his family," she says, referring to my father. "We have just returned from a funeral in the city. There are no buses, so we are walking to the village." The soldier ignores her and comes closer to my father. "What's in your bag?" he asks in Pushtu. My father replies in Pushtu, "Nothing much." We sit helplessly, not knowing what is going to happen. They order my father to empty the bag. "Candles, matches, blankets, all the things for running away," says one of the men in a loud voice. "We are just returning to our home," I manage to say in Pushtu. "Where are you from?" he asks with a smirk. From behind the burqa, I stare at his face. "I'm from Wardak," I say. The soldier laughs. "But your Pushtu accent is not Wardaki," he says with confidence. I shouldn't have spoken.

An army officer, in full military uniform and hat, appears at the middle of the hill. "What is going on?" he asks. The soldier near my father stands straight. "Sir, they are escaping to Pakistan—looks like two families from Kabul." We protest, insisting that we are from Ibrahim Khel. The soldier laughs. "Who are you trying to fool? We can tell Kabulis from the way they walk. Here, everyday, we see a lot like you, posing as villagers." The officer arrives at the foot of the hill. "Let them go," he says, brushing his thick moustache with his right hand. "They will rot in the dirt and heat of Pakistan. They will regret it." He fixes his military hat. We sit in silence, watching the officer walk away. The soldier orders my father to gather his things and leave.

Naseema helps my father put the candles and blankets back into the bag. "Walk slowly," says Naseema. "They sometimes shoot if people move fast." Like people already dead, we walk down the centre of the road, in slow motion. We hear more gunshots. "Don't look back," Naseema advises. My father looks tired and broken. A once influential man, he's being reduced to a powerless creature, humiliated over and over again in front of his family. There was a time when his words were taken seriously by both his employers and those who worked for him. Neighbours always greeted him respectfully. But now, the road to Pakistan has left him as helpless as the rest of us. He walks with hesitation, knowing he cannot go back.

The sun is brutal. It feels as if our rubber shoes are melting onto the sun-bathed road. At sunset, we arrive at a village. I've never seen anything like it. Houses are built onto the side of a hill. A high semicircular mud wall separates the village from the hill and its outskirts. Everything is the colour of dust. There is no road, only a dirt track.

A group of women with long black embroidered dresses and head covers come out to greet us. They all know

Naseema, who now has a cheerful smile on her face. They take us through a tall wooden door into a house. For the first time in hours, we take off our shoes, our feet still sweaty and numb from the touch of rubber. There are a few cushions leaning against the mud walls, and a single bed. Over it lies a white embroidered cover. Naseema politely tells my father he can sit on the bed. "I'm fine," he says, sitting on the floor like the rest of us. It feels strange. After the checkpoints and guards, we are now at the mercy of villagers with whom we have nothing in common.

As she takes off her burqa, Naseema tells us this is her sister's house. She pulls a bright pink scarf loosely over her head. "There are no other men in the house," she says. "You can take off your burqas and relax." An elderly woman, the mother of the family, called Anna ("grandmother" in Pushtu), sits near the door and smiles at us warmly. Her bony face, pointed nose and deep eyes are striking. She has a streak of white hair on each side of her head, kept away from her face with a set of long, coloured hairpins. Her black scarf barely covers half her head.

Two younger women arrive with a large pot of milk and some glasses. "They are our brides," says Anna, pointing at the two women. One is Naseema's sister. Anna pours us milk. "Tell them to drink," she says in Pushtu, asking Naseema to translate. "Milk will help get rid of your tiredness. I just milked the cow this morning—tell them it is fresh." Naseema informs her that my father and I can speak Pushtu. My father learned to speak the language while working in the Afghan countryside. Though I learned Pushtu in school, I've never had a chance to speak it. My first few words were the ones I uttered today, with little success.

My father asks if the milk is boiled. "No, but it's fresh," replies Anna. Naseema explains our concerns, and Anna immediately sends the pot of milk off to be boiled. My mother wants to find some water to wash the glasses, without offending the family. I have a look at the hands of the women and conclude that the milk is not clean. "I'm going to close my eyes and drink it," says Samera.

Mejgan is fast asleep on the bed. A chubby woman comes with a pot of wild berries floating in cold water. More women arrive, most bringing something—dried fruit, freshly cooked bread, butter and cheese. Each one welcomes us in her own way. "You must be very hungry," says Naseema's sister. She insists that we eat.

The dilemma for us, of course, is how can we eat? All the dishes in our home were cleaned several times before they were brought to the table. The utensils were sterilized in a pot of boiling water. Fruit and vegetables were soaked in a potassium mix and rinsed with fresh clean water. Mother Fatema was famous among our relatives for cleanliness and care. She never entered the kitchen without washing her hands, as is the routine in most city homes. But my father always demanded that extra attention be paid to hygiene, nutrition and health. And now, just a day away, here we are—so-called modern, urbanized people—driven out of our clean, tidy house into a world of which we know nothing. With our city attitudes, we think we are above even the kindest and most generous of people simply because we use knives and forks, eat on separate plates and sit around a dining-room table. In reality, we are lost between the two worlds.

Strangely enough, our hosts also treat us as if we are better than they are. The women who arrive all speak of themselves and their gifts as unworthy of city people. They observe our behaviour with a kind of fascination. They respect Naseema and view her as a link to the city, to a different life.

I don't touch a thing. I watch my parents as they drink their glasses of milk and swallow some berries. Samera tries to drink some milk, but can't. She eats some bread. Naseema shows us the toilet. It is on the other side of the empty yard, a tiny room with a hanging curtain as its door and a hole in the centre of the floor. We carry a lantern and watch our shadows as we walk in and out of the toilet. There is a water carrier outside. We pour water over each others' hands to wash. My mother and I—the most health-conscious of all—empty the entire water jug just to wash our hands. Our behaviour is embarrassing, but there is nothing else we can do; we are terrified of falling sick.

We wake up to the sound of roosters and the murmur of wind passing through the thick sycamore trees. The sun is already up. More freshly boiled milk and pots of tea are brought in, along with newly cooked bread and a plate of plums. I find our package of dried fruit and eat some with a piece of bread. I search for water to wash a cup so I can drink tea. My father tries to be reassuring. "Anything boiled and well cooked is fine," he says, giving me a meaningful look. Habibullah is the only one accustomed to rural living. The rest of us are prisoners of our own upbringing. Mejgan is too young to know better. She follows us by example rather than by words.

Two boys of eight and nine come in. One is Naseema's brother, the other a second cousin. They have brought two of our bags from Shafiqa's house. I quickly look inside. The tea set, several fabrics, the silver teapot with medication, and another package of dried fruit are still here. They have also brought news about the road. "There were lots of soldiers on the way," says Naseema's brother. "They were searching everything and everyone." My father asks how they managed to bring our bags. "We told the soldier that our brother was a military doctor and was recently killed in the war. We were taking a few of his belonging to our village for the family," says the other boy. "Did they believe you?" I ask. Both shrug, as if it doesn't matter any more. Another neighbour comes by with news that there are soldiers all over town and near the village. "It's better if we stay one more day here," says Naseema. "We can leave at night or very early in the morning—before sunrise."

The fear of the road, of the army checkpoints and of further humiliation comes over us again. Habibullah sits on the corner of the bed, deep in thought. As if in mourning, we all sit in silence against the mud wall. Anna has the eyes and gestures of an ancient wise woman, like the ones who exist in fairy tales. She immediately notices our grim faces. "It is better to wait," she says. "You can stay here as long as you want. This is your own home. It's very hot in Pakistan right now. Pass the summer here, and go in the autumn." My mother explains that we want to see my brother and Samera's husband as soon as we can.

Anna encourages us to join her daughters-in-law in preparing bread. Samera and I sit near the circular kiln, which is built into the ground, to learn how to cook bread. It appears such a simple thing. "Do you want to try?" asks one of the women. I take a piece of the soft dough, spread it over the kiln frame and attempt to stick it to the wall of the hot oven. The heat nearly burns the skin off my hand, and the dough falls into the fire. The women laugh. I try again. After losing four potential pieces of flatbread, I finally manage to stick the dough to the wall. In a few short minutes, the cooked bread comes out. It's not as thin and crisp as the ones the village women bake, but it is appetizing. The smell of freshly baked bread spreads fast. I'm so hungry I begin to feel faint.

"Would you like to eat fresh plums with your bread?" asks Naseema's sister. The smiles on our faces is the answer. We take some bread and climb to the roof, following the two women. Plum and apple trees tower over the clay roof, the fruit hanging from the branches. I have to touch them with my own hand to believe they are real. "The apples are diseased," says Naseema's sister, biting into one to show us the tiny worm inside it. Samera and I watch her as she spits out the piece she's bitten. Greedily we collect some plums, rubbing them on our clothes to clean off the dust, as Naseema's sister shows us. How soon we've forgotten the cleanliness of our city life. Not until after I've wolfed some down do I remember that they are not washed.

By now, I've gained enough confidence to speak Pushtu. I even try to translate for Samera, who says one word in Pushtu and the rest in Dari, laughing at herself. With my broken Pushtu and Samera's sign language, we manage to talk to the two women. They tell us that their husbands are fighting with the mujahidin forces on the top of a mountain, pointing at a peak that Samera and I cannot distinguish. Naseema's sister is a couple of months pregnant. Samera's eyes brighten. She wants to know how Naseema's sister got married and how long ago. The two women speak cheerfully about their weddings and, running out of breath and Pushtu words to translate, I suddenly realize that they are communicating in a strange way, as if there is a universal language of happiness. Naseema's sister speaks in Pushtu, Samera in Dari with some Pushtu words, but they understand each other.

Shortly after sunset, they serve dinner. As we sit around the tablecloth spread at the centre of the room, Anna tells us about her husband. "He was a mujahid," she says proudly. "He died in the war against *kufar*s [infidels]. Now my two sons, the husbands of these two"—pointing at her daughters-in-law—"are on the mountain. They are fighting the *frangies* [foreigners]. *Inshallah* [God willing], they will be victorious." She lifts both her hands to pray for them. Out of respect, we join in.

Naseema tell us that, since her husband's death, Anna has looked after all family affairs—a small stretch of land, a cow and the house. "Her sons come occasionally to visit for a few hours," Naseema says. "But it's not always safe, so they stay on the mountain." We also learn that the two rooms—one of which we've been using—belong to her sons and their wives. Anna sleeps on the other side of the yard, in an empty room that is like a storage shed. "Most nights I don't sleep," Anna says. "I keep guard, in case the Soviet or the government army shows up. My sons have entrusted their wives to me. I'm an old woman. I don't care if anything happens to me. But I must protect these young ones." She says the last words with a long sigh.

The next morning, Naseema wakes us around 3:30. "It is time to go," she says. Like lost souls, we put on our shoes and burqas. Anna has already prepared breakfast. "Eat something," she says kindly. It is too early to eat. We thank her for everything and make for the door. Naseema tucks some bread in one of our bags. We follow her. We can see the light gradually rising on the horizon. There are no villages, just one hill after another spread out in front of us. My father has thrown the largest of our three bags on his back. He looks like one of those *joalies* (weight carriers) in Kabul who tote sacks of flour or barley. Naseema has another bag under her burqa. I'm carrying the smallest one, dragging it on the ground when we climb the hills.

At midday, we pass through a beautiful valley. In ordinary times I would have loved to sit on the grass here, but we only stop briefly to drink some water and eat dried fruit and bread near a narrow river. Then we wade through the water. The riverbed is muddy. "Take off your shoes," Naseema instructs us. "It's soft ground underneath." She throws the smaller bags onto the other side of the river. Then she helps my father cross with the heavier bag. Wrapping our burqas around us, lifting up the skirts and the bottoms of our baggy pants with one hand and holding our shoes in the other, we make our way to the other side. Following Naseema, we rub our feet on the grass to clean off the mud.

The rest of the way is dry land. But my mother is falling behind, tired; my shoes are hurting me. We are not used to walking across such rugged landscape. There are no army checkpoints. By going through villages, we are intentionally avoiding them, says Naseema. At sunset, we arrive in a village where we're going to spend the night.

Naseema knocks at a door, and a little girl in a red dress opens it. She runs inside as soon as she sees Naseema, calling to her mother. Naseema follows her and returns with a key. The guest room has proper cushions and pillows and a nice red carpet; the family must be rich. Naseema brings two plates of cooked spinach and potatoes with a stack of bread and drinking water. We are so exhausted that we've no appetite to eat. Naseema hands us a couple of sheets, saying we can use them to cover ourselves.

We leave early the next morning, as soon as the roosters call. It's a hot day. After three hours of walking, we encounter a government checkpoint. A soldier orders us to stop. "Where are you going?" he shouts from a distance. "Home," Naseema shouts back. The soldier walks towards us, holding his rifle. "We were at a wedding and are going home now," Naseema explains. "Where was the wedding?" asks the soldier. "Ayoub

Qala," we say collectively. This is the name of the village where we just spent the night. "Wait here," says the soldier. He returns to his post, a mud room with a broken window. We sit on the ground, waiting for his orders. The two other officers are watching us. The soldier comes back. "Your family?" he asks my father, pointing at us. "Yes, my wife and daughters," he says. "I have to see their hands," the soldier says. We stick out our hands from behind the burqas. I notice how dirty my nails and hands look, as if they haven't been washed for days. But it is not enough to satisfy the soldier. He sends out a boy of eight or nine to call a woman from the nearby village.

After some thirty minutes, an elderly woman arrives to examine our faces. She pushes her long black scarf away from her face as she pulls back our burqas to look. Naseema is talking to her, trying to find out what's going on. "He thinks you've got a man under the burqa," she says. When the woman lifts the burqa from Mejgan's face, she laughs loudly. "She's a little girl, ah, a little girl," she says to the soldier, who's standing a couple of metres away. "You must have walked so awkwardly that he thought you were a man," says Naseema to Mejgan. Naseema explains that men escaping conscription sometimes use the burqa as cover. She then follows the other woman and the soldier to the room. We sit again, helplessly, waiting. It is only the fourth day of our journey, yet it feels as if we've been on the road for years.

Naseema returns. We are free to go. The anxious boredom of sitting at the checkpoints, the fatigue of walking kilometre after kilometre along dirt tracks and hilltops and through mud, through countryside we don't know, has drained our energy and the hope of making it to Pakistan. At no other time in my life have I wished the sun to disappear from sight—not just because of the heat, but because sunset means we can stop walking. As we leave the checkpoint, Naseema says this is the last government post. "The rest is mujahidin country." She says these words with happiness.

"How often do you travel this road?" asks my father.

"Often," she says.

There is silence.

"It's very dangerous," says my mother.

"I help a lot of families leave," Naseema says.

"It's a difficult job," my father adds.

Naseema doesn't reply. Since we discovered her age and saw her face for the first time, we've been wondering why she does this. Money is an obvious answer, but there are thousands of people like her who make more money spying for the KhAD. Maybe she spies for the KhAD too—how would we know? These days, people do anything to survive.

The following day we are waiting along the road for a wooden bridge to be repaired. The area is called Durrani, a place we've never heard of before. We sit on the grass, under a tree. There are a few other families. They, too, are escaping from Afghanistan. A pickup truck full of watermelons is waiting for the bridge as well. The driver stands by his car, watching us from a distance, and then brings us some watermelons. Each family gets one or two. It's like a free picnic. We lift the burqa covers from our faces, breathe the warm air and eat warm watermelon hungrily.

As we sit under the shade of a wild berry tree, my mother asks Naseema how many brothers and sisters she has. "One older brother, and one younger—the one who brought your bags," she says. "I've got two sisters—one you saw in the first village." Her older brother is a mujahid and is currently in Peshawar, Pakistan. "Where are your parents?" asks Samera. There is a pause. "Some years ago . . . ," Naseema begins, and then swallows the rest of her words before beginning again.

"Someone had shot a Russian soldier in our village," she says. "Villagers were worried about the punishment from the government. They even sent a man to the committee to tell them we were not responsible for the Russian's death. One night, the army came. It was late at night, totally dark. We heard a sound, and by the time we got up, the soldiers were already over the wall and in the yard. They had surrounded the village. The man who had gone to plead on our village's behalf was with them. My father saw him and walked out to find out what was going on. They shot my father right in front of the door, before he could say a word. We saw him fall on his back. My mother ran to the door to help him. He was not dead. We could hear him crying from the pain.

"The soldiers walked towards the house. I took my baby brother and went to hide behind the curtain, where my mother kept extra blankets and pillows. My older brother covered my two sisters with sheets and went to help my mother. 'Don't move,' he told us. A soldier hit my brother on the head, and he fell unconscious. My mother held the soldier's leg, screaming, 'You killed my son, you murderer.' And then they shot her too." Naseema stops. She has torn the rind of a piece of watermelon into tiny bits while speaking. She throws them to the ground.

"Later I discovered that the Russians had orders to shoot anything that moved. Maybe that's why they shot my dad in the first place. Who knows? I saw the face of the Russian soldier who walked into the room where we were hiding. He said something to the others. They ran a torch over the wall and the window. Then they walked out. Someone had put a knife into my father. When the raid was over and the villagers came together to bury the dead, we found the knife in his body. Our neighbour thought it had been done by the village man my father had recognized in the yard, standing with the soldiers." Naseema stops again.

We all need a break. Naseema wipes the sweat from her forehead and fixes her burqa. Her expression is helpless, innocent. Samera looks like someone who's just been to a horror movie. Eyes fixed on Naseema's face, she's waiting for the happy ending. There is none. "Helping people leave the country is my revenge for my parents," says Naseema in a determined voice. "I was eleven when they killed my parents. My brother was thirteen. He went to the mountain, then to Pakistan. My uncle took us to his home in Kabul. I raised my one-year-old brother and my sisters there. After my uncle died, his wife kicked us out of the house." Naseema shakes her head.

"She asked you to leave? Where did she think you'd go?" asks my father.

"She made our lives miserable, complaining that we dirtied her home, insulting my sisters when I was away. So I rented a place and moved out."

It's hard to think how to divide the blame between the Russians who shot her parents, the man who betrayed her village, and her uncle's wife.

"With the help of God, I've married off one sister, the one you saw." Naseema looks up. Warmth has returned to her face. "God willing, I'll marry off the other one soon as well."

"What about yourself?" I ask.

"I'll never marry," she says. "I have to avenge my parents' blood. I saw them die with my own two eyes." She points her finger to her face. "I still have to look after my younger brother. He's like my son. I've raised him, you know." She sounds proud. "Him and me, we work together."

The bridge is fixed. Naseema brushes the dust from her dress. On the other side is a countryside of trees and fields. "This is Logar," says Naseema as we cross. I remember Noriya, my classmate, talking about this place. Her family was originally from this province. She'd be stunned to know I am here. It has been years since they've been here, because of the war. We walk along a rough track beside a roaring river. Where the water is shallow, and with Naseema's help, we ford the river on a bed of stones, and then trudge through a deserted town. There are several empty, half-destroyed houses. The land hasn't been worked for years. "Russians bombed this place," says Naseema. "The people here were the first to oppose the government. All the men are now fighting in the mountains."

We take refuge for the night in another small village. A woman is our host. "She's cooked some goat meat," says Naseema. As the meat is served, our host proudly explains how last autumn she had to kill her last goat. What we are offered to eat is the last of that goat's meat, she tells us. "You should have kept this for your family," says my father. "You're guests," she says. "There is nothing better than a guest." Later, as we cross the yard to go to the toilet, the woman shows us a hanging wooden stick. "That is where we dried the goat meat."

"I'm going to be sick," says Samera. "I wish she'd never shown us that stick. God knows how many flies and worms visited that piece of meat." I remind her it was cooked.

None of the women we meet in these villages has any formal education. They treat us with great respect because Naseema tells them that my mother is a teacher and that we have been to school.

For a change, a lorry is going to take us a few kilometres. "Their neighbour is going our way, so I asked him to give us a ride," says Naseema. We climb into the back of the lorry. As it starts to move over a mountain road, I slide from one end to the other, screaming for help as the lorry bounces over the uneven road. "Hold on tight to the sides," Naseema shouts. "Try to sit firmly on the surface." It's hard steel. "God help us," says my mother, telling my sister to hold on to my father if she can't keep a hand on the side bars.

We are travelling at the base of a mountain, along a line of silver birch and oak trees. "He used to work for the ministry of construction," says Naseema about the driver. "He used to transport stones in this lorry." Now he works with the resistance. "If it weren't for the bandits on the road, the mujahidin territory would be safe for travel," says Naseema. "People are kinder, especially when they know you're going to Pakistan. There are no checkpoints to worry about." The lorry stops. "We've got a few hours' more walking before the next village," Naseema says.

After eight days on the road, we can't believe we ever wanted to go to Pakistan. My mother is the first to express regret: "If I'd known it was going to be this hard, I would never have left Kabul."

"Too late," says my father. "I tried for years to tell you that. We're going to Pakistan—what else do you expect?" He is very upset. But he doesn't say another word, and Jamila doesn't reply. They are too exhausted to argue.

Far away from any town or village, we walk through a desert. There is no use keeping our shoes on. Holding our shoes in one hand and lifting our burqas with the other, we drag ourselves along. There are bones half-covered in sand. I see a skeleton I'm convinced is human. Naseema says it's a dead horse. Farther on, we see an animal skull. "See?" says Naseema, kicking the skull with her feet. "This is the head." Over the hill, we can make out the sunken carcass of a large truck, its yellow cab and part of its windshield still visible— and a skeleton close to it in the sand. Naseema is silent now. This is a man, not a horse, I say to myself.

A minibus moves slowly over the sand. I feel as if I'm dreaming. As it gets closer, Naseema waves so we can get a ride. "Only women," says the driver. "Men have to walk." The driver is concerned that if the weight is too great, the car won't move in the soft sand. We jump inside the bus, taking the bag from my father. I sit in the back seat to watch from the window. A group of men catch up with my father. They are all walking. The engine of the bus screams as the driver shifts gears to keep it moving. We drive down a slope, and my father and the other men disappear from sight. We tell Naseema to ask the driver to stop and wait for him. "The car can't stop—with its weight, it'll just sink into the sand," Naseema says. "Don't worry, there are other men; they'll be with us soon." When it reaches a hard patch of land, the bus stops. The driver sprinkles water over the engine to cool it down. We sit in the bus, waiting. Finally, the group of men arrives. My father is with them. They all get on the bus.

We continue the journey, up a mountain, with the desert behind us. "We're lucky to have seen this bus," says Naseema.

As we drive, she points to a set of stones a couple of metres from the road. "That's the graveyard of forty people who were killed not long ago." In a vain attempt, I try to count the tombstones. "The government planes fly over this area and drop bombs if the pilot spots a bus or a car. They know that people are leaving the country, so they try to stop them. Those forty were killed by a bomb. That's why cars don't come this way. This driver is very brave."

"This is it," says the driver. "This is the end of my territory." Naseema tries to persuade him to go a little farther. He shuts down the engine.

As we resume our walk, she explains that these areas are divided into territories. Different groups control each portion of land. The drivers can't go past their own line. "What if they do?" asks my father.

"Either they are shot at, or they have to pay a lot of money to buy the right to travel in the next territory."

This is a product of war. Afghanistan was once a country. Now, it has been chopped into clandestine states that belong to warlords, mujahidin groups or bandits.

After two more days of walking, just once getting a ride on a cart pulled by a tired donkey, it feels as if we'll never make it out of this austere land. Our rubber shoes have become coffins for our lifeless feet. It's impossible to put the shoes on or take them off without crying with pain.

On the tenth day of travelling, we arrive in a town. There is a large stockpile of flour—layer after layer of sacks—on the side of the street, partly covered with a sheet of plastic. There are also piles of wood. "How come no one takes anything?" asks Samera. "The area is controlled by the mujahidin," says Naseema. "I'm sure they're guarding everything."

A lorry goes by. Naseema lifts her hand to stop it. It drives on a few metres and then halts. A man holding a Kalashnikov is sitting in the back. He helps my father get aboard, then the rest of us climb up. After an hour, the driver stops for a break. A young, slender man, holding his right leg to keep it above the ground, hops out of the front seat, trying to walk beside the lorry. His friend, shorter and better built, gets out to help him. The young man sits on a stone, resting his right foot carefully on the ground. My father asks him what's wrong. "He's got a *chara* [a piece of shrapnel] in his foot," says his friend. The young man is in pain. His face would normally be very handsome, with high cheekbones and honey-coloured eyes. But his skin has a yellow cast. His eyes are tired, with dark lines underneath them. "We were on the front line. He was throwing a hand grenade, and a rocket landed nearby. A piece of shrapnel has gone inside." The young man's right foot, covered with bandages, is three times its normal size. "We're going to Peshawar so he can have it removed." They say they are fighters with the Harakat Islamic Party. My father asks if they have proper medical supplies with them at the front. It turns out they don't even have a doctor.

The guy who's been doing all the talking has long curly hair and a kind smile. He brings water to my mother so she can wash her hands. "How old are you?" asks my mother. "Nineteen," he replies. My mother asks him about his family. "It's been three years since I was last home. I've got a mother and a sister her age," he says, pointing at Mejgan. He is from Sangi Safid, a town near Logar, explains Naseema. "It's far away," he says. My mother complains that we've not been able to sleep properly, nor eat or wash up. He laughs, touching his curly hair. "How long do you think it's been since this hair has been washed, mother?" he asks. We are silent. "Three months," he says. I look at his greasy curls. They reach to his neck. "When I first joined, I was laying mines for the Russian tanks—anti-tank mines. You had to be very careful. One day, I reached for the back of my head to scratch it. I had lice in my fingernails. I nearly screamed. It's like that at first, but you get used to it. When you're at the front, you're lucky to live, you don't think about washing and shaving or a haircut."

The lorry is ready. The two mujahidin offer us the seat next to the driver. My father refuses, saying the patient has the priority. He searches in the silver pot and offers the wounded man a few painkilling tablets. "To help you get to Peshawar," says my father. The man looks at them suspiciously. Then his friend asks if the armed man in the back is with us. "We thought he was with you," says Naseema. "No. He's probably with some other group," the curly-haired man replies. Naseema explains that my father is a doctor. "Why don't you come and work with us?" asks the wounded man. "We need a doctor." My father says he has to take his family to Pakistan.

We drive on for four more hours. At one point, the gunman in the back bangs on the side of the lorry, asking the driver to stop. He jumps out of the car, and the lorry moves again. After a few kilometres, the driver stops. This is the end of his territory. The wounded man and his friend stand on the side of the road, waiting for another vehicle. The wounded man shakes my father's hand, showing his gratitude for the medicine. We say goodbye, wishing them luck. They smile. Later, I turn and spot both men in the distance, still on the side of the road, waiting for a ride.

* * *

It's getting dark. Naseema is becoming nervous. We are in Zazhi, she says. The tall mountains covered with trees are breathtaking in the early evening light. "We have to find a place to spend the night," she says. "It's not safe to continue walking in the dark." Zazhi is famous for its beautiful women and handsome men. And, during the war years, for revenge killing and banditry. On a hilltop, Naseema spots a half-ruined building. We head in its direction.

It turns out to be an abandoned café. It has a roof, but one of the walls has half fallen. There are some people already inside, each claiming a little space to spend the night. Most are already asleep, or pretending to be. There are still the remains of a large kiln, a few shelves and a stove. We gather in one corner, spreading our blankets on the ground. In the dark, we chew the remainder of our dried fruit, sip water and prepare to sleep. My father suggests we use our bags for pillows.

I can't fall asleep. I notice a door near where we've laid our blankets. Carefully, I open it. It leads to a small balcony. The stars are shining so brightly that I feel I'm in wonderland. There is a half moon. In the dark, I push the headgear of the burqa back over my shoulders, wearing it like a shawl. I can hear the sound of water. Why is the night so haunting? I press my fingers against the balcony's floor. It is soft soil. My fingernails sink into it. My mother slips through the door. "What are you doing here?" she whispers. "Come and sleep." I look at my hand. Bits of moist soil are falling off my fingers as I lift them from the ground. I wish we could stay here a few more days.

"This is the last night before you cross the border," Naseema says as I walk back into the café. I realize I've been saying goodbye to my country. I've never thought of it like that before—never thought about being so attached to anything. "The whole world, the universe, wherever we go, it is all the land of God's creation," I've heard my grandmother say. Why does it make any difference, then, to leave this place for another?

Inside the café, sleeping bodies lie in rows. Some have pulled burqas over themselves for cover, others woollen shawls; a few men have only checkered scarves over their heads and faces. I sit between my mother and Samera on the tiny rectangular space that is going to be my bed for the night. It feels like a grave.

In the morning, we walk along the river I heard the night before. We are close to the border. "I'll be turning away after that curve," says Naseema. Naseema has become a part of our family. We feel as if we've known her for years. She is polite, kind and intelligent. We've told her about my brother Hassib and Uncle Wahid, who are in Pakistan. She knows about my father's recent illness. She let Mejgan put her head on her shoulder while walking, when she was too tired to stand on her own. She's told us how she smuggles arms, bringing guns to the underground fighters inside Kabul. She hides the hand grenades and pistols amid spinach and lettuce in a basket. But she constantly changes her methods of hiding and transportation. She's also made friends with lots of guards; she bribes them, and they leave her alone.

"If I had a choice, I'd study medicine," Naseema says. "God only knows how many more times I'll be crossing that desert." There's not much hope in her voice.

It's midday. There are high mountains ahead. My father gives Naseema a note to be taken to my grandmother, informing her of our safety. She kisses my father's hands and our cheeks. "The car will take you from here," she says. "The driver is paid. Take good care, and good luck." She pulls her burqa over her face and walks away. We stand and watch her in sorrow and admiration. She's the bravest eighteen-year-old I've ever met, and also one of the most resolute. All the way, the only person who didn't complain about pain, hardship or problems was Naseema. Her determination to fight the Russians has made her my heroine. Like Malalai. I'll always remember her name.

We get in the back of the navy blue pickup. The road is an unpaved track, two parallel lines of dirt with a yellow-green patch of grass in the middle. The dust stirred up by the tires burns our throats. The hard seats of the pickup feel like rocks. From where we are sitting, we can look only backwards, to the land we are leaving, to the place where Naseema is returning with our note. The grit swirls around us. At one point the pickup stops, and two men climb into the back. They are dressed in traditional Afghan clothes and have small beards, like all the men in mujahidin territory. One is a skinny, tall man with greenish eyes and thick eyebrows. Two of his front teeth are missing; the rest are a bright yellow.

The tall man asks my father where we are going. My father mumbles a few words about our journey to Pakistan. The man, who introduces himself as a mujahid belonging to Gulbuddin Hekmatyar's Hizb-i Islami (Islamic Party), laughs loudly. "So we finally forced you out of Kabul," he roars. "Our rockets are working." He grins. He tells my father that he is responsible for firing rockets into our city. He turns to his friend. "When I finish firing the rockets, the next day I go prowling to see how many people I've killed." His friend smiles.

My father asks him how well he knows the targets he is shooting at. The man laughs loudly again. "The city is the target. That is where we send the rockets. They just seem to hit the right spot." I remember the bus station, the blood on the road, the officer's hat, the hanging hand and purse. "One evening, several of the rockets missed," yellow-teeth says. "They hit a graveyard." The dead, it seemed, were killed all over again. He speaks so coldly about it, the counting of casualties a kind of scientific operation. And yet he is driven by passion for a Russia-free Afghanistan, much as I am. Why is this man so proud of launching his rockets on Kabul? Those of us who lived in Kabul were not all Communist Party members. "You support the Communist government by continuing to live under their rule and work for them," yellow-teeth replies.

I want to protest that I was a member of a resistance group that harmed the government more than it helped it. Instead I remain silent. His logic in justifying violence is not much different from mine when I proudly threw stones at the military vehicles and government cars. None of the soldiers and officials in those vehicles was individually responsible for the Russian occupation. They were not all Communist Party members. But I was angry, and I believed the Kabul regime would fail if these people quit working for it. Of course, there is a difference between throwing stones and firing rockets— the first is an act of civil disobedience, the other is a crime— but the motives are identical. What is it about occupation that makes us able to justify anything?

"Two SCUDs landed in Parachinar," says the mujahid. "That's where you'll be arriving on the other side of the border. They hit a restaurant and killed three people. You'll see it when you go down the mountain." My father asks if the restaurant belonged to Afghans. "They are Afghan," the man replies. His friend explains that people from this side of the border have moved to the other side, and now they're running all the businesses there.

The pickup truck stops. The driver tells a Pakistani border guard that we are Afghan refugees. The officer then taps the vehicle and says, "Welcome to Pakistan" in Pushtu, with a smile. Tears run down my cheeks. The two mujahidin jump out of the vehicle. Our pickup turns along a sheer cliff and bumps, skids and twists down a narrow road.

Something is hurting inside me. I think about my books, and the little things that have been precious to me: the silver Parker pen given to me as a birthday gift, the faces of family and friends. All those I remember have a kindness attached to them. I think of Dyana and Mir, my grandmother and Aunt Shafiqa. All of a sudden, a real border is now between us, and they are out of reach.

9

A HOUSE OF MARTYRS

Let's cry
For the bitter lives of refugee women,
For the silence of closed and broken doors.
For the memory of too much grief and too little
      happiness,
For the dark days and nights, for the death of art and
      poetry.
Let's cry
For love, for beauty,
For the white stones on which we've engraved our
      memories,
For remembrance—the fleeting moments—
For the prayer call of freedom,
Let's cry.

                  Qahar Ausi, 1989

THE SMOGGIEST, WARMEST SUNSET I've ever seen. Peshawar at the height of its glory. Once part of the eighteenth-century Afghan empire, it's now a place of refuge for thousands of fleeing Afghans. After a six-hour car journey from the border town of Parachinar, we have arrived in downtown Peshawar. Cars, rickshaws, buses with musical horns, strung in bright red, green and orange lights, horse-drawn carts and bicycles move in a haze of dust and smoke.

I have heard many Pushtu traditional songs praising Peshawar. But today it's overcrowded, polluted and dirty, a forgettable place if not for the jubilant moment of reuniting with Uncle Wahid and my brother, Hassib. It's a scene from a typical Indian movie. Against the background of a busy street, familiar faces stop to stare at each other in utter disbelief. "It's you! My God," says a voice. "So we found you," we say in reply. We greet each other with smiles and tears.

As darkness spreads over the city, we arrive in Latifabad, a poor district of grey walls, one-storey concrete buildings and barren, garbage-strewn land. This is where Uncle Wahid and Hassib have been living with an Afghan family. Qasim, the eldest son, is Uncle Wahid's best friend. We meet everyone, but given our state of exhaustion, it's difficult to remember who is who in the family's chain of command. We will stay with them until we find a place of our own.

They serve us cups of tea and ice water. We sit in a large room, where two ceiling fans circle over our heads. "There is only one bathroom," says a tall woman—one of several ladies in the house. "But there is enough water for you to take a shower." The relief and pleasure of feeling water running over my skin for the first time in almost twelve days are sensational. We sit around a large tablecloth—spread on the ground—to eat a dinner of rice and potatoes. An overwhelming fatigue has succeeded fear. We complain about the pain in our bodies. "As if I've been beaten with a stick," says my mother. Knowing that we don't have to get up in the morning to walk yet again is comforting.

All night, I dream of the road, travelling that treacherous

frontier track over and over again. The heat of the Peshawar summer is unbearable, even at dawn. In Kabul, there was always a breeze in the early morning and evening. The heat makes me impatient, irritated with my own family. I feel suffocated in the room, desperate for air in a place where so many people are sitting. I hear my father talking to our host about the cost of living in Pakistan. Uncle Wahid and Samera are chatting with Qasim's grandmother. My mother is recounting the tale of our long trek across Afghanistan. Too many conversations are going on at the same time. I leave the room.

Qasim's mother is washing something in the yard, which is surrounded by high concrete walls. I walk to a door in the outer wall and open it a crack to look outside. Before my eyes can get used to the open space—which looks like a field—I hear a gunshot. It takes me a few seconds to react and slam the door. Turning my head, I see Qasim's mother running towards me in terror, pulling me back towards the inner part of the house. "Don't you ever do this again," she hisses. What have I done wrong?

Now the entire family is in the yard, forming a circle around me. "They will shoot," one of them says.

"They already did," replies the mother, turning towards me.

One of the girls tries to explain. "Women are not allowed to leave the house without proper cover—if we go out, we go in groups, or else a man has to come with us." She grins. "This is Latifabad, in Pakistan—not Kabul," she says. "You'll get used to it."

The words whiz by my ears like bullets. "Was someone shooting at me?" I ask. "Was someone trying to kill me?"

"No," the girl replies. "They are warning you that if you peek outside the door again with your hair uncovered, you'll be in trouble."

"Who is doing this?"

"The mujahidin forces."

"But why would the mujahidin do this?" I ask.

"You've got a lot to learn," the father says.

I am led back inside feeling even more suffocated. One of the women sprinkles water on my face—something traditionally done to a person in shock. Another hands me a glass of water.

But it is what I'm hearing, not the gunfire, that is shocking. Are these the same mujahidin who fight the Russians? The freedom fighters, the resistance to the occupation? There must be some mistake. Why would they shoot at refugees?

"This is mujahidin-controlled Peshawar," insists Qasim. "Here, you're a prisoner—like being in Puli Charkhi, especially if you're a woman."

His brother, Fareid, quips, "Unfortunately, you pay for your own lodging." Everyone laughs at the joke.

"The tragedy," adds my uncle, "is that this is true."

I had been excited to move to Pakistan—the place where my mujahidin heroes were based. Pakistan is one of our friends in the war against the Russians. There's a distance between Peshawar and Kabul, but being in Peshawar meant I was closer to the seat of mujahidin operations. I could be directly involved. But my journey has not ended with my arrival in Peshawar. There seems to be a different kind of distance now—an ideological one—separating me from those whom I've idealized all these years. Am I not one of the mujahidin? I have supported them with my life. Why are they prepared to shoot at me?

I follow one of the family's daughters into the kitchen, offering to help with the dishes. She is a high-school graduate, but here in Pakistan she stays at home. Her two older sisters, also educated, stay home as well. Her elder brother,

Qasim—a civil engineer—works as a bus conductor. Her younger brother, a high-school graduate, sells used clothes in a market. The daughter shows me her long Pakistani shawl, which she puts around her, covering all of her face except for her eyes.

"Don't you get bored staying home all the time?" I ask.

"It is hard at first, but then you get used to it," she says. "It's because of the jihad."

It's impossible for me to accept that the people I admired so much could actually force women to stay at home. All those brave women in the villages, Anna, Naseema . . . They were all mujahidin. The first victims of the 1980 uprising in Kabul were mujahidin—women who received bullets in their chests for refusing to end their protest against the Soviet invasion. Mir's friends and the underground Islamic youth group I was part of were mostly female fighters. There was no imposed dress code. So what is wrong with these people in Pakistan?

I leave the kitchen and find my father and the others discussing how to find a place to live. I sit next to my father and tell him that I'm going back to Afghanistan. "You can't do that," he says. "We've only just arrived here."

"I don't care," I reply. "I'm not going to live under these conditions." I get up and stand against the door. I'm so used to my personal freedom I cannot bear the thought of being locked up behind the walls of a house.

Everyone gathers around me by the door. Qasim's father suggests we should go to Islamabad. "The mujahidin don't have much control there, and there are courses, schools that women can attend."

My uncle explains that my father's chances of finding a job as a doctor are much greater in Peshawar than in Islamabad. "All foreign-aid agencies are based in Peshawar."

"Let's go to Islamabad," my father says, looking at me.

After we get our money in exchange for the piece of paper we brought from Kabul, a car arrives at the gate of the house, and we are on our way to the capital of Pakistan.

Only a three-hour drive away, Islamabad looks much more like a city than Peshawar does, with wide tree-lined avenues and proper road signs. But even here, there are restrictions. In Islamabad, women go out wearing a Pakistani-style shalwar kameez and head cover similar to the ones I saw in Peshawar, but with some hair showing.

We go to the house of one of my father's relatives. After dinner, we talk about what happened in Peshawar that morning and who might have fired the shot. The family thinks it must have been Gulbuddin Hekmatyar's people. He is one of fifteen different mujahidin leaders. "He's disliked by all refugees," says Najeb, our host. "He's America's favourite, and the most powerful. He was the only mujahidin leader to receive Stingers from the States." Najeb tells us that during the reign of General Zia ul-Haq, Hekmatyar's sphere of control reached as far as Islamabad. "Now, with Benazir Bhutto in power, he's been limited to Peshawar and region."

As we settle into the modern G10 district, a newly developed suburb of Islamabad, we learn more about Hekmatyar and the other mujahidin groups. "The CIA paid more than 3.1 billion U.S. dollars to create and support Hekmatyar," says our neighbour, Qalanderzada. "As for his religious attitude, Hekmatyar is very close to the Iranian leaders. It's ironic that the West thinks the Iranian leadership is theocratic and fundamentalist, but keeps Hekmatyar and his Islamic Party on their payroll." Qalanderzada is a poet and writer, an old friend of my father. He moved to Islamabad with his wife, son and daughter several months ago, and divides his time between writing and treating refugees' psychological problems through hypnotism.

He is slightly shorter than my father, and a decade older, with dark skin and snow-white hair. In his spare time, he discusses poetry and politics with us. In addition to Hekmatyar, he tells us, the CIA also supports Yonous Khallis's all-Pushtun, anti-Shia Islamic Party. "It's mainly because of his high body count against the Russians," Qalanderzada says. Khallis is as radical in his propagation of an Islamic ideology as Hekmatyar. There is also a third group, Sayyaf's Islamic Unity. Abdul Rasul Sayyaf is directly supported by the Saudi government and wealthy Arab donors. He promotes the Saudi brand of Islam called Salafi. "Together, this triangle of ultra-conservative mujahidin groups provides a source of inspiration for the Arab Islamists; their members are America's foot soldiers in the Cold War." Qalanderzada shakes his head. There are several other Muslim parties, but none has enough legitimacy to form a government. So, with the help of the West and its Muslim allies—Egypt, Pakistan and Saudi Arabia—a coalition of various mujahidin groups has formed an Afghan interim government-in-exile. In the future, the coalition is supposed to replace the communist government in Kabul. "They'll be no better than the communists, maybe worse," says Qalanderzada.

In Kabul, I was unaware of these religious and political rivalries. I didn't know that each foreign country that opposed Russia's presence in Afghanistan supported its own chosen Afghan Islamic group. I didn't know that these groups fought each other for power. I was fascinated by the word "mujahidin." Because they were fighting the Russians, I supported them all, unconditionally. Their ability to intimidate the communist government in Kabul was proof of genius as well as courage. Now it appears that, like so many of my friends and classmates, I was staring at a looking glass. The mujahidin I believed in are no longer a reality. I'm beginning to see a different face of jihad.

"The Afghan jihad leadership is corrupt," I write to Mir. "Refugees live in places of desolation, with little water or electricity, in fifty degrees of heat. They are crammed into the poor districts of Peshawar and into the refugee camps near the border. The leaders of the jihad and their cronies live in large homes with walls of marble. They drive the newest model Toyota Corollas; the refugees walk long distances because they cannot afford bus fare."

But Sayeed, the man who's going to take our letters, says it's too risky to carry mine. People who take messages to Kabul accept only safe notes and, occasionally, a picture. Like many untold stories, my letter remains unsent. "Why don't you write about the weather, the city and the market here?" Sayeed asks. "I bet your friends in Kabul would like to hear about the Atwar bazaar in Islamabad."

I go with my father to the Atwar (Sunday) bazaar, early in the morning when the heat is still tolerable. The market is about thirty minutes' walk from our flat. I look at all the books spread over a cloth on the ground. "I bring them from Iran," says the bookseller, a tall, lean man in his late twenties, with a short brownish beard. He watches us with green, slightly narrowed eyes. "If you want a specific book, I can try to find it on my next trip." His display reminds me of all the books we left behind. But my father urges me to leave. "We'd better get home before it's too hot," he says. I know he's thinking about the books as well, but he prefers not to remember them any more—like so many other things in life that we now wish to forget.

As we cross the road, a young man with dark skin, thick black hair and a beard comes close. "Do you call this *hijib* [head cover]?" he asks. I continue to walk. "Is she with you?" he asks my father loudly.

My father stops. "Yes."

"Aren't you ashamed to see her dressed like this?"

"What is the problem?" I ask of this young man.

He turns to me and points at my head cover. "We've been fighting a holy war, spilling our blood—but not for this, not for our women to be dressed like this."

I'm dressed in a Pakistani-style shalwar kameez and have a head cover on, but my hair is still visible underneath my scarf. I look the man up and down. If he is so keen on what he calls "Islamic attire," why doesn't he look at himself in the mirror? His own tight jeans and T-shirt don't seem to fit his description of the mujahid he hopes to represent.

"I'll have to take you to the committee," he says, showing us his Kalashnikov.

I want to tell him that if he is so brave he should go to the front line or go and live under the barrage of rockets in Kabul. But my father intervenes. "We only arrived here a few days ago," he says. "She'll be properly dressed in the future." I hate my father's sheepish reply.

"You better make sure of that, or she'll be in trouble," says the man, staring at me as if I'm naked. We walk away with his eyes still fixed on us.

"Why didn't you let me answer him?" I demand of my father.

"What would you have said?"

I wanted to tell this man that I have always thought foreign occupation was an invasion of my personal rights, a violation of my integrity as a human being. That's why I hate the Russians. What he is doing is exactly the same thing. I wanted to tell this young man that the occupation obviously hasn't ended for me; that it's continuing in another form, which I will also resist. I'm running out of breath. My father is walking too fast.

"And you would have said all of this before he shot us, or afterwards?" he asks, mockingly. "You can argue with someone who uses words but not with someone who uses a gun."

"You were scared to go to his stupid committee," I accuse my father.

"No, I was afraid he'd shoot you or worse." My father stops. He cannot bring himself to say the man might have raped me. He doesn't understand that the man had already robbed me of my dignity and freedom. "Anyone who allows himself to preach about a dress code in the name of God is mentally disturbed—you can't reason with people like that."

My mother later takes his side. "If he killed both of you on the street, no one would've stopped him. Men with guns can get away with anything."

Mr. Saifi, who used to teach at the Lycée Istiqlal in Kabul, is visiting us from Peshawar. He was my brother's teacher. He joins my parents in warning me about "the jihadis," as he calls them. "There is no tolerance for any kind of debate," he says. "The first time I was stopped by them for wearing trousers and a shirt, I tried to explain to them that the Afghan jihad was not about clothing. This young man who was twice my size responded by reaching for my neck. He lifted me up a few centimetres from the ground. I didn't know what I'd done wrong. But I didn't like his reply and decided that I'd never argue about anything with them again." Saifi smiles. "Having a sense of humour helps," he says. "Otherwise the reality here is too painful to take."

Like everyone else, he now wears traditional clothes and has grown a beard. He says that he still sees himself as a dedicated mujahid—anxious to maintain the school in Peshawar that he helps run. "If we give as much attention to fighting about clothes as these radicals do, then we are no different from them." Saifi says that, in Peshawar, Afghan women who've made the mistake of working for a foreign-aid agency are sometimes kidnapped or assassinated—to teach others a lesson in morality.

With little to do in a two-room flat in Islamabad, I write letters to Dyana almost every day, even though I usually can't send them. But I hope she'll get to read them one day. I have learned to write in coded language in case Sayeed agrees to carry any of these letters to Kabul. So I write: "I'm living in a city where laughter is considered a crime; where the word 'death' rules over everything—the password is 'grey.'" I'm telling her that we are not allowed to be happy. "Two stones" is my code for "two eyes" (which means knowing things), and "a rock for a heart to pray" means having a heart of stone to survive. "A city where bullets are reasons, gunfire is an answer to all questions we cannot ask. A pinch of dust is our worth; a city where our human voice is never heard."

"I'm lucky to live in Islamabad," I write in another letter. "That is what I've been told, but I don't feel it. I've left a part of me behind in Kabul—not only in the memories of you, Dyana, and with my grandmother and my books, but also every step of the way on our journey. I've left my heart in mud villages where women await the return of their husbands and sons."

No matter which side of the border you're on, Afghanistan is a tragedy. Page after page of my cheap Pakistani notebook is filled with words of disappointment, nostalgia and unhappiness. I tell Dyana about our neighbours and the people who visit us—old acquaintances and new friends. "Monier is a young intellectual with an air of carelessness about him," I write. My father met Monier recently in the Atwar bazaar. He used to live in Iran, but moved to Pakistan more than a year ago. He's brought some books with him that he's lent me to read. It's not a bad collection, from Persian classical poetry to modern politics. "You would've liked the poems," I write Dyana.

Monier was a member of the Harakat Islami mujahidin group, one of the eight Shia parties based in Iran. Now he's as disillusioned about jihad as the rest of us, though he still keeps in touch with his old mujahidin friends. "I support an Islamic government in Afghanistan—but not with these groups," he says. His sixty-five-year-old mother has come from Kabul to encourage Monier to marry his fiancée and move to the States. But Monier is trapped. His mind may be in the States, but his heart is not. He shows us a picture of his fiancée. Dressed in a glamorous pink party dress, she looks cheerful. She's been living in the States with her family for several years. A relative did the matchmaking and she came to Islamabad for the engagement party. Since her return to the States, she's been sending him gifts, has finished his immigration paperwork and is waiting for him to join her. "Wouldn't you like to go?" my mother asks Monier. He beats around the bush. "It's not that," he says. "I like her, but I've got things to finish here." It's the wrong answer, and we feel sorry for his fiancée.

* * *

Uncle Asad and his family arrive one day in the late afternoon. Our small flat is quickly filled with noise—people we barely know, luggage, suitcases, Iranian blankets and clothes. Uncle Asad, his wife, Rona, their five daughters, four sons and a daughter-in-law, and four of Uncle Asad's in-laws have all left Iran for Pakistan. "We are going to America," he says over dinner. One of his sons has emigrated to Florida and has promised to bring the entire family to the States. My father says there's a four-bedroom apartment for rent down the road. "I'll speak to the real estate office tomorrow morning," he says. "We only need a place to stay for a couple of months," says Rona. "We will be leaving soon for the U.S."

It's hard to believe this is the same Uncle Asad who fell out with my father over the communist government in Afghanistan, and who then returned a few years later as a devotee of Iranian ayatollahs. Uncle Asad has trimmed his beard and changed his Arab-style abaya for a set of unironed trousers and shirt. His wife, though, carries her long black chador, a token of Iranian influence, wherever she goes.

I have little in common with their children. One of the sons has brought a box full of cassette tapes of Iranian pop songs, and he listens to them all day. "These songs are banned, but easy to find in the black market in Tehran," he says, while shaking his head to a tune by the Iranian singer Moheen. He encourages my brother and me to listen to Moheen. It's a cheerful dance song, with a fast drumbeat and loud keyboards. My cousins all speak Dari with an Iranian accent.

"Iran is an awful place," says Uncle Asad. "The Iranians treated us badly. They used to call us 'dirty Afghans.'" Rona tells us how they had to move from one house to another as Iranian landlords stopped renting to Afghan refugees. "During the Iran-Iraq war, when we waited in line to buy sugar, tea, bread or oil, we were constantly pushed out of the line because we were Afghans," she says. Rona is torn between her admiration for Iran's modern culture and infrastructure and her hatred of the Iranians who treated her with disrespect. "My three daughters were born in Tehran," she says. "They are Iranian by birth, but their country didn't want them to stay. The Iranian government closed down all our businesses and wanted us to leave."

My mother is now busy with Uncle Wahid and Samera, who has given birth to a baby girl. Given the ordeal she has been through, it's amazing the baby has survived. Samera's youngest brother now lives with them. A recent messenger from Kabul brought the news that Ali has been released from detention and is thinking of fleeing to Pakistan as well. There are more people arriving from Kabul every day. Mikhail Gorbachev has ensured that all Soviet military and economic support for the Kabul government has ended. But the mujahidin are still fighting, and those who arrive from Kabul say the rockets and bomb explosions, as well as the shortage of food, are worse than ever before. They also predict that Najibullah's rule will soon come to an end.

Uncle Asad and his family have occupied our flat for a week. I haven't been to the Atwar bazaar since the day of the encounter with the mujahid, but now our own home resembles the chaos of a market. After breakfast, my uncle, his two sons, his brother-in-law and his father-in-law leave for *hada*, the bus station. Jointly, they have bought a couple of Suzuki minibuses. "They've got to work," says Rona. "Even when we go to the States, they'll have to work."

All day they drive passengers, returning home late at night. There is no time for lengthy conversations, speeches about dress code and ayatollah-type rituals. They have been refugees for a long time now, living this every day for nearly a decade, Rona says. We are just discovering the hardships of this life. Uncle Asad is nagging my father that he, too, should invest his money in a minibus. "You have a young son," he says. "I'll drive the car; he can be the conductor until he learns to drive." My mother is unhappy with the proposition. "They're jealous," she argues. "They want my children to stop studying and work instead." Hassib is attending a weekly French course to keep up with his language studies, and a Pakistani neighbour has promised to help him enter a computer course. "You can have a lot of money, but if you don't have an income, it'll be gone in no time," says Rona.

My father worries that she's right. For several months now, we have been spending our savings without the prospect of any income. My father struggles with the fear of running out of money, and the conundrum of our future. "We'll be going to America," says Uncle Asad. "You've little chance of getting out of here any time soon. You've got to think of the future."

Despite my mother's wishes, my father decides to follow his brother's advice. Fourteen-year-old Hassib spends his days as a conductor in a minibus. He doesn't like it, but he's excited about learning how to drive. He's promised to teach me too.

For Uncle Asad and family, it's time for America now. And the West comes to our doorstep when their son Faoud shows up in sunglasses, Levi's and a Mickey Mouse T-shirt. "In the States, I'm a dishwasher," he says. He doesn't know how to say "dishwasher" in Dari—neither do we. I don't even know if there is an equivalent word for it in Dari. We are all impressed. He shows us an album full of photos of him in front of well-lit buildings, fancy shops and beautiful parks. "This is my car," he says, displaying a shot of himself behind the wheel of a red vehicle. He also shows us a stack of cards—health and insurance papers, a driver's licence. "I've applied for my green card, but it will be a while before I get it," he explains. Instead of the dream-come-true answer, he gives his parents a reality shock. "I can't sponsor you all at once, so you'll have to wait." How long? He shrugs his shoulders. No one knows.

"Standing in the passageway of old memories, I wave a torn flag," I write to Dyana. That flag is the symbol of my existence these days. There was a time when my heart wept for my ruined future, the missed chances and lost hopes. I used to have nightmares that I was going to lose something precious to me. Now I've woken up to the realization that I lost it some time ago. I've already sent three letters to Kabul and haven't heard a word back. It's as if we don't exist for those on the other side of this bloody border. "Life," I write again, "is an empty road."

To ease my depression, I attend a sewing course. It's the rainy season, a welcome change from the overwhelmingly hot weather of the past few months. When it rains, we go up to the roof of the building to soak in the water. The moment it reaches the ground, it dries up. "The soil is even thirstier than we are," I write to Dyana. Will the waiting season ever end? It's hard to motivate ourselves to leave the flat. The Pakistani shopkeepers stare at us as if we are for sale. There's the fear of being stopped by one of the mujahids who occasionally patrol the streets. But the classroom is a form of escape. Thinking about measuring and cutting, sewing and hemming can take the mind off negative thoughts. "Writing has become a silly preoccupation," I tell Dyana.

The sewing course is operated by the Jamiat Islamic Party—one of the relatively moderate mujahidin groups. Every morning, we begin by learning a verse from the Quran—it's part of the regular curriculum. Fareeda, a kind woman in her mid-twenties, teaches us to read and interpret the holy text. This is the first time I actually understand the meaning of the verses. If I had had a better knowledge of the Quran, I could have recited some verses in defence of my argument to the mujahid who lectured me. Fareeda laughs. "The kind of people who stop women on the street and brag about jihad don't know how to read the Quran, let alone understand its meaning." She advises me to learn the Book, and to give up fighting the mujahidin. "It's not worth it," she says. "Use your energy for better things in life."

Uncle Asad and his family have finally moved into a separate flat in the next building, but they still spend a lot of time in our home. Faoud has returned to the States. There is still no news from Kabul. The sewing course is nearly over. The winter's humidity is unbearable. Every day, young and old, we complain about aches and pains in our legs, arms and backs. Cursing life has become a new form of entertainment.

—

I'VE BEGUN TO TEACH in one of the mujahidin-run schools. After writing an exam, I was hired to teach Persian literature to grades five to twelve. The school receives direct support from Saudi Arabia. The principal is an elderly Afghan woman—a former teacher from the north. There are three Saudi women who teach Quranic recitation, Arabic and English as a second language. Their husbands have joined the Afghan jihad. We don't exchange a word with these women—they only arrive just in time for their classes. I stare at them curiously. They barely smile. One has a tiny baby she brings with her. The principal says her brother was killed in the jihad and her husband has been inside Afghanistan for several months.

The school has a rigid dress code: all teachers wear long black coats with head and face covers and white gloves. No jewellery is allowed. Students are provided with a dark grey uniform. Other than a *chawki dar* (doorkeeper) who also sells cookies during the ten-minute break, no man is allowed to enter the school premises, even though we are fully covered all the time. "You're not allowed to discuss religion and politics in any of your classes," the principal instructs. "How can you teach literature and not discuss these subjects?" I ask. There is no interest in debate or dialogue. "Just do as you're told," advises Roahafza-jan, another teacher. Silence, silence, silence!

The only consolation is working with students who are so eager to learn. They are young and enthusiastic. They don't have enough textbooks. They borrow each other's pens. Some students are so poor they can't afford to buy a notebook. "Why haven't you done your assignment?" I ask Malika, a grade seven student. "If I do all my assignments, the pages of my notebook will be finished," she explains, eyes on the ground. "My mother can't buy me another notebook any time soon."

Malika, the only student who wears a black coat and head cover like the teachers, is very intelligent. Her sister was also a student at this school, but was given in marriage two years ago to a man in Saudi Arabia. "My sister sent me this outfit from Saudi," says Malika. "Her first and last gift." She is in tears. "Her husband is very cruel. He doesn't allow her to be in touch with us any more." Later, Roahafza-jan, who knows all the gossip about everyone, tells me that Malika's sister has disappeared since her husband took her to Saudi Arabia. "Only Allah knows the full truth, but from what we've heard, he locked her up in a basement. Some say she escaped to an unknown place; some say she's become a prostitute. To save face, her family says her husband doesn't let her contact them." Malika tells me that, a couple of months ago, her thirteen-year-old brother went missing too. "My mother nearly had a heart attack," she says. "My mother's health is fragile, especially after my sister went."

A few days after her brother vanished, a mujahidin group contacted Malika's family, asking for ransom. "They think that because my sister married a Saudi we must be very rich." She sighs. "My mother pleaded with the mujahidin, and it seems there was some disagreement among them because they let my brother and another boy go without getting any money." It's a common fear among the refugees—that their young boys will be kidnapped and released after being raped. "My brother is still in shock," says Malika. "He was kept in a dark room, hands tied. They beat him up. He didn't want to talk about it until my mother saw the bruises on his arms. He's not going to school any more. He is afraid to leave the house." Malika is lost in thought, staring at the blackboard. Then she picks up her cotton bag. The skirt of her long black coat sweeps the dust off the floor as she rushes out of the classroom.

Soraya and her sister are in grade six. They're the only two women from a household of orphans and widows who are learning to read and write. Every teacher—even the dry-mannered, rigid principal—is impressed with the sisters' progress. They are below average for grade six—particularly in Dari literature, because their mother language is Pushtu. But because of their ages—thirteen and fourteen—the principal decided to let them sit in the class. They make an effort to keep up with all the schoolwork. "My brother is a good mujahid," says Soraya. Because he's the only male left in the family, he's been allowed to spend more time in Islamabad. Wali doesn't want to marry because he's afraid to leave a widow behind, as his seven brothers did. Instead, he looks after his father's two widows, eight children and three grandchildren.

We visit Soraya's family on the anniversary of her father's death. He was recognized as one of the great mujahidin fighters of his time. He was the first, but not the last, in the family to die for God. Her home is a house of martyrs. "We've given seventeen martyrs to the jihad," she says. "Both our mothers and all our sisters and sisters-in-law are widows." Like statues, perfect and dignified, the widows and orphans kneel on a carpet, staring at us in total silence. A shake of their heads is a

Soraya, Nelofer and another teacher at the Imoutelmoumeneen School.

sign of welcome. But the order of tragedy must not be broken by words. A permanent look of sadness lies across the faces of these young women, who are in constant misery. "We are women," says Soraya's mother, breaking the heavy silence. "Allah has created us to suffer. We accept Allah's will."

Invoking Allah's name has become the answer to everything rational or irrational—it is the same for dying, pain or suffering. I don't think the Allah I'm discovering in the Quran would be pleased with all this. But for this household of decorated war heroes—their framed photos hang on the wall—and their beautiful widows, gaining Allah's favour in this life and the one to come is the ultimate satisfaction. There is little else they can do.

In each class, students compete to be the first to read as soon as I give them a new lesson. I ask Mariam to come to the front of the class and read. She blushes. "I can't," she murmurs underneath her breath.

"Come to the front and read!"

"I can't read," she says.

"Louder! Speak louder. I can't hear you."

"She can't read in front of the class," says the girl sitting next to her. Mariam is silent.

"Why not?" I give a lecture about the importance of having the courage to walk to the front of the class. Everyone is silent. The echo of my own voice scares me. I ask Sahra to come and read. She obeys immediately.

Mariam is absent for two days in a row. On the third day, her mother is waiting at the school gate to talk to me. Poverty screams from her cast-off clothes, her patched-up head cover. As she speaks, nervously pulling her head cover over her forehead, I notice her hands. The fingers are hardened, the nails dirty. "Mariam loves school. She loves studying," she says. "Her eyes have turned red from so much crying in the past two days. She is not going to return to school. She is afraid she'll fail because you asked her to read in front of the class and she can't." She pauses. I'm lost for words. She picks at her fingernails. I prevent myself from telling her to stop doing it. I ask her what the problem is. "My husband became a martyr five years ago," she replies. "Mariam was six. I've raised her and two smaller ones all by myself. I've been feeding, clothing and raising them by cleaning Pakistani homes. Yet I can't afford to buy her new shoes. Not this year." She pauses again. "A Pakistani woman gave me a pair of shoes for her. I told Mariam to wear them to school. But they are too large for her. When you ask her to come to the front of the class, she's afraid the others will notice her large shoes. She is embarrassed. Allah helps us all." I tell her it's okay. But she sobs and says I won't give Mariam good grades. "She's always been the first in her class. She is a hard-working orphan." I promise not to ask Mariam to read in front of the class again. There is a tired smile on the woman's face as she leaves.

Mariam stands by her desk and holds the pink-covered book in her tiny hands. She reads with an undeniable passion:

> You're the star in our dark nights, Mujahid.
> You're the guardian and the guide, Mujahid.
> You're our honour, our light, our hero.
> With your dagger you tear into the enemies' chest.
> With your gun you defend our land.
> You're the true saviour, worthy of our praise, Mujahid.

I wonder if she's thinking about her father when she's reading.

* * *

All the stories and poems in the textbooks celebrate the mujahidin's bravery, exonerating them for killing and destroying the *dushmen* (enemy), the Russians. They are all battle songs, chants for a war that's already cost over a million lives. Every word, every page is dedicated to jihad, the martyrs of the war, religious duties, morality and piety. These texts are printed in Pakistan with financial aid from Western governments and non-governmental organizations such as Oxfam and UNICEF. Little wonder there is no room to discuss politics or religion. I ask the principal if I can use an old Dari literature textbook. "I've got to see it first, then Hojee-sohib [the head of the school, who lives in Peshawar] has to approve it," she says. "Normally we don't allow anyone to teach anything outside these texts."

The decade-long Soviet occupation has not only produced death and destruction, it has given birth to a militarized culture of jihad and justified violence. This invisible product of war has now cloaked every aspect of life, including education. Not only in history and literature but also in mathematics and science, the equation is jihad versus everything else. "There are eight Russians in a tank. A mujahid fires an anti-tank missile and burns the tank. Two Russians escape. How many Russians are dead?" asks the grade four math book. "This is normal," says Nazefa-jan, who teaches grades one to five math. "The communist government brainwashes our children with its ideology; we have to protect these young minds from this by teaching them about the values of Islam and jihad."

It's no surprise that Hojee-sohib is venerated by some of the teachers. He is the ultimate authority. When news of his visit reaches the school, everyone panics. Before his arrival, the principal gives us a lecture on how to behave piously. We are to cover our faces, except for the eyes. "Hojee-sohib dislikes the sight of women's faces; he hates flirtatiousness," she warns. "So be careful."

The doorkeeper announces his arrival. A well-built, bearded man with knotted eyebrows enters the main office, followed by a fully covered woman. He watches us—all female teachers—with an affectionate, lustful gaze. He smiles profusely, waiting for us to thank him for his visit. As I start talking to him, the partial face cover slips from my nose, revealing my entire face. Hojee smiles widely. Two other teachers suffer the same unexpected fate with their face covers. It seems that Hojee doesn't actually mind seeing our faces. We note this, but don't have the courage to ask why, then, there was such a fuss over *hijib*, why such double standards. His wife, a slim woman with a long pointed nose and keen eyes, moves frantically around. She is his deputy. Hojee-sohib has a second wife who never attends these public events.

The school has designated days for which we organize various events. We condemn the day of the Saur Revolution, the hated day of Karmal's arrival in Kabul, by lining up students in the schoolyard to recite poems and jihadi songs and to chant slogans. "Down with the communist regime. Death to Najibullah and his supporters. Death to Russians," everyone has to shout. Days of celebration include Mujahid Day, Afghan Jihad Day, and the death dates of a few mujahidin commanders—people I've never heard of before.

Hojee and his wife are here to take part in the celebration of Jihad Day. The schoolyard is turned into a temporary camp, with seats, a podium and a microphone. Green and black banners decorate the stage. First there is the Quranic recitation. Then the principal welcomes Hojee-sohib; he, in return, congratulates the principal. A few individual students read essays; groups recite poetry and songs. No music is allowed.

Nelofer on "Jihad Day" celebration at the Imoutel-moumeneen School, Islamabad, Pakistan, 1989.

Then we teachers follow Hojee-sohib to the main office for a meeting. "There is a shortage of funds," he says. "Your efforts are appreciated by Allah and your mujahid brothers." We haven't been paid our monthly salary of five hundred Pakistani rupees for the past three months. Hojee praises our hard work, our pious behaviour in and out of school. "I've not heard a single criticism about your attitude and Islamic clothes." That is what the principal wants to hear. "Your principal has done a wonderful job of teaching and training you for such piety." Hearing this, I feel cheap. It sounds as if we are the principal's call girls. She sits triumphantly behind her desk, smiling from ear to ear.

My father has begun to work in one of the mujahidin-run clinics in Islamabad, which offers basic medical services for Afghan refugees. Now that my father has a job, my mother asks my brother not to work as a conductor any more. That doesn't go over very well with Uncle Asad and family. They are also upset because Faoud has told them there will be further delays before he can sponsor any of them. "He says the best he can do is to send money to help with the expenses," says Rona.

We receive three letters from Kabul. One is from the family—Aunt Najmeya writes on my grandmother's behalf, describing their hard life. A letter from Mir explains in coded language that his brother has finally been released. He and his friends were sentenced first to death, then to life in prison. There is no mention of the fate of his friends, but Mir is pleased that his brother is out of danger. Dyana's letter is brief and tells me only that she is well. But it includes a poem:

> There is a floating river,
> A mountain, and waves of clouds
> Standing between us.
> From words and memories,
> The petals of daisies and roses,
> I'll prepare a bridge,
> So we can cross this great distance.

This happens the same week we discover that Hojee-sohib has gone to Australia. All the teachers circle around the principal, demanding an explanation.

"He must have been sponsored," says Zarena.

"I'm sure you knew," says Roahafza-jan.

"By God," swears the principal, touching her head as a sign of her innocence, "I didn't know anything." She looks embarrassed.

"What about our unpaid salaries?" asks Najeeba.

"My son has gone to Peshawar to find out," says the principal.

This gives everyone a chance to talk about the double standards practised by the mujahidin authorities.

That evening, we are enjoying the autumn breeze, sitting on the stairs to the roof. Qalanderzada is in a weird mood. "The fifteen-headed monster"—his epithet for the coalition of mujahidin groups—"has been using religious rhetoric to rule." The implications of this, he predicts, are much greater than anyone can imagine. "The Indian poet Rabindranath Tagore wrote a series of letters to Mahatma Gandhi," says Qalanderzada, smoothing his white hair with his fingers. "He warned Gandhi not to mix politics and religion in his fight against the British. He called it 'spiritualizing politics.' But Gandhi failed to understand the significance of what Tagore was saying. So by the time Indian independence was achieved, the Hindu-Muslim conflict was already destroying India as a country. In Afghanistan, too, we've mixed religion with politics in our rejection of communism, without realizing the danger." Qalanderzada pauses. I remember that Shariati talked about the politicization of religion, but as a form of self-awareness. What we're seeing in Pakistan is manipulation of Islam for political self-interest. "I have a premonition that you will go to a far corner of the world," says Qalanderzada, abruptly placing his hand over my father's shoulder. "It's better to get away from this place and all these stupid politics," he says, shaking his head in frustration.

And Qalanderzada's prediction proves correct. We are going as far as it is physically possible to go from Pakistan, from the mujahidin and from Afghanistan. Canada has accepted our family as political refugees. My father applied for refugee status a year ago. Now a letter has arrived from the

Canadian embassy in Islamabad, telling us that we will be leaving in two days. It's so sudden that we can't believe it's true. Only fourteen months, and I am already tired of living in Pakistan, tired of the hypocrisy of the mujahidin, disillusioned with the jihad. I no longer believe this will bring us a free, independent Afghanistan. I no longer want to fight with guns. I want to educate myself and to fight with words. No such opportunity would ever be open to me in Pakistan.

I don't know much about Canada. I have heard it's cold. I once saw a map and a picture of men in snowsuits called Eskimos. I think this is how most Canadians probably dress. When we write the name "Moncton" on our newly bought suitcases, we don't even know how to pronounce it. I can't speak a word of English.

The night of our departure—October 12, 1990—is chaos. Neighbours gather to say goodbye. Everyone in the building is jealous that we are leaving, particularly Uncle Asad and his family. They follow us to the airport in one of their cars.

Before I can worry whether the news of my departure has reached my students, or what their reaction to it may be, we land thousands of kilometres away, in a small, picturesque town in a province called New Brunswick. From the air, Moncton looks like an earthly paradise, with colourful wooden houses, and leaves that mix red, yellow, orange, green and brown, against kilometres of empty land. Every image is a postcard shot.

From the heat of Pakistan we arrive in the cold autumn weather of Atlantic Canada. From a life surrounded by visitors and guests, stories and gossip, to a place out of time, a place of silence, where the only visit comes from the local

Nelofer, Habibullah, Hassib, Mejgan and Jamila in our new Moncton home, 1991.

multicultural association. I find myself in a land of shopping malls, seventy TV channels and grocery stores with a hundred varieties of rice, milk and cereal. "If only a quarter of this was available in Pakistan, the lives of most of my patients would have been saved," my father says, gazing at the shelves of food. The people here are kind and generous, but they are surprised when, asked what I like about Moncton, I say it is peaceful. "Peaceful?" they ask, at a loss for words. For those lucky enough never to have experienced war, the word "peaceful" has little meaning.

As we settle into our new hometown, we become preoccupied with our mailbox, checking it several times a day. We wait for letters from family and friends. My parents spend most of their time reading and writing letters. From eight different countries around the world—Germany to Australia, the United States to Pakistan—we receive long letters, all handwritten in Dari. And we write diligently—word by word—about the experience of living in Pakistan, our sudden departure, the new city and the challenges of a new life.

I O

SEASON OF GRIEF

Blood will flow from the sky
Flames will cover the universe
Hell must burn its height of fire—
And this gives just a tiny picture of life in Kabul
Qahar Ausi, 1992

IT'S JANUARY 1991. Trees are mirrors of ice. I
write to Dyana about the snow and cold in Moncton. I've
started to learn English in high school. I carry two thick
English-Persian and Persian-English dictionaries. I look up
words in one of them so I can speak to my classmates, and

they show me words in the other to help me understand what they are saying. People are unaware of Afghanistan here. The other day, a girl in school asked me why I wasn't as dark as other Africans. When I said I was not African, she gave me a puzzled look. "Isn't Afghanistan in Africa?" I wish I could speak English so I could explain.

I wait for Dyana's letters. Her replies come in tiny handwriting, careful and neat, on thin green, pink, yellow or blue coloured paper. " . . . This coffin of treachery has been going around far too long—it's time it was buried," Dyana writes of the communist government. "If you thought life was a tragedy in those early days when you were here, then we have to invent a new meaning for the word 'tragedy' in order to describe the situation now. We don't know what's going to happen to us. People are hurrying to get married and have children because it's the only thing that gives us a feeling of certainty and happiness. We live as if it's the last few days of our lives. Last week was my uncle's wedding. We laughed as if it was our last laughter. Too bad you weren't here . . ."

A year later, another note, dated February 1992, to which she attaches a poem.

When the song of separation
Echoed in my heart's ear,
My eyes—the sources of pure water—
Went dry.
Only when I realize that life
Is nothing but a sad memory
Do I begin to weep.

Two months after this—Dyana's most recent letter—the mujahidin at last topple the Afghan communist government. A coalition of mujahidin groups forms an interim administration, each leader agreeing to rule the country for two months at a time. My father moves around the house with his new portable shortwave radio to listen to the news about Afghanistan. We call each other to the living room to watch the news on Canadian TV. The report shows a map of Afghanistan, a few fast-moving shots of Kabul and then a meeting of the mujahidin. No wonder my classmates at Moncton High don't know much about life in Afghanistan. But we are grateful for the news—even in its briefest form.

And certainly the news of peace in Afghanistan is brief. "My heart beats from fear and fury again/ Another night has prevailed before we ever saw the morning light." Dyana quotes a classical Persian poet in her letter from Kabul, which reaches me six months after she wrote it. A couple of weeks after the takeover by the interim government, Gulbuddin Hekmatyar, who has been appointed prime minister, bombs the city. He must be the first prime minister to attack the seat of his own government. The American-supported militia leader wants to be president and has no interest in sharing power with anyone else. To communicate this, he sends planes to bomb the Presidential Palace and stays in his military headquarters outside the capital. Learning from Hekmatyar's example, a defecting mujahid called Abdul Rashid Dostum declares himself the representative of the Uzbek minority group in Afghanistan. He emerged as a bandit and militia leader fighting the Russians in the north. Later, he joined the communist government and was given the title "General" by Najibullah. Now he, too, wants to rule the country. Burhanuddin Rabbani, whose term as president of the interim government for two months has ended, refuses to hand over power to his successor. This provides an excuse not only for Dostum, but also for the leader of the Wahdat Party—an ethnic Hazara group—to launch their own attacks on Kabul.

Bitterness has arrived, knocking on the door
Like a dagger; each stab hits my chest.
Bear it, or die, but don't give way,
Because if it enters the heart, it'll burn the soul.

Dyana begins her letter with this short poem. These days, she writes frequently, more freely and with more detail.

. . . I can't begin to describe what we are suffering. You're lucky not to be here. We have three families in our home now because the west, south and east of Kabul are all under attack. I was writing a letter to you by candlelight—there is no power at all—when my aunt and her family arrived. They used to have a beautiful house in Selo [West Kabul], but had to abandon it as they ran for their lives. At sunset, a group of Hazara militiamen from the Wahdat party knocked at the door. Before the family managed to open it, a few of them had already jumped over the wall. They made everyone, including the children, kneel on the ground, tying everyone's hands behind their backs. As one of the men pulled a knife to kill her husband, my aunt pleaded, saying, "God won't forgive you for the death of an innocent Shia Muslim." At first, the militiamen said they didn't care. Then one of them asked my aunt to recite the names of the twelve Shia imams. She was so scared that she started making mistakes. Then the husband began to recite the names, as did their children, one by one, to prove they are Shia Muslims. Finally, after several hours, they were set free. They were told they should leave if they wanted to stay alive. In just their slippers and casual clothes, they walked for at least three hours before making it to our home. They were saved only because they remembered the names of the imams. Hundreds of other innocent people are dead. My aunt went home after a week and found bodies lying all over the road, in front of the houses. There was no one to bury them because all those alive had escaped, and those who'd stayed were dead. My aunt's home was totally looted; even the window frames were gone. . . .

Dyana's letters are a litany of pain, a record of my city's tragedy.

September 1992. Kabul.
I wrote this letter a while ago but, because of the fighting in the city, couldn't send it sooner. Someone's leaving for India, so I'm sending this letter and a couple of poems.
. . . We are badly stuck here. May God embrace us and destroy these mujahidin—that's our prayer every day. Last night, they announced an Islamic *hijib* for women, once again. Islamic *hijib* means a long, baggy coat that reaches our ankles, a head cover and no makeup. We are all infuriated. The first few days after the establishment of an Islamic government they made a dress code mandatory. When the fighting intensifies, *hijib* and everything else is forgotten. We can go out without a head cover and no one seems to care. Then, when there are a couple of days of

truce, they start picking up on women's clothes again, as if there is nothing else to worry about. We prefer not to have this restricted dress code, but it comes with a heavy price—house-to-house fighting. Some days the war is so bad that leaving home is like committing suicide. But I've become like you. Yes, you can say that. I go out even on very dangerous days. My heart shrinks when I sit home for one day. I need to get out—despite the danger. Last month, for a whole week, I sat and stared from behind the window into the blue sky as the mujahidin were firing at each other—from bombs, to rockets and bullets. But then I lost patience one day and left to go for a walk. Going to school, university or the office is like a joke. They are open one week and closed the next. Three different groups are fighting each other inside the city. We keep moving to relatives' homes from one district to another—all people do that. But there is not a safe corner left.

Neither have I got the will to move,
Nor a wing to fly,
And my hands are shorter than all the walls.
You say, leave this city,
Look for the gem of your happiness somewhere
else.
But can't you see
That high mountains surround my city,
I cannot move,
I cannot go,
Neither a wing nor a leg is left.

9 January 1993. Kabul.
I'm so pleased to get your letter after a year and a half—it's

been a long time, and I thought you might have forgotten about us in destroyed Kabul. I don't blame you. These days we'd like to forget about ourselves. . . . Every moment we await our death. There is no security. Our neighbours were about to leave, but a rocket tore their sixteen-year-old son to pieces. Day or night, all we hear is the sound of rockets, tanks and bullets. We are like the walking dead. I was so upset to see people becoming indifferent towards this situation. They were laughing in the street as if war were a free picnic or a silly party. I wanted to cry. Then I realized that it should be like this—we should laugh at everything, because there is nothing else we can do. We are so helpless. We must laugh at our helplessness, at our fate, at the tragedy called our life. Our laughter at all of this is more bitter than any tears. . . .

Several of Dyana's later letters have no date, but are written with even more fury at the new rulers of the country and the civil war that's engulfed Kabul.

. . . It's been a week since we've had water. I always knew life without food was going to be difficult, but never considered that life without water is hell. We've managed to find some drinking water, but we can't go to the bathroom inside the house any more. People are using bushes, street corners, gardens and fields to relieve themselves. This is the most disgusting face of war—if not the most dangerous one. I'm sorry to be disturbing you with all this awful news. I'm so happy you're not living here. Your parents were smart to leave. Wish we'd done the same. There is no mercy for us. If you come, you won't recognize Kabul—the city has been destroyed by bombs—what the mujahidin's rockets couldn't accomplish from far away has now been achieved under their direct rule. Dostum's barefoot militias, as they are called, have robbed most districts in the city. They've kidnapped a lot of women. We used to say, "God save us from worse days." But we have been living worse days for a long time, and no one, including God, has saved us. . . .

"Solitude"

You and I are the memory of a story,
The story of a long night
That won't be forgotten for a long time.
For years, I've been thinking,
I wish life was without memories.

. . . The Wahdat Party has finished destroying West Kabul. They've used people's homes as their strongholds in the street fighting. They are pushed back one day, and gain a few more inches of the city the next. Civilians are the real casualties. The area is pretty much levelled now. My aunt is living with her in-laws in Khaier Khona [North Kabul]. Dostum and Hekmatyar have taken care of Kabul South and East. Rabbani, who's still holding on to the presidency, has established bank accounts abroad, like most of his commanders, who have a collection of cars and wives here in Kabul. His chief commander, Ahmad Shah Masoud, is the defence minister and is in charge of the government. His men say they are innocent, but it's hard to believe that word any more. If they haven't directly robbed, kidnapped or killed, they've very closely watched it happen. They have occupied the tallest mountain—the TV tower mountain—

and from there, they can see everything. They are actually happy to see other mujahidin groups fight each other. It's to their benefit, so they can have the government to themselves. But they don't know that no one wants them any more.

The glorious days of the mujahidin are gone. The mujahidin have disgraced themselves. In the old days the word "mujahid" bore a sense of respect. The word has become an insult now. When people in the bus or on the street get into a row, if one person wants to belittle and insult the other, they say, "Hey, you mujahid." One would think this was embarrassing enough. But they are so locked into their pillage and destructive rule that they don't seem to care. God punish them for everything they've done to us. We can only wish; but we do wish that this brutality that's been brought upon us—by anyone, any power, any country—would be bestowed upon each and every one of them, exactly the same. So they'd know what it's like to suffer. . . .

. . . It's been four months now since this wicked, bloody war quieted down. After three years, schools and the university have just opened. We have lived through some horrific times. I've decided not to write you about the war any more because it must be very boring for you to read the same thing all the time. Besides, I'm sure you see the reality of our suffering in the news there in Canada. Do you? But there are times that I can't help it, and I want you to know. It's as if I feel relieved thinking that there is one person—if no one else, at least one person, my dearest sister and friend—who knows and cares to know. Anyhow, it's been a year since we returned to our home again, after circling the city for a safe corner to spend a night in, or a few days at a time. I hate living here now. But ours is not living any more; it's just survival. We try to stay alive. It's as if we're living behind a wall called life. People on the other side live, and we wish to live.

A rocket killed Qahar Ausi, the poet we used to know. He'd become a good friend. Accepting his death has been very difficult. His wife had just given birth to a baby girl. He was so excited about it. But God took him away. Why is the world so cruel? Is God so angry that he can't stand our innocence? Do we all have to be corrupted or die so we may be forgiven? People say innocents die—that's true. Otherwise, why aren't these criminals, from Karmal to Najibullah, from Hekmatyar to Dostum, even injured, let alone suffering a terrible death?

Like a dagger, Dyana's words and the news of Qahar Ausi's death tear my heart. I feel wounded, in pain. I cry all night. I remember his mischievous smile, his bushy hair and beard, his piercing eyes, the look of happiness on his face when he held the first printed copy of his book that was later banned. A couple of years ago, I received a handwritten note from him: "Do you know when I walk the streets, when I watch the dusty sunset of my city, what I think about? About our country, history, culture, and about our intellectual geography that the traitors have torn into pieces . . . I hope you'll study, learn a new language and return as a responsible caretaker of your own culture." Then I received two of his books—*Prelude to the Red Rose* and *My Poem, My Sorrow*—which had been published after I'd left Afghanistan. His poems and note became friends in my long nights of studying as I attended Carleton School of Journalism in Ottawa. Ausi had escaped to Iran with his wife and baby girl, but in August 1994 he'd returned, saying he couldn't stay away from his land. Less than a month later, in September, the land he loved so much took him forever. He was killed by rocket fire two days after he celebrated his thirty-eighth birthday.

In winter 1994, Dyana writes about a possible marriage to an Afghan abroad.

> There were several Afghan suitors from Germany, Australia and the States. My parents refused them. Now my mother regrets it. If there is a good man in Canada whom you can recommend, I will consider marrying him. My mother says she trusts your judgment. I don't know what you would say about this. Knowing you, you'll be laughing at this, but don't laugh. I'm serious. . . . Please write when you can. Nowadays, letters reach Kabul from Europe in two weeks. I am waiting for yours.

> 24 August 1995. Kabul.
> . . . Will we ever meet again? I'm afraid the past has become a memory, an unforgettable memory, a dream that may never be repeated. Walking that school road, reading poetry under the soft spring rain—it was such a long time ago. But somehow I still have hope that one day you'll return and there will be peace. We'll talk about war stories—as old memories. We'll walk that road again. . . .
> My mother is hoping I'll get married. There is a guy— wish you were here to meet him and tell me what you think. . . . I don't know if my father would ever agree. It is hard to think of love when there is so much chaos, poverty and ugliness around. But we must, I tell myself. I know you'll tell me the same. I'm so proud that you're studying

journalism. I feel I'm with you in spirit. I'm glad I finished my studies, despite everything. Being in university is wonderful, especially where you are. You must have access to all sorts of books and research material. We had to study under the barrage of rockets and with the sound of tank shells . . . write soon if you can.

I write, but get no reply. Months go by, and there is no news from Dyana. My mother says maybe she got married and is now busy with her new life. Then I get several letters— one saying her father refused even to meet the suitor, insisting it was not time for Dyana to be married. Another letter speaks about something more disturbing than her father's comments.

1996. Kabul.
. . . Imagine one morning you wake up and get ready to go to work. But when you open the door, a group of young men, dressed in dusty and filthy clothes, push you inside the house with their rifles and say you're not allowed to leave. Imagine your younger sister wants to go to school and your mother has to go grocery shopping. Your sister is told she doesn't need any education, and your mother, though fully covered, is beaten or sent back home if she's not accompanied by a man. Imagine that your income is essential for the survival of your family, but you're told with indifference that you are not allowed to go to work. Imagine all of this happens to you only because you're a woman. What would you do if all you could do was stare at the walls inside your house as a substitute for living a normal life?

With this letter comes the shock of what she describes as life under the rule of a new group called the Taliban, who have established control over most of the country.

> . . . It's not that we had an easy life with the mujahidin, but this is a different lot—a weird group of people, lots of young boys with kohl on their eyes, long hair, long beards, turbans and *perhan-tombon* [the Dari word for Pakistani-style shalwar kameez]. They beat men, taking them to the mosques to pray. They have forced all women to stay home. They've banned all music. Not that we had much electricity to watch TV, but once in a while it was a good distraction. Now we can't even watch that. They've smashed all TV sets. Can you imagine? If we are sick, we can't go to the hospital. The stupid mujahidin with their infighting paved the way for these animals. . . .

There are no more letters for another six months. Then I receive another brief note that was written four months before it reaches me. It begins with a poem.

> "Hope"
>
> From all my wishes only,
> I worship silence,
> Because in silence,
> I hear the sound of laughter,
> In silence,
> The vision of happy memories visits me frequently,
> And asks how I feel.

December 1996.

. . . In winter, nights are longer and days are shorter. But for those of us who live in darkness, it doesn't make any difference. Spring, autumn or winter, day or night, it's all the same. When we began work, one of our co-workers said she didn't mind when the mujahidin were fighting amongst each other because we were free to wear what we wanted. We used to mock her, saying we were ready to follow any dress code so long as there was no war. Now there is no fighting in the city, but with it has come another war—a restricted dress code, the beating of men and women on the streets, stoning to death and forced marriages. It's like being in a prison, without the chance of release. . . .

We get news that my poor blind grandmother, my uncle and my aunt have escaped to Pakistan. "They brought me here," says my grandmother's faint voice on the phone from Islamabad. "It was really bad in Kabul. So we left." My mother is happy that her family is out of danger. "You did the right thing," she keeps saying down the line to Islamabad.

Then I receive a whole series of letters from Dyana, most with a poem attached, each continuing to talk about the pain of life under Taliban rule. It seems as if Dyana wrote a letter every week. In one she said that, since she had no other occupation, she would write more letters. She apologized if this was wasting my time and expressed the fear that the letters might not reach me at all because it was getting more difficult to send mail, even though the Kabul postal system was operating. Each letter is a reflection of enormous pain and suffering.

I plead with various women's organizations at my university in Ottawa, showing Dyana's letters—trying to find a way to help her. There is a little interest in the plight of Afghan women, but largely there is just complacency. What the Taliban are doing is regarded by some as a part of everyday Afghan culture. There is a strong sense of unease about condemning their actions. "Do we have the right to criticize the culture of another country?" says a woman in November 1998 at a "peace-building" conference, hosted by the Canadian government for non-governmental organizations to talk about the future of Afghanistan. Most international aid agencies argue that it's not so bad to work with the Taliban. "They've brought peace," argues the Red Cross delegate at the conference. The few dissenting voices—including mine—are ignored.

I return home holding a stack of Dyana's letters. She is right—there is no help. In a moment of despair at the world and its indifference towards the suffering of an entire people, I tear to pieces all the letters from January 1997 to February 1998. Then I search the shoebox in which I've kept most of her letters, and others from my grandmother and aunt—letters dating back to 1990. After reading a few lines here and there, I watch the letters turn to ashes—one by one—in a silver tray. When I'm done, my hands are covered with dark smoke and ashes. The smoke detector starts screaming. I jump up and knock it to the ground.

The letters I quote in this book are the only ones that survived, either because they were not in the shoebox, or because when I got tired of burning letters I kicked the box around and some of them got scattered. After March 1998, there were no more letters. The last ones she sent made it clear she was tired of her life and was ready to end it.

13 February 1998.

. . . Sometimes I think I'm going to die from loneliness and grief. I continually think that I've become a useless and hopeless thing. Or we are forced to become like that. Sometimes I laugh with bitterness when I see I'm living in a city of lost people. If the current situation continues, I'll lose my mind completely.

March 1998.

> Leave me, for I'm destroyed.
> Leave me, for I'm lost, gone with the wind of
>   memories.
> Don't hurt me any more with stories from the green
>   loving days,
> Don't remind me any more of those memorable
>   nights.
> Let me be, for I can't bear any more pain.
> Growing, laughing requires a season;
> I don't have the ability to live.
> I've become a flaming house of pain,
> The cold song of loneliness.

My dearest friend, companion of long years of misery,

What can I say, for my heart is pressed with sadness. I think about the time when we used to go to school. The time when we had hopes and aspirations, thinking about the future. You may find this very odd, but I've been living in those memories for all this time now. What I was and what has become of me now. The past runs like a movie in front of my eyes. I remember the past moment by moment, I live in it—there is no present, there is no future. It feels as if I've lost something and I'm searching for it . . . The walls are closing in; life doesn't have the same meaning any more. Music doesn't sound the same. I'm tired of reading . . . I'm happy for you—happy that you're going to have a life, and a future. Please forgive me for this. I know you'd say, I've gone mad. You're probably right. If only I didn't understand what was wrong with life, if only I could be indifferent like so many other people. But I guess it's better to be sad and mad than to be indifferent. I'm sure you'll agree. I want you to enjoy life to its fullest. Don't deny yourself any happiness. I want you to live a life full of pleasures, adventures, things we loved, being independent, carefree, with lots of laughter. I want you to live for me, and for you . . . for both of us . . . and live it as we wished life to be.

Your sister and friend, as ever,
Dyana

This is where all smiles must end.

—

I TRIED TO GO BACK TO FIND DYANA. I was fearful that she would commit suicide. In May 1998, I did manage to cross the border. On a spring day, after a car journey of nearly two hours through a barren land, we arrived at a set of domed mud houses. A few kilometres ahead, a tree trunk was placed across the road to block traffic—apparently the Taliban guard had gone for a lunch break and afternoon prayer. Other than our old navy pickup, there were no cars around. "We must stop here," said Samad, my kind smuggler. Under cover of a burqa, I walked to one of the houses, where a woman was cooking bread in a smoke-filled room. The only sources of

light were a tiny window and the fire, over which she was
turning balls of dough into round, puffy bread. I sat with the
woman inside while Samad went to check out the road. We
were on the outskirts of the city of Herat, which since 1995
had been controlled by the Taliban. It was cozy enough
inside, with the smell of freshly cooked bread and the shim-
mering of the orange fire highlighting the dark skin of the
bread maker.

I had just finished drinking my sweetened tea when
Samad returned. "We must leave now," he said, breathless,
his beard shaking as he spoke rapidly. The woman offered
him bread and tea. "Another time," he said. "They're hanging our men in the square in the city. I must go back to
Mashad right away." He kept looking out the tiny window.
"It's not safe for me to be here. It's not safe for you to be
here either. We must return." He opened the door. I followed him to the car, and we drove away. I could still see the
tree trunk on the road—a Taliban checkpoint, a militia road-
block or a trap? It was hard to say. Samad drove like a
maniac over a road that war and weather had brutalized,
leaving craters, potholes and long stretches where the
asphalt had completely disappeared.

Despite my disappointment, I could understand his fear.
He was a member of a mujahidin group that had controlled
parts of western Afghanistan before the Taliban's takeover.
When the Taliban mercenaries arrived to capture the city,
some mujahidin defected; the majority went into hiding,
while others fled to Iran. Occasionally, disguising himself as a
merchant, Samad would return to bring information. But he
never expected to arrive in Herat on the day of his friends'
public execution.

By dusk, I was sitting in another Afghan home, this time

Nelofer in Tehran, June 1998.

in Iran, sipping another cup of tea. Samad had already gone to report the awful news of his comrades' deaths at the hands of the Taliban in Herat. "You can wait here a few days, and when the situation improves, you'll be able to go back," said one of the women, trying to comfort me. I stayed three days. The situation was not going to change any time soon, and I returned to Tehran, broken and lost, trying to find alternative routes to Kabul.

In Tehran, I became part of the furniture at the Pakistani embassy, pleading for a visa. I even visited the Afghan embassy where the staff from the old mujahidin Islamic regime sat around idle, all words and no action. "You can't go to Kabul now," they insisted. "Have you heard of the Taliban?" What was I to do? Try to cross the border illegally again? My Iranian visa was due to expire. All I could do was return to Canada.

* * *

After reading and rereading Dyana's last letter for months—
I think I actually mourned, fearing she was already dead—I
finally received a note from Dyana's uncle in Dubai. It was
towards the end of winter, 1999, and it brought the good
news that Dyana was alive. Her family had moved to the city
of Mazar-e-Sherif, in the north.

"They're probably hoping to escape to Uzbekistan," my
father concluded in a moment of shared relief. Dyana's father
had always opposed fleeing to Pakistan. Her elder brother,
she had told me in one of her letters, had been sent to
Moscow a few years earlier. Though I hadn't yet heard from
Dyana herself, her uncle assured me in a second letter that
she and her family were fine. "They don't have an exact
address in Mazar," he wrote. "As soon as I get any news, I'll
let you know." Look out for any letters from Dubai, any of the
former Soviet republics or even Moscow, I told my parents.

I completed my MA research on Afghan refugee camps in
Iran and Pakistan. As I was preparing to write my thesis, I
received a call from Mohsen Makhmalbaf, whom I'd met in
1998 in Tehran. He asked me to return to Iran to help make a
film about Afghanistan. So in November 2000, I found myself
back at the border.

II

LEAVE MY DAUGHTER ALONE

Moments, holding daggers in hand,
Moments announce danger and death
The end of your bitter journey is yet far from sight.
Listen, co-traveller,
In such a passing trip,
Don't forget your ancestral land.

Qahar Ausi, 1991

A STRONG AUTUMN WIND is sweeping through the desert along the Iran-Afghan frontier. Mohsen Makhmalbaf, his assistant, Kova, and I are walking between the clay walls of Niatack. About five hundred Afghan families have built homes in this refugee encampment, replicas of their houses on the other side of the border. The wind is slapping us with dust, fine sand and bits of straw mixed with dirt. Not the sort of welcome I'd expected from the border of my country, but milder than the reception its current rulers, the Taliban, have offered. "If we see your cameras inside our territory, we will shoot you," a Taliban representative told Makhmalbaf. The storm is blowing ever stronger, and we shrink deeper inside our woollen shawls.

And so, once again, I find myself within kilometres of the country I left twelve years ago. I thought I had left the tragedy of war behind me. But it's in front of me once again, like a misty, half-broken mirror in which I can see shadows struggling to escape. This time, I'm to play myself in a film based on the story of my failure to reach Dyana. Nafas—the character based on me—is an Afghan woman whose family fled Afghanistan a decade ago. Her younger sister, who was left behind, has become depressed living under the Taliban. She's written a letter saying she intends to commit suicide at the last eclipse of the century. Now an Afghan-Canadian journalist, Nafas is at the Iran-Afghan border, hoping to go inside Afghanistan to rescue her sister.

Because the attempts to gain permission to film inside Afghanistan—where the Taliban now control about ninety-five percent of the country—were in vain, Niatack has become the substitute location for the film; its refugee residents and their stories are to become part of the plot. But even here, we have no protection, no help—either from the various mujahidin, militia and smuggling gangs that roam around in their cream and beige Toyota Corollas, or from members of the Taliban who travel in their Chevy four-by-fours across the border into Iran. The Iranian government, nervous that our film will depict them as uncaring and indifferent to Afghan suffering, has sent a message to us, warning us that if we don't present them with a detailed script they'll send soldiers to shut us down. For their part, the Afghan refugees have taken little interest in our project. As we head back to our hotel in the city of Zobul, about twenty-five minutes from Niatack, we are lost in thought.

The hotel where we are staying is a dodgy place. A sole receptionist sits in the lobby, watching dramas on TV until late into the night. There is not enough water to wash the sand and dust from my ears, face and hair. In the morning, as I open my eyes, I see a footprint on the floor. Has someone been here? I jump out of bed to look. As I walk, my own footprints remain on the bed of dust on the thick Chinese carpet. The room can't have been cleaned since it was furnished.

At the Afghan-Iranian border during filming of a scene from Kandahar, *with director Mohsen Makhmalbaf, actor Hassan Tanti and members of the crew, December* 2000.

I hear the sound of cars arriving, doors slamming and men talking. I look through the dust-thick curtain. Several fancy cars are parked just outside my window. Whoever they are, fear is creeping into my mind. It's best not to think of any Alfred Hitchcock films.

When we return from another day of scouting around the stormy refugee village, the cars are still there. A group of men dressed in nicely ironed white shalwar kameez, with long turbans and beards, are sitting in the lobby. The television is off. One of the waiters says there is a meeting between Iranian politicians and Taliban representatives. At about one in the morning, a group of tall, armed men get into the cars and drive away. What is going on? Are they members of the same Taliban that attacked the Iranian consulate in Mazar two years ago, killing all but one of the ten people there? The same Taliban that provoked the Iranian army to advance to the Afghan border? For months, the two armies stared at each other along the frontier, guns ready. President Khatami's government managed to avoid hostilities. Now we are discovering that the Taliban cross the border to cut deals with the Iranian government. We hear that Iran has helped restore the telephone lines in Herat. Is this the same Iranian government that recently sent military supplies to Ahmad Shah Masoud in the north of Afghanistan, in an attempt to undermine the Taliban? As one of my professors back in Canada used to say, there are no permanent friends or enemies in politics, only permanent interests. Iran is doing what Pakistan has done in regard to Afghanistan for decades—it is looking after itself.

The eight-hundred-kilometre border between Iran and Afghanistan has become a smugglers' haven for everything from narcotics to household supplies. It takes only a short walk to the Zobul bazaar to see the effect. On the street, people sell brand-new electronic appliances and equipment—digital cameras, CD players, Japanese television sets, VCRs and cassette recorders. They are cheap and tax-free, originally purchased in Central Asia, smuggled through Afghanistan and sold in Iran. And they pass right through Taliban territory, where television sets are ritually smashed as unislamic, where music tapes are hung from trees and cameras forbidden. But that's for ordinary people. The smugglers, like the narcotics dealers, are exempt from these rules. In Taliban-controlled Afghanistan, the criminals have become the hangmen, and the innocents the condemned.

When loads of these goods reach Tehran, the price doubles—as with the opium that crosses the Afghan border into the Asian republics. "The turnover of drug money from Afghanistan after it reaches Western cities is over eighty billion dollars a year," says Makhmalbaf. The Afghan farmer who cultivates poppies makes a meagre living from his work, while the cross-border mafia and their collaborators reap the benefits. The local Iranian economy suffers. When people can buy a Japanese VCR for the same price, they won't buy the low-quality Iranian version. The Iranian government wishes to control this black market, but the mafia runs deep and wide.

Life in these territories is cheaper than the VCRs. A few kilometres down the road from the mafia-run market, people live in filthy huts, with no sewage system, no electricity, no clean drinking water. In Niatack, families share their homes with their animals. The children play in the dust. In the dry land of dirt and clay, there is no vegetation, no sign of anything green, other than the women's traditional clothes and the pieces of ribbon tied to the unwashed hair of their children—tokens to keep the evil eye away from them. Evil itself should be on the run from a place as deprived and destitute as this.

I walk inside a house to talk to the women. A goat and two sheep lie sick on the ground. Skinny chickens are eating a few crumbs. "This is our life," one of the women says.

"Why do you keep the animals here?" I ask.

"Where else can I keep them?" she replies. "We've got to keep the goat for its milk, and we want to sell the sheep. But no one buys them any more. They say animals from Afghanistan are diseased." She insists that her chickens and sheep are fine. "It's a nice, well-built sheep." She runs her hand over the back of one of the animals. "Do you know anyone who can buy them?"

The sheep stare at me with curiosity. Do they know that they, too, are unwanted refugees?

We have a meeting at the office of the Iranian authorities in Niatack. It's a large, empty concrete room with three wooden and two rusted iron chairs and an iron desk. We are supposed to meet the Afghan leaders from the three different Afghan communities in Niatack—two Pushtu-speaking tribes and several households of Hazaras, who speak Persian. Each community has its own mosque and its own mullah, who also acts as its leader. Self-appointed or chosen by the community, they are now in charge.

Two representatives from one community are present; no members of the other two communities have shown up. A man with a beard and hair that's been freshly coloured with henna begins to apologize. "I was not well, you see," he says, faking a cough. "I was going to talk to people, but I've got this cold." Mullah Qader, who's the leader of his community, says they need a few more days to talk to people. Their motto for the past week has been "hopefully tomorrow." When I utter a few words of Pushtu, the two men all of a sudden take a keen interest in my presence. When they learn that I've come from Canada to help with the film, they complain about lack of money, lack of medicine and shortage of food. But here is your chance to earn some money, I tell them. We'll talk to the authorities to see if we can help bring a doctor and medicine.

"You're one of our own," he says. "So you understand that it's against our tradition to do these things." I ask what they mean by "these things." They repeat our words—"making a film"—without having any idea what that means. "No matter what a film is," says the henna-haired man, "it's against our religion to let strangers see our women and talk to them. You know all this very well." It turns out they haven't spoken to anyone about the film; they admit that they've never seen one. Assuming that the film is an Iranian government project, they're afraid to say no directly. Therefore, they've been delaying us with excuses.

They have no intention of helping us, I say to Makhmalbaf as we walk out of the office. It's better to talk to people directly. If the majority of these people have never seen a film, why would they be any more willing to help? The least we can do is show them a film. So Makhmalbaf sends Abual Fazel and Hassan, our crew, to buy a large-screen television, a VCR and copies of several films.

The afternoon is spent negotiating with the Iranian authorities to let us use one of their spare rooms in the office compound as a makeshift cinema for the refugees. The authorities are concerned about the kind of films we are going to show. We can only show those Iranian films that are not banned in Iran. Showing any film or TV drama in Pushtu is out of the question.

*   *   *

We've moved out of the creepy hotel into two compounds with enough room for the entire crew. I wake up around 4:30 A.M., when I hear Abas-agha preparing breakfast in the kitchen. At 5:30, as the morning light breaks, we start work. Ten-year-old Zahir, an Afghan refugee from another border village, helps Abas-agha with his daily tasks. Zahir's father, whose real name is Gulbuddin but who prefers to be called Qoutb, arrives every morning to go with us to Niatack, where he guards the minibus with the equipment and serves us cups of tea and water.

Qoutb was a fighter with Gulbuddin Hekmatyar's Islamic Party. But he feels that Hekmatyar betrayed him when he gave his men and territory to the Taliban militias. "It's because of this that I changed from my old name, which was the same as Hekmatyar's first name," says Qoutb, who's a tall, good-looking man with dark curly hair, long eyelashes and green eyes. "Before the drought, I used to plant enough vegetables in my farm on the other side of the border to feed my family," he says. "There was also help from the Islamic Party. But now, it's all dried up, both the land and the party." And so he works at odd jobs. Every evening, he collects our leftovers to take home for his family.

Zahir is the eldest of his six children. Zahir is very intelligent, and Abas-agha has been teaching him how to cook and clean, make tea and wash the dishes. It's good training. "Men can do these things," says Zahir, sounding a little surprised. Zahir says he likes to study, but there are no schools in their refugee village. "In the village, we dig in the mud to get water," he says. "It's yellow, not the colour of water here. If you let it set, you can see the mud at the bottom of your cup. We are always sick with stomachaches and diarrhea." The

Iranian government opposes the building of a water pipe because they're afraid it would be an incentive for refugees to stay in Iran.

The brutal wind has died down and has been replaced by a touch of sunshine. We arrive to set up the first screening. Abual Fazel and Hassan have worked hard to clean the room, spread a carpet and even hung curtains to stop the light from intruding. It's mayhem outside, with hundreds of curious children and teenagers gathered at the door. At ten A.M., they are all allowed in and are directed to sit on the floor, facing the television. *The Cyclist*—Makhmalbaf's 1980 film about Afghanistan—comes on the screen. This is the only Afghan-related film we can present.

I sit in a corner, watching the faces of the spectators, whose eyes shine with excitement and fear. As soon as a scene changes—or where the film has been edited—they get up to leave. "It's not finished," screams Hassan, asking them to sit down and be quiet. I realize that for those of us used to watching films, the edit point is seamless, but for these refugees, watching the screen for the first time, each edit is so noticeable that they assume it indicates the end of what they are watching. But they learn quickly to stay for the next scene. They've lost their innocence, I tell myself as I walk out for fresh air.

A few women standing by the wall of their mud houses ask what's going on. They are dressed in traditional clothes, with black head covers that barely reach to their foreheads but hang loosely down their backs. In my broken Pushtu I manage to explain that we've organized a cinema. "So good," says an elderly woman. "We're bored here all day long. It would be nice if we could see what those kids and teenagers are watching." Her daughter-in-law, who is holding a little baby, asks if women can go to the cinema. Of course you can, I say. "But our men won't let us—unless it's only for women," the elderly woman says. We'll organize a day for women, I promise.

Hassan is having a hard time getting some of the children to leave the room. "It's time for a break now," he says to those who are insisting on staying and watching more. "Later in the afternoon, we'll have another showing." For these children, it's been love at first sight. They sit like little birds in front of a water pond, without blinking—all eyes, ears and minds given to the screen. They don't want to miss a second. They remind me of myself when I used to watch films as a child, lost in that dreamy world where the power of images and sound takes over everything else. "Can't I just stay here?" asks a little girl. "No," Hassan replies gently. "I've got to lock the room." Disappointed, she stands up and walks to the door, holding the hand of her young brother.

Since Hassan cannot afford the time to look after everything in Niatack as well as our production needs, a young man—one of the few refugees in Niatack who knows how to operate a television and VCR—is being paid to run the cinema. He is a member of the Hazara group. As more children from the Hazara community show up, the Pushtun fathers and brothers prevent their own children from entering the cinema—some even using force, beating those children who want to go and watch the film. "Our children won't mix with the rest," says an angry young man. "He only lets in his own community," complains another. The Hazara man in charge of the cinema denies that he is favouring his own ethnic group. The dividing lines here run deep—physically as well as metaphorically—and it's hard to determine who's right. In this flat land, these three Afghan refugee communities live in isolation from each other. Houses belonging to one community are built far away from the others—with miles in between—as if still separated by the natural mountains of their homeland. Here, mountains of fear, ignorance and hatred have become the barrier. And no one from any of the communities bothers to talk to or even smile at members of the others.

The only solution is to try to rotate the use of the cinema between the communities. But the refugees don't trust each other, and no one is willing to take responsibility. Where there is poverty, there is little chance for tolerance. So the cinema—though loved by the majority—is now transformed from a place of collective education to a site of sectarian and ethnic violence. To avoid making the cinema yet another source of animosity between the rival communities, it's better to close it down.

The children walk mournfully behind the television and the VCR as they are taken away. It's like a funeral. "Are you bringing the cinema back?" asks a kid, holding on to Hassan's leg. Hassan looks more sorrowful than the children. We hope the adults in the community somehow learn to share. Perhaps then the younger generation will have a chance for a better life.

Mullah Zahir is a Pushtu-speaking leader with great sympathy for his community, and an open mind. A slender man in his forties, with a black beard and kind features, he's the only one who has spoken to his people about the film and come back to us with an honest answer. "If your film can bring attention to the tragedy of this displaced population, then you can film inside our mosque and among our community," he says. "Young boys and girls will be there, but I can't promise any of the community's women will show up." He introduces his daughter, who is in grade five. She will be present on the day we shoot.

This is a breakthrough. After days of endless negotiations and attempts to gain the support of a people lost in their own destitution, we are finally filming. The children are excited at the sight of the camera and sound equipment. They are curious but intrusive. They gather around us like flies sticking to cotton candy. By the third day of shooting, almost every member of the crew has lost his voice from shouting and screaming, trying to keep the children at bay to complete a single scene.

Mullah Zahir has opened the door. Mullah Qader comes forward next. Young men in his community, he says, will take part in the film. But no women will participate. He says, however, that he can send me among women, in any household in his community, to talk, film or take pictures. "You're an Afghan," he reminds me. "You understand our culture, that foreign men are not permitted to talk to our women." I try to argue that these men are all Muslims, that they have no bad intentions when they talk to women, that filming would take place in the presence of husbands, fathers and brothers. "You understand," he insists. "It won't be possible."

"Where is your husband?" Mullah Qader asks me. I shock him with the news that I'm single. "Where is your father?" I tell him that my father is in Canada, and that he supports what I'm doing. He has a moral problem. On the one hand, he says, he respects me. On the other, I'm an Afghan woman, and if my father has no problem with me travelling and working with a group of men, then what should he think of my father? "What should he think of himself?" I ask. He has no answer, but now believes that I've become his responsibility. "How old are you?" he asks. Twenty-seven, I say. "Couldn't your parents find you a good Afghan man there?" he asks with a smile. As I try to find the least embarrassing way to explain that my parents would never do such a thing, he continues with his stream of thought. "We can find you a suitable husband here," he says. "No thanks," I say. "But you're getting old," he says, seriously concerned about my age. "When are you going to have children?" Not only do I represent his honour, but I've now become his source of concern. His offer of help is genuine. Several women in the village, hearing that I'm an Afghan—often as I start speaking Pushtu with them— show similar concern about my situation. They would be happy to find me a husband, they say.

Many girls in Niatack are engaged or given in marriage by the age of ten or eleven, and most have a baby by the time they are fourteen. Girls of ten are no longer innocent children, unaware of the cruel world around them. They like to wear makeup. They shy away from boys who are a year or so older than them. They flirt consciously; their gestures, their smiles, the way they touch their hair, stand in a corner, steal a smile or a gaze from a young boy—it is all intentional. Their culture has conditioned them to become little women. They giggle and tease each other about boys. Most already know how to hold a baby.

Nourjahan, whose name means "light of the world," can tolerate only a split second of light in her left eye, and her right eye is blind. She lost her sight as a result of some unknown disease in early childhood. She places her tiny hand over the eye that has a little vision but can't stand normal light. She sings an Iranian song in her heavenly voice: "My groom, why are you late? It's our wedding day, why have you been delayed?" Other girls sitting around her in a circle answer for the groom. "My love, I was gone to the market to buy you lipstick. I was gone to the market to buy you a watch." Like angels they raise their hands as they whisper the words.

"How old are you?" I ask Nourjahan.

"Ten or eleven," she replies with a warm smile. She often gets help from another girl to walk.

"Ten or eleven? Which?" I ask.

"I don't know," she says.

She is not the only one. The majority of refugees in Niatack don't know their exact age—even their parents are just guessing. They are what the rest of the world was centuries ago. They are our past—and ironically we can't seem to stand it. Do we impose our chain of time and our consciousness of it upon them just because we wish to help them?

We are filming in Araify's community, among the Hazara households. The film calls for a refugee camp near the Afghan-Iranian border, where the head of the camp, played by Araify himself, is looking for a family to take Nafas to Kandahar. A man agrees to take her with his family as his fourth wife. A young girl named Zarbibi—who is playing a member of the family—hasn't returned for her second day of shooting. Akbar (a member of the crew), Kova and I start our search. We find her house among Mullah Zahir's community. I knock on the patched-up, rusty door. A woman answers. "Can I talk to Zarbibi?" I ask. "She's not here," says a man standing in the yard. But I see Zarbibi, who is about ten, sitting amid purple and blue pillows and blankets in the corner of the room. I smile as our eyes meet. "She's not well," says her mother. I sit on the ground. Akbar and Kova are waiting outside.

I try to explain that yesterday we shot the film with her in it. If she refuses to help us, we'll have to throw out all the work we've done so far. It doesn't seem to mean much to the family. "She doesn't want to go," says her father. Zarbibi is staring at me sadly, playing with the corner of her green head cover. "She can't go to the other side," explains her mother. "They'll beat her up."

Apparently, a couple of Pushtun girls who went yesterday afternoon to check on the film crew were chased by Hazara kids. Though Zarbibi was not among them, the word has spread in this community that their children will be beaten up if they cross the invisible line. There is a long stretch of bare land between the two communities—in their imagination, it's a rigid line, rooted in mistrust, betrayals and hatred instigated by years of war.

As I assure the family that I'll take full responsibility for Zarbibi's safe return, the father kneels in front of me, his hands extended towards me. "Please leave us in peace," he says. Then he reaches for his turban and holds it underneath his bushy black beard. It is a sign of begging in Afghanistan. "Please, please," he pleads, "leave my daughter alone. There are others who can help. She's afraid." He pauses. Zarbibi is watching us carefully. "We are afraid," says her father. "We've lost our entire livelihood, our home, our land, our cattle, our families and children to the war. Let us now at least keep our dignity and honour. Please let us be." The man begins to cry. The quest for pardon in his dark eyes cuts right through my heart. What can I possibly tell this broken man? What can I possibly offer? Zarbibi is sobbing too—now rubbing her eyes with her green scarf. I don't know whom she's feeling sorry for, herself or us.

If I wished to define beauty, I would point to Lawangi, a fourteen-year-old Baluchi woman with a face of goddess-like perfection. "She'll make a world laugh with half a smile, and turn an army of heroes to tears with one sad look from the corner of her eyes," says Kova. She's slim, with skin the colour of honey, wild black eyes and a walk that would turn any head. "She doesn't walk like the others," says Hassan, quite taken by her presence. "Her heels don't touch the ground; it's as if she moves with the air, like in a dance." She's barefoot, wearing a blue dress and a brown cotton head cover. Holding a little boy's hand, she comes forward to be on camera. With ease, she puts her scarf aside to wear the cream-coloured burqa we've given her for the scene. Then she stands, tall and dignified, to be filmed. She is to play the role of one of the old man's wives.

Lawangi shows up for the first two days, and then disappears. When we ask around, a boy of about eight says he's her cousin and can show us where she is. As the rest of the crew prepare the scene, Kova, Akbar and I once again set out to find an escapee. The boy takes us to his home, where a group of women circle around me to talk. I promise that I'll return to have tea with them and hear their stories, but right now I need to find Lawangi. Pulling up her see-through blue head cover, Lawangi leans against the mud-brick wall. "Here she is," the women laugh. Lawangi walks forward to leave with us, giving instructions to her little brother to wait for her return. It's encouraging to see a willing participant. Like a horse ready for a race, Lawangi jumps into the back of our pickup with her cousin. It seems so natural for her to be like this—carefree, wild and simple.

On set, Lawangi is happy—enjoying the attention, the camera and the admiring gazes of everyone around her. "You're fourteen and not married? How come?" I ask. "Two years ago, my mother and one brother died of tuberculosis," she says. "I have two younger brothers. My father doesn't have money to take another wife, so he's kept me at home to look after my brothers. He goes to work in the city, so I take care of the house."

Dr. Shafchic, who's a friend of Makhmalbaf, has come to help the refugees in Niatack. For a week he's gone door to door, examining young and old in the village. We have spent at least ten thousand U.S. dollars on medicine for the refugees, which Dr. Shafehie has been patiently distributing to the people. Tuberculosis, he says, is one of the main killers of refugees in this area. "At least ninety percent of them have the disease," he says. "I've written over two thousand prescriptions in the past week. And that's only for those for whom we don't have the right medicine." He is convinced that Lawangi has tuberculosis. "Unless she's treated," he says, "she will die—just like her mother and brother."

"You must be seen by a doctor," I say to Lawangi in the morning. She's feeding a piece of bread to one of her brothers and is not paying much attention. She has brought both of them—boys of three and four—asking them to sit in a sunny corner near the wall while she's acting her part. It's a tough start to the day. I can't get my mind off tuberculosis, and the people around me, who may die from a disease that was controlled in the West decades ago. I can hardly keep my eyes open in the light.

As we break for lunch, Lawangi says she must leave. "I've got to go home. My father has returned from work. I must go," she pleads. "My father is on his way here." She shakes my hand, as if hoping to wake me from the sleep of ignorance. "You don't know—he's crazy. He beats me as if he's mad." She has the look of a slain lioness as she shows me her bruised arms.

"Would it help if I came to your home to talk to him?" I ask.

"Talk to him? If he knew I'd told you this, he'd kill me at once."

"Lawangi! Lawangi!" calls her cousin, pointing towards the end of the alleyway.

"He'll be here soon," she says, walking backwards, still facing me. Her expression is a cry for help. She would love to continue working with us, she says, but it's not possible.

"Should we try to talk to your father?" I ask again. "Would he listen to anyone? Your aunt? The Iranian authorities?"

"It's no use," she says. Then she lifts her right hand in a gesture of goodbye, with a bitter smile that would make the world cry.

I look around to find someone from the crew to pay her day's salary. They're crowded around us—young men, children and teenagers, chewing their cheese and bread, spitting the pits of consumed dates to the ground, sipping their cups of tea. Lawangi picks up her younger brother in her arms, walking behind her cousin, who's pulling the hand of her other brother. Dust rises as she walks—barefoot, with the lightness of a wind, yet with hesitation. After every step, she turns her head, staring at the crowd and me. Then she turns away in slow motion, as if wanting to memorize it all. The last time she turns to look, her eyes seem watery. But she lifts her chest high and holds her head straight. She doesn't seem to care that her head cover has fallen over her shoulders. She disappears from our gaze, and we never see her again.

Several days later, we send Lawangi's money home. Her cousin is the messenger. "She's not going to return," he says, scratching the back of his head. "Her father won't let her leave. She hasn't even come to visit us."

Not only does more film now have to be discarded, but we also have to find another woman—preferably one who is Lawangi's height, if not with her exceptional looks. The crew is convinced they'll never again lay eyes on anyone like Lawangi. "At least not for a long time," says Hassan. He has fallen so hard that he's willing to pay any price for her. "You can't marry her," says Kova. "She is just a child—only fourteen." Hassan is forced to think twice. "Not to marry her, but to take her out of the yoke of her father's tyranny," he says. I'm ready to plead with anyone who can offer her a roof and a chance to grow up. But Hassan is discouraged. Qoutb says that, while Baluchi women are much freer in their movements once they are married, they'll never marry an Iranian. "Her father will marry her off to a Baluchi man," he says.

Hygiene is a problem in Niatack. None of the mud houses I've been to has a bathtub. Women complain that they don't have enough water to wash their children, let alone themselves. "Could we build a couple of public bathhouses?" I ask. The Iranian authorities show us a public bathhouse. It's for men only. "Our women don't go to public baths," says a man, fixing his square hat over his curly hair. "It is a question of our honour." But no one can see them inside a closed bathhouse, I say. "No, they can't, but knowing that women are inside the

307

bath, other men—men who are not their husbands—can imagine that they are naked. It's a dishonour."

I have never heard such an argument, condemning not just immorality, but the immorality of imagining being immoral. Yet for the men in this village it is such a persuasive argument that they don't care if their wives or mothers die from lack of proper hygiene, so long as they are not seen—or even imagined being seen—by other men. One thing these people certainly don't need is the Taliban morality police. They police themselves better than any Taliban, especially when it comes to morality and women.

Sadullah is Mullah Qader's nephew. He is eleven or twelve, he says. With his dark skin and sharp eyes he has a vengeful look, but a kind heart. The first time we hear him sing, we are electrified by the music of his voice. He is the eldest of six children. "Their father became a martyr for Allah," says Mullah Qader. Sadullah—who's called Sado—is the only breadwinner in the family. He buys a few kilograms of dates from the market in Iran, walks to the other side of the border and, once inside Afghanistan, walks around the villages, shouting, "Dates, sweet Iranian dates." He returns before sunset with a little money and whatever else he can collect on his way. In the film, he's playing the role of a boy who's been kicked out of a Taliban school for lack of discipline and is hired by Nafas to guide her in her journey to Kandahar.

Ever since Sado was heard singing, boys in the village have been bullying him, teasing him and calling him names. "I'm not going to sing again," he says. "Why not?" I ask. His younger brother tells me the boys say Sado sounds like a woman when he sings. Sado is upset and doesn't even want to work with us any more. Mullah Qader manages to convince him to finish the sequence. Sado is making more money by working with us than by crossing the border, but he's unhappy, he says. "You'll all leave," he contemplates, "and I'll have to deal with the insults." The pressure from people in the community—who are at best ignorant and at worse jealous—is very strong. I ask Sado if he'd like to become a musician. "Musician?" He reflects for some minutes, and then answers with a question: "What is a musician?" Once he knows, his eyes grow keener, his manners softer. "I'd like to." He smiles. But how? Where?

We've taken Nourjahan to a doctor because of her eyes. The doctor said that after surgery she'll have vision in one eye. She'll be able to see and won't have to place her tiny hand over her troubled eye. She, too, could become a singer. How can we fix the problems of Niatack so that children like Sado and Nourjahan can grow up?

We are walking across a sand mountain, filming a sequence in which Sado pulls a ring from a corpse, singing a Pushtu song into Nafas's tape recorder. Sado stays close by me. We walk back to our bus together, talking about his family. He would like to have a sister, he says. His mother has six boys and no daughter. When we get inside the bus, he sits quietly in the back. It's often a few kilometres' walk to the bus because we can't park on the sand—the bus would disappear fast. If we stopped moving, we too would disappear under the sand, which moves on the surface of the earth so rapidly that in just a few hours we discover a soft mountain where there used to be dry, hardened land.

"These used to be wheat fields," says Qoutb, handing me a cup of tea. Qoutb knows this region. Just on the other side of the border lies his hometown of Helmand. "That"—he points at the white ground—"was a river." After four years of drought, the riverbed has disappeared and the wheat fields have turned into dry sandy hills.

Day by day, Sado is growing kinder and more concerned. He waits for me to catch up with the rest of the crew as we walk over the soft sand. He offers a helping hand when I need to climb a sand mountain. He knows I'm an Afghan. He, too, feels responsible for my protection.

And day by day, we are getting closer to the danger zone— the smugglers' road. Motorcycles and strange cars are becoming frequent. In a desert, where the only moving things are the wind and the sand, it feels odd to see a shadow following us from the top of one hill to the next, to notice an armed man keeping pace with us, to come across a group of men who don't take their eyes off me. Walking towards the car, I become conscious of myself as a woman. As I sense the strangers' eyes following me, I automatically reach for the covering of my burqa. We are inside Iran—no one here is imposing a burqa on me. When we are not shooting a scene, I usually push the cover away, so I can breathe, see, function as a normal human being. But for the first time, I feel in need of it. I feel safe underneath the garment, and less conscious of being an object.

The two previous times I wore a burqa—when we left Afghanistan more than a decade ago and when I tried to reach Dyana two years ago—I didn't mind it so much. It was a tool of escape, something that concealed my identity for a purpose that had greater meaning: survival. However, since the Taliban made the burqa mandatory, I have begun to despise it, concluding that it is one of the worst symbols and tools of women's oppression. Reminding myself how much I hate the burqa, I push the cover away again. But after a few more steps—and though I know Sado is walking slowly behind me—I once again draw it over my face. I fear the gaze of those strange men standing in the distance, watching me walk. Oddly enough, I feel protected by the burqa. My relation to this bizarre Afghan creation has suddenly changed. I no longer dislike it; the burqa offers a sense of immunity, however false, in a land that's so much in need of peace and security.

Gulolay, a young woman in Niatack, asks me if we would give her a burqa instead of money if she works with us.

"What do you want a burqa for?" I ask.

"I want it for the night of my wedding," she says. She explains that, among her tribe, wearing a burqa is a sign of sophistication. "Brides wear them on the night of their wedding. Especially when the groom arrives to take her home, she likes to be dressed in a burqa," she says. "It makes the bride more mysterious and desirable." One person's symbol of oppression is another person's tool of protection, and someone else's means of seduction. Where do you draw the line?

The burqa is an urban phenomenon, I learn later. In rural Afghanistan, women once moved freely within their own communities. Dressed in their traditional clothes, which included a modest head cover, women were respected in a society where everyone knew each other. But when rural people began to travel to the city, either for tourism or for employment, women found themselves outside their protected territories. To feel safe, the women created a cloak that provided them with the privacy and security they'd once enjoyed in their village compounds—the burqa. A rural woman who travelled would return home wearing a burqa as a sign of prestige—showing that she'd been to the city. Given the remoteness of Afghanistan's landscape, not everyone could travel outside the village. So the burqa became a symbol of city dwelling, city visiting and a city lifestyle. At a time when women could not move around easily in cities, the burqa provided them with the freedom to do so. It became a tool of their liberation from the shackles of a patriarchal society that didn't favour their presence outside the house, that didn't want them seen in a hostile environment like the city.

In the cities themselves, the burqa was gradually discarded in favour of smaller scarves—which conveyed both modesty and modern looks. In the villages, women continued to work on farms, gather firewood, carry water and take animals to pasture wearing their traditional clothes—regarding the burqa as a sophisticated outfit worn only in cities. For my mother's generation, the burqa became a sign of rural rather than urban living. The women who continued to wear a burqa were either elders who had no formal education, or those who came from villages.

When I was growing up, the number of burqa-wearing women increased, as most people fleeing their small towns took refuge in Kabul. No one seemed to pay much attention to the burqa at the time. It was just another item of women's clothing, similar to some men's turbans or *chapans*. Burqas were more a class marker than anything else. Women from the upper or upper-middle classes wore modest but Western-style clothes. Women who wore burqas were referred to as *chodaridar* (burqa-wearing) and were seen as having a traditional mindset.

Despite sympathy for Gulolay's tribal tradition and her bridal wish, I cannot bring myself to offer her a burqa as a wedding gift. "Not on my watch," I say. "I'll give you money as a gift, and you can buy whatever you want." She is disappointed. She doesn't have any incentive to be in our film now, she says. Only if we give her a burqa will she participate. "I can't find a burqa to buy in Iran," she says. "And I can't go to Afghanistan to get one." I tell her we call the burqa a woman's prison. "Do you want to be in prison?" I ask. It's irrelevant. She wants it. "Why should it be a prison when you want it?" she asks. Perhaps I don't understand.

As we move still closer to the border, farther away from Niatack, we discover starving families. Six families—all women and children—are hiding inside a ruin. Like animals scratching the face of the earth, they are crawling over the ground. I lift up a girl—probably twelve years old. She crumples like a fallen leaf. I try to lift her again. She seems lifeless. I try to get her to drink a sip from my water bottle. Makhmalbaf calls on the production manager to rush her to the hospital.

These families have walked hundreds of kilometres, for days, without food or water. They are victims of a recent Taliban attack on the city of Bamiyan, in central Afghanistan. Bamiyan is home to Hazaras; it's the home of the two giant Buddhas; and it was once the corridor through which pilgrims travelled from Central Asia to China. My father and his friends used to go to Bamiyan for picnics and historical explorations. Now it has become a valley of death, as one of the survivors describes it. "The Taliban killed all the men," she says. "We managed to escape, but some died on the way."

We have no authority to provide them with shelter. They will be considered illegal refugees and won't be allowed to stay in Iran. The only thing we can do is provide them with food. We head to the market, where like mad people we buy cartons of fruit, juice, bottles of water, blankets, a gas stove, pots and glasses, and warm clothes for the children. Akbar takes the supplies to them.

We sit around our tablecloth, where Abas-agha is serving dinner. We look at each other, at the delicious saffron rice, the chicken kebabs and salad. No one has an appetite. "If you don't eat," says Zahir, "you won't be able to work." We know the logic, but we can't get our minds off the starving people we saw this afternoon. We go to bed feeling full without having touched the food.

Two days later, the twelve-year-old girl is released from the hospital. Akbar, who goes to bring her back, asks the doctor what was wrong with her. "She was not sick," he told Akbar. "She was hungry."

One of the women becomes part of the film—she plays a woman who, thinking she is ill, sees a doctor and is diagnosed as being hungry. When we finish the sequence, we go to check on the six surviving families from Bamiyan. They've been found by the Iranian authorities and have been taken to another camp, from which they'll be deported back home to face their tormentors. A vicious circle of cruelty dominates the lives of these people—and the civilized laws of other countries make sure that that order is not broken.

The feeling of helplessness is overwhelming. It's not just one problem, one obstacle, one grievance that we can help fix. As we peel away one layer, another set of difficulties emerges. And there are no simple solutions. Some of the problems are centuries old, others have been created or compounded by two decades of war, yet others are the result of a life passed in exile.

A scene from Kandahar. *Nelofer with Sadullah, at the border refugee village of Niatack, November 2000.*

As I walk near a well—we're shooting a scene in which a group of women are washing clothes when Sado and Nafas arrive to drink some water—I hear a voice. An elderly woman is shouting at me. "Go home, you shameless woman," she screams, holding a stick in her hand. "Do you have no honour, to speak to men in public and work with them like this?" She insults me and curses me. I feel like crying. What is wrong with me? Being an Afghan? Or having sympathy for Afghans? What have I done to deserve this?

Gulbuddin, a fourteen-year-old refugee from Niatack who's been assisting the camera team, tells me I should ignore her. "She lost her son in the war, and she can't think straight," he says. "Don't think about anything she said. Everyone knows she's not well." I appreciate his kindness. This is the first time he has spoken to me. He is a very shy person, hard-working and loyal. "I brought my sister to work on the film," he says, blushing. "My father said it was not good for her, but I told him I was around. Besides, you're an Afghan. I watch you work with men. My sister can do the same." He calls his sister to introduce her to me.

Shreen is twelve or thirteen. She is skinny, with green eyes and a pointed nose, and is very shy. As I sit inside the bus to talk to her, Qoutb brings me a cup of tea and a square of sugar. A little girl is watching us from the corner of the wall. I call her to come closer. Barefoot, with a runny nose and hair that looks as if it's never been washed, she comes forward. She must be five or six. I offer her the sugar. After a little hesitation, she takes it, placing it in the palm of her hand with care, as if it's a diamond. She looks at it as if it's the most precious thing on earth. Eat it, I tell her. She is still looking at it with great curiosity. I show her how she can eat the sugar cube by eating one myself. Slowly, she brings the sugar crystal closer to her mouth. Then, with the tip of her tongue, she touches the sweet square. Gradually, she develops a taste for it, liking it more and more. Finally, she places it between her lips and chews it gently. Then she smiles—as if I've given her the world. The excitement on her face is astonishing. "That may have been her first taste of real sugar," says Qoutb. In some parts of the world, we give children so many toys—all sorts of sophisticated things—and we can't inspire even a smile, let alone enthusiasm and satisfaction.

—

MAY 10, 2001. CANNES, FRANCE. It's the world premiere of *Kandahar*. Months after Niatack and its stories of poverty and despair, we are standing in front of the stairs of the Palais des Festivals. Walking up the steps, over the famous red carpet,

On the red carpet at Cannes. Nelofer, Mohsen Makhmalbaf and the crew at the world premiere of Kandahar, May 10, 2001. (Photo: Amir Assefi)

is a dream for any director, movie star or producer. Makhmalbaf, the crew and I are greeted by the director of the world's most popular and prestigious film festival. In a place where directors and stars spend thousands of dollars on their dresses, hairstyles and makeup, Makhmalbaf is in black jeans and a T-shirt; I'm wearing a worn, traditional red dress that my sister made and a pair of old slippers, pieces of which are literally falling off as I walk. This is my revolt—however silly, helpless or absurd—for Niatack. The commercial world that engulfs our energies, turning us into good consumers in a daily life that's ever more comfortable, has also made it possible for hundreds of Niatacks to come into existence.

The past four days have been madness, with interviews every ten minutes. The photo shoots make me feel as if I'm an exotic animal in the zoo. "It's part of the game," says Makhmalbaf. "This is our chance to talk about those starving people." A French reporter is upset that we showed land-mine victims running with wooden prosthesis legs in the film. It's not upsetting that these men have lost their legs to the land mines, or that our governments in the West helped litter Afghanistan with these explosives—no, what is disturbing is that we are showing these victims to a world whose sensitivities should not be offended.

A French film critic suggests that the film uses English as its narrative in order to gain a better market. He fails to realize that I've lived and been educated in an English-speaking country for over a decade. "Why didn't you speak your own language?" asks another reporter. I did—Dari, Pushtu and English are my languages, and I speak all three in the film, I explain. They are not interested in an Afghan woman who can learn and think. They are rather unhappy that I've dismantled the boxed image of an Afghan woman—submissive, oppressed and able to speak only in a native tongue. "Would you have been less upset if I spoke French instead of English in the film?" I ask. There is no answer.

At a press conference, a reporter asks why we made a film about an "unimportant subject." The comment indicates that Afghanistan is a forgotten land. It lost its relevance for the West after the end of the Cold War. Perhaps, but not for long.

Four months later, I arrive at the Civic Hospital in Ottawa to check on my sister, who was in a car accident on her way to work. As my eyes search among the patients in the emergency waiting area, I notice that everyone is watching television. What sort of action movie is being played that's captured everyone's attention? I wonder. I see a shot of two skyscrapers, one of them in a shadowy glaze of smoke. At the bottom of the screen it reads "CNN." I stop moving. As I watch, a plane hits the second tower. It's like being in a movie theatre, where the spontaneous reaction to a moment of surprise is a simultaneous gasp from the audience. Our mouths literally drop open. "What the hell was that?" says a man in a wheelchair with a bandage around his head. It is the morning of September 11, 2001.

As my sister lies in bed at home, recovering from the shock of her accident, I sit in front of our television set in tears, thinking of all the innocent lives that were so brutally destroyed in New York, Washington and Pennsylvania. The map of Afghanistan is becoming a frequent image on television. "What are they going to do?" my mother asks nervously, as pictures of the Taliban and Osama bin Laden are interspersed with footage of a country we used to call home.

I first heard Osama bin Laden's name in 1995, in a letter from a family friend in Peshawar. He said that a group called the Taliban—men who describe themselves as an army of peace—had swept through the Afghan southwestern provinces. "They carry a white flag—as a sign of peace," he wrote. "They may be Pakistani, but their true identity is yet to become known." He asked whether I'd heard of a man called Osama bin Laden. "He's an Arab who is said to have men and weapons in Afghanistan."

After reading his letter, I remembered that, in 1989, my friend Daoud—who'd been at the camp of Ahmad Shah Masoud, one of the mujahidin commanders, before visiting us in Islamabad—had told me that a rich Saudi had sent a group of Arabs to Ahmad Shah Masoud with lots of gifts. "The gifts were copies of the Quran, produced in hardcover in beautiful crimson and gold, with golden designs on every page," said Daoud. Masoud met with the messengers. "Then he sent them back with all their gifts, saying he was fighting the Russians to free Afghanistan, not to subjugate it to Arab sheikhs. The Arabs left very angry." Almost twelve years after that meeting, Masoud was killed in a suicide bombing on September 9, 2001—two days before the suicide attack on New York. Two Arabs, who arrived at Masoud's camp on the pretense of filming an interview with him, detonated explosives hidden inside the camera only minutes after meeting him.

Back when we lived in Pakistan, I didn't pay much attention to bin Laden. Later, I heard him described as one of the Arabs who was instrumental in defeating the Russians. But inside Afghanistan, and even in Pakistan, nobody I knew spoke of him. During the days of the Afghan jihad, we discussed the mujahidin parties, the names and characters of all their leaders. Bin Laden was an obscure guy, at least among the people I knew. While in Afghanistan, I dismissed any news about Arab fighters as propaganda from the communist government. When I saw the wives of some of these Arab fighters at the school in Pakistan, I realized the extent of their involvement in the Afghan jihad. But their presence seemed more of an anomaly than a cause for alarm. Like most Afghan mujahidin, they too were supported by the West.

Trying to distract myself from the misery in the United States, I decide to plant some lilies along the driveway of my family home. My parents moved to Ottawa several years ago to be close to us—their children—as we all went to university. I live in Montreal now, my brother lives in Quebec City and my sister lives at home. The lilies are to be in memory of those innocent people who were killed in America. They will also represent my hope that civilians in Afghanistan won't be killed in revenge for their deaths. But lifting several heavy packages of gardening soil leaves me with a back injury. In pain, I walk around the house, answering calls from reporters, film festival officials and distributors of *Kandahar*. All of a sudden, everyone wants to talk to me about Afghanistan, about the film and about Dyana.

Where is Dyana? I have been hoping for months now, especially since the release of the movie, that she might get in touch. What would she think of the film? And how is she reacting to the sudden attention being given to the tragedy of Afghanistan, and in particular to the lives of women who—after being ignored for years—are now emerging as a matter of intense Western interest?

As I travel with *Kandahar*, I am treated like a movie star—limos and taxi cabs, five-star hotels, and press conferences packed with reporters and cameras. "Are you one-hundred-percent Afghan?" asks a journalist in Thessaloniki, Greece. "Are you sure you don't have any royal family connections?" asks another in Rome. The questions from the press say more about the journalists than about me. But I appreciate the chance to express my thoughts. In the midst of the world drama, where battles of "good" against "evil" are being fought, and the triumph of destruction and death are taking place, I have unwittingly become a spokesperson for a cause. I ask audiences to see the world for what it is, to think of the millions of deprived people who are ever more frustrated, ever more distressed over the failure of their corrupt governments to deliver on their promises of prosperity, freedom and democracy. And I ask people to remember the bankrupt Western policies that protect these governments.

In October 2001, I tell an audience of over four hundred people at Columbia University, in New York, that Afghans nowadays are perceived as either victims or villains. The first are to be pitied, the second feared and despised. I tell them I would like to speak to them as an equal. A young woman with short blonde hair raises her hand. "Are you telling me I shouldn't believe those mad guys on my TV screen who are shouting and saying they want to destroy America?" Another woman says her neighbour's son was killed in the twin towers. "How can I explain to her that we don't need to avenge the death of her son because Afghanistan is a poor country?"

Marisa Berenson, an American actress who is also here to speak, tells the audience that her sister was in the second plane that crashed into the tower. "She was a mother of two, a kind woman," says Berenson. "My sister would never have wanted anyone to die in her name." A dead silence. In the United States there seems to be more complacency than elsewhere, coexisting with fear and disillusionment. People don't appear to connect American foreign policy to the situation in the Middle East, or to the U.S. involvement in Afghanistan during the Cold War. As American aircraft start bombing Afghanistan and the death toll of civilians rises, there is neither an outcry for the 3,670 innocent Afghans who are killed after September 11, nor any sympathy for the two million dead and missing Afghans of the past twenty years.

Back at my family home in Ottawa, we hear news of attempts to bring King Zahir Shah back to Afghanistan. I ask my father what he thinks. "Like the British in the nineteenth century, the Americans are trying desperately to install an Amir Abdur Rahman Khan to bring some stability to the region," he says.

"It could mean prosperity for some Afghans, but not necessarily justice or democracy for the nation." He pauses, rubbing just above his left ankle, where he was hit by the bullet in pro-democracy protests in Kabul. With his arthritis, the spot, a small dark patch, tortures him with a nagging pain.

"You have the mark of a bullet on your leg," I say to him. "You fought against the monarchy once. What do you think of the attempt by the democratic world to bring the king back to Afghanistan?"

"It's symbolic, of course," he says, still massaging his ankle. "Zahir Shah is too old and too uninterested in the affairs of Afghanistan to do anything. Frankly, I don't think he ever *was* interested in the affairs of the country, even when he was king. I don't approve of monarchies—they are at best corrupt, at worst self-indulgent. If the Russians hadn't invaded Afghanistan, there wouldn't have been any mujahidin or Taliban. But with all this, we've regressed in time, sinking below year zero. If the monarchy means a starting point, it's not so bad." He shakes his head, trying to justify his argument. "We have to start somewhere," he says. "Don't we?"

12

DYANA

Remember me when I am gone away,
Gone far away into the silent land;
When you can no more hold me by the hand,
Nor I half turn to go yet turning stay.

Christina Rossetti

ARIANA AFGHAN AIRLINES FLIGHT 404 from
Dubai lands at Kabul International Airport, a rough landing in
every sense of the word—it's my first time home since my family left Kabul thirteen years ago. Stepping onto the tarmac, I
do not recognize my country. Playing in my head, like a

jammed tape, is the sound of explosions, the 1989 night when an arms depot was set ablaze near the airport. I look around. The "international" airport is a mockery of itself: the runway— what is left of it—is surrounded by bushes and stretches into overgrown grass. A smashed DC-10 lies in a corner next to two burned-out helicopters. A decrepit military plane, the Soviet red star still shining on its tail, is spread-eagled on its belly. The blue-and-white tail of an Ariana passenger aircraft sticks up from a pile of broken military and civilian aircraft.

Inside the terminal, arriving passengers struggle towards a tiny window behind which a stern-faced officer in an old Afghan military uniform sits checking passports—here, at least, is the face of a familiar, stifling bureaucracy. Elderly porters carry massive suitcases on their shoulders. An old man nearly collapses under a pile of luggage. One at a time, I say. He ignores my call and rushes to pick up more. Poverty is written across his face; when he smiles he shows a set of darkened teeth with several gaps.

Amid the bomb ruins of a city square, Afghans sell watermelons from a wrecked van. July 2002.

On the drive from the airport to the city, I stare at the men crossing the road: tough-looking unwashed faces, bold eyes, long beards, messy hair, all dressed in shalwar kameez, with their shalwars rolled up to reveal their bony ankles, their rifles casually held at their sides. There are a few burqa-shrouded women and crowds of children, some selling water, others begging for money. This is not the Kabul I remember—even in its most miserable days. Where have these men come from? It's not until I see my own uncle—one of my mother's brothers, whom we used to call Uncle Sweet because he made us laugh—that I understand. I realize that every man has been reduced to the state of a mad militia-man. He looks as though he has just climbed out of a trench; he, too, has an unironed shalwar kameez, a long beard, messy hair and rough hands. The only thing missing is a rifle. "If it were not for the international peacekeepers, I would've had to have a machine gun to survive," he says. "There are many thieves in the city." He's just returned from Pakistan with his family. "Why is everyone dressed like this?" I ask. "Clothes are the least of our worries," says one of my cousins. "People are returning from Pakistan and Iran and have no place to go to. There is no electricity. The whole city smells of sewage."

I recognize the grey walls surrounding my old school. The yard looks the same; the main building gleams under the sun in its new coat of pink paint. A sign says the school has just been repaired by UNICEF. There's a handwritten poster—the work of a student—on the "importance of the Loya Jirgah [the Grand Assembly] in Afghan history." In excitement, I run into the hallway to look for the school library, a place from my past, a sanctuary. I knew that room so well, every dark wooden shelf on which I replaced one newly read book after another. But when I open the door, I see an almost empty room. One lone iron shelf stands against the wall, and another colourless wooden shelf holds some textbooks and a few tatty volumes in English donated by a UN agency. Instead of desks and chairs, most classrooms have only a plastic sheet on the floor for students to sit on.

Dyana and I had engraved our names on our wooden desk. But there's no point in looking for it. "They have all been burned," says a teacher who recognizes me. "The lab has been totally destroyed as well." As a student, I saw a human embryo in that lab. Now everything is gone. The Taliban have seen to that. Everyone comes to school wearing a burqa. It is surreal. A crowd of burqas walking in and out of a place that for me was a symbol of modernity. There *were* women with burqas then, but only a few, and they were in the streets. Dyana and I would have burst into laughter if we had seen a burqa-clad teenager arriving at school. Now it is a necessity. These women fear for their lives. Security is a fragile layer of ice, spread thinly over a river of anxiety and destitution.

On our street in the Taymanie district, everything is rotten. The corner of the street, where Dyana and I used to meet, is a mountain of rubbish and dirt. Piles of garbage have replaced the grass and flowers along the walls. It is evening. I push open the old iron gate of my home. Hardened dry land has taken the place of our lawn. The pond is empty, the water pump broken. The upper floor has been shelled to bits in the war. Below live three refugee families whose own homes have been destroyed. I walk into the living room, where I used to read my poetry books. The stonework in the wall was designed by my father, and it is still there. But there is nothing left of my past. All the books have disappeared. I ask the woman who greets me about them.

"I've heard about your books, but God punish us if we've touched anything," she swears. I ask about a black-and-white framed photo of my parents' engagement that was on the living-room wall when we left. "I've never seen it," she says. The curtains, the chandeliers, the furniture are all gone. The windows are broken. I touch the garden wall, which I used to climb to watch the Soviet tanks rumbling down our street. A little girl's paradise—my home—looks smaller than I remembered it. Years of drought have turned my father's garden of flowers to dust. But my mother's fig tree has grown. It towers now over the single-storey house, a symbol of something that has survived in our pulverized world, its branches shaking in the harsh night wind that blows down from the mountains.

I have come home to a place that is no longer home, to a city that is no longer mine. I long ago became a refugee—a lucky one, with my family safe in Canada. "We've no place to go," says the woman, walking behind me around the house. "My cousin is living in your maid's room." She points to what used to be Mother Fatema's home.

"Has anyone seen Mother Fatema?" I ask.

"Her younger son, Joma, was killed in the war," says my uncle. "Haywaz, the elder son, has gone missing. I saw their poor father one day on the street. He was begging. As soon as he recognized me, he turned away. He was embarrassed. He said his wife was sick, heartbroken."

Outside in the street, neighbours gather round me. Some have just returned from Iran and Pakistan. "I saw your film," says Hassan, who used to fly kites with my brother. "I've just returned from Iran." He pauses. "Are you moving back?"

"I don't think so," I say.

"Is the doctor coming back?" asks another neighbour.

I have no answer.

Sikander, my father's cousin, visits with his daughter. "I'm glad you left," he says. "When the communists detained me, the officers who brought me to your home asked a lot of questions about your father. I was worried they'd get him too. I spent almost two years in prison before they let me go. I've inherited arthritis from that bloody prison. They tortured me by running freezing water over my legs." I tell him that my father has the same problem because of the tortures he went through. "Do you have with you any medication for this?" he asks. With his white beard he looks older, but he is still tall and slender. I'm happy to see his eyes haven't lost their spark.

His daughter, like the majority of women in Kabul, is a widow. "My husband was a mujahid. I'd just given birth to my daughter when they brought his body home. I married his younger brother, mostly because of my child. He was a good man. He was killed in a bomb explosion. I'm an unfortunate woman. I've survived two young deaths and am still alive."

I begin to realize that the psychological damage done to this country will take a long time to heal. Physical reconstruction depends on how long the international community is interested in helping Afghanistan. Kabul is the only protected city in the entire country. International forces— Turkish, German, French and Canadian—patrol the streets of my old home city in their flimsy Jeeps and ponderous armoured vehicles. It's not an army of occupation, but a legion of foreigners on special behaviour. American CIA men operate here; Americans also supply the bodyguards for

President Karzai, an unhappy precedent Afghans have noticed with growing concern. But more than a few thousand foreign soldiers are needed to restore peace and security here.

Kandahar is four hundred kilometres southwest of Kabul. A former Taliban stronghold, it's a city on the verge of an explosion. It was once a place of harmony and culture, of wealth and beautiful gardens and music and poetry. Several great Pushtun poets came from Kandahar. The city was famous for its pomegranates. The blossoms of pink and red roses, which Kandaharis still cherish around their windowsills, are a memory of this beauty.

But cultural extremism has cast a shadow over the life of this city. Mullah Omar, the leader of the Taliban, has carved his name in black on the white marble wall of the biggest shrine. Inside the large silver-and-gold room lies the grave of Afghanistan's founder, Ahmad Shah Durrani. An ex-Taliban soldier shows me around, along with a man loyal to Wali Karzai—a brother of Afghan president Hamid Karzai and the head of one of the powerful tribes in the region. They take me to a small, secret door, behind which several deep steps lead to an underground chamber where Ahmad Shah Durrani is buried under a massive stone. There are men sitting there, reading the Quran.

It was in the gateway to this shrine that Mullah Omar stood in 1996, holding the cloak of the Prophet Mohammad. Omar told the Kandaharis that he'd had a dream in which the Prophet had asked him to lead his followers. It was here that he declared himself Emir of the Faithful. The Taliban, whose name means "students of religion," shrewdly combined religious symbolism with the region's historical memory. No one dared challenge such a powerful combination in a place of discontent, superstition and bloody history.

Forty kilometres west of Kandahar stands the baking desert town of Maiwand, site of the great British defeat, where Afghan warriors called *talib*s cut down the British grenadiers in the Second Anglo-Afghan War. It was here that Malalai rallied her menfolk before dying under British gunfire. At 4:45 A.M., a golden line spreads along the far edge of this desert. It looks as though the earth and the sky meet on the horizon, merging into one single line of light. The dark, deep blue sky above my head has such clarity that—as they say in Afghanistan—you can see through it to eternity. Towards the light, where dawn breaks, I walk on the dry, hardened ground.

When I was a schoolgirl, the very word "Maiwand" used to make me feel proud. Now, looking at this place, I feel angry and sad. I'm amazed at the power of history. It is about human folly. But it is also a corridor—however narrow and dark—to a partial understanding of our existence and behaviour, our relationship with the rest of the world. In search of the past, I have travelled halfway around the globe, from Canada to Afghanistan, from a world of peace, material comfort and technology to a country that lives in the shadow of its history—a place whose only relevance to the rest of the world depends on the value and extent of a Westerner's life and "security." It may be illusionary, self-indulgent or bizarre, but I still think digging into the grave of history might lead to an understanding of the present.

As the golden light rises slowly, the small, flat town emerges, with its mud houses, a few scattered green fields, the peak of a hill at the far end and a desolate cemetery. It looks ancient, abandoned, out of touch. The Maiwand of my imagination was a large garden where brave souls grew instead of trees, and the poetry of young women blossomed like flowers. The real Maiwand looks grey and forlorn, as shabby as any of the other dirt-poor villages in the area.

They say in Afghanistan that once a battle has been fought, the sound of a marching army will always echo on that spot. And this ground has witnessed many battles. I sit on the ground to hear the sounds of the past. I have heard it said that cries of pain and agony, the roar of anger, the cheers of victory from a battlefield, mixed with the dust and wind, remain in the memory of the soil. It transforms itself into a sad melody, known only to those who know the sounds of the desert. They say the ghost of the past hovers there forever, that the stories of battle, victory and betrayal are told and retold with the changing seasons. Children hear them and, growing old, take them to the grave. Open the ground's battered corpse, and you can see its wounds. While we script the human losses in our books as the "main event," the places where wars are fought remain as marginal reference points. I sit motionless in this desert to see how, dancing in the haze, all that happened at Maiwand comes alive—the soldiers, the officers, *ghazis*, horses and guns, cries, wounds and blood. What about those souls whose immediate resting ground lies beneath my feet? What compelled those men to turn this place into a slaugh-terhouse, to fight, to lose all? What reasons did they have to choose battle and death over their own lives?

Now, the only sound is of the wind. It's odd the way we explain battles, as if it's just about winning or losing, victory or defeat, or—to sound politically more sophisticated— about control of power. We look at wars as a kind of theatre, a drama of trickery, backstabbing, lies, mockery, betrayed loyalties, heroism and tragedy. But ultimately, war is about death, decay and destruction. It is about human folly laying waste to lives. How we count on the soil—the deep, dark ground—to hide it all. Countless narratives of pain, disaster and misery are hidden underneath this piece of land. But on the surface, the desert is just a bath of heat, a dun-coloured haze of innocent sand. A yellow glow surrounds it with a holy light. The sun is not fully out, but I can already feel its suffocating heat. Could this place have looked the same more than a hundred years ago, in July 1880, when the British and Afghan armies fought here? Could this place have been the same twenty years ago, in January 1980, when the Russians tried to fight their way into this bastion of resistance to foreign invasion? How did this place look a year ago, in December 2001, when the Arabs, Pakistanis and their Afghan allies—the Taliban—were running for their lives under the American B-52 bombers?

Why should a small, poor country like Afghanistan become a permanent battleground for proxy wars and political rivalries? In the 1980s, the Russians and Americans turned Afghanistan into a war zone. Meanwhile, the Saudis and Iranians, two rival powers within the Muslim world— Iran propagating the Shia Muslim sect, Saudi Arabia promoting the Sunni Wahabi faith—have been fighting a Muslim cold war in Afghanistan. Two other competing enemies, Pakistan and India, have used Afghanistan as a battlefield for their power struggle. Afghanistan has lost more than two million lives for the benefit of presidents and kings, policy makers, criminals, arms manufacturers and dealers, not to mention the new "war against terror." On July 1, 2002, about forty innocent people died near Kandahar when Americans bombed a wedding, mistaking the celebration shots of the party for terrorist fire. Even momentary happiness here is condemned by death. The desert and the sun are the only tangible links between the past and the present, the two silent witnesses to what has happened here. They have ownership over a story we can only attempt to understand as it shifts in our history books from the official British inquiry of a defeat to the myth of an Afghan victory, from the formal accounts of Russian failure to our tales of Afghan triumph, and from concealed documents of secretive Western deals to our untouched dossiers of those Afghan criminals who have made these wars possible.

At the far corner of a local cemetery, Arab fighters are buried by the hundreds. Two Afghan gunmen guard their graves, trying vainly to prevent people from turning them into a shrine. This is the al Qaeda cemetery. "They were killed in the American bombardment," says one of the guards. "We buried them—men, women, children—five, ten bodies in one grave." He shakes his head. "We did our Muslim duty to bury them," he says.

"When the Arabs were here, they used to give people many gifts," says another man. "I didn't have any direct contact with the Arabs, but I know they didn't do anything to disturb the people."

A woman arrives with two bright green sheets. "My cousin sent these from Karachi to spread over the graves of this woman and her two children," she says in Pushtu. "Their son was blind. Someone took earth from these graves for him, and he got his vision back. So she asked me to thank the martyrs by covering their graves with these sheets." The graves are piles of dust without stones or names. The guard helps her spread the sheets over them. She offers a prayer and leaves. It reminds me that I, too, once visited the grave of an Afghan *shaheed* in Kabul.

Back in Kandahar, a turquoise dome atop a tall white pillar reflects the dwindling last rays of the sun. Three polished artillery pieces stand on three sides of the pillar, protected by a white fence. They are relics of the Second Anglo-Afghan War. The dedication on the stone beside the cannon is in Dari: "To honour those brave souls who fought for freedom and independence." An odd combination of political propriety and nationalistic pride, the monument is a reminder of the glorious history of the region. At night, the place swims in a frenzy of green and white neon lights, a well-lit stage for a new episode of *Star Wars* in the middle of a rugged, dusty, dangerous city. Like legends, monuments, too, are central to the politics of this region.

Kandahar is now a city of extremes, a place of men and guns, expensive cars and starving children. It is oven-hot, a dry blowtorch heat that sucks colour out of the landscape. Even in post-Taliban Kandahar, there are few signs of women. Those who venture out are covered from head to toe, whether in burqas or in long, Arab-style black coats and head scarves that also cover their faces, except for the eyes. The wealthiest and most powerful men drive the latest model Japanese cars, watch sixty channels of television on satellite—favouring a pornographic channel and MTV—and frequently cross the Afghan-Pakistan border to engage in smuggling.

If Afghanistan has been "liberated" by the United States and its allies, Kandahar is a poor advertisement for the West's concern. The poor have to survive by begging or through back-breaking labour: brick-making, heaving massive wooden carts loaded with iron, scrap and carpets. I watch two eight-year-old boys wolf their way through a meal I and four colleagues have ordered: three heaping plates of rice and three plates of meat and potatoes with bread. When we offered

335

them a meal—they were watching us hungrily through the window of a Kandahar restaurant—I thought they would probably eat a little of the food and take the rest home. But they can't have eaten for days. In the city's Mirweis Hospital, there are children malnourished to the point of starvation, with sunken cheeks and protruding ribs; stunted infants rasp for breath next to their mothers.

There is one option for survival in post-Taliban Kandahar: give your loyalty to a powerful and influential man. General Ghul Agha Sherzai, Kandahar's bearded, fat-faced governor, is said to have the largest number of men in his camp. Wali Karzai, who has no official title but is well respected, has a large following. Also sharing this pyramid of power is Pashton Kholid, who, like Ghul Agha, is another former mujahidin commander, now known—and despised—as a close ally of the American security forces.

On the surface, of course, law and order reign. Shared economic interests and the American presence may be dominant for the moment, but there is no guarantee things will stay that way. American Special Forces agents in four-wheel drives cruise the highways, cradling pistols and automatic weapons, dressed in jeans and mismatched camouflage blouses and bright shirts. Kandaharis accept the American presence—for now. They are "guests," my driver insists. "But if they are going to build a permanent military base or interfere with the everyday life of the people, then we will not tolerate them."

America's biggest base—at Kandahar Airport—looks all too permanent, a great desert enclosure of prefabricated barracks and Apache and Chinook helicopters, of trucks and tanks and armoured vehicle parks, of radios and wire prisoner cages. The Soviets used the same airport as their base during their occupation of the country.

In theory, the Taliban have been vanquished. Listening to some Kandaharis, it is hard to believe. At a carefully pre-arranged spot, a former member of the Taliban council agrees to meet me. "Mullah Omar was a good man," he says. "He responded to the people's demand to put an end to the law-lessness that prevailed in this city." From the window of the room, I see a black Toyota that once belonged to the man who declared himself the "Emir of the Faithful." The black car, now owned by one of the new government's supporters, was one of twelve vehicles given to Omar by Osama bin Laden. After Mullah Omar's disappearance, the new government administrators divided up his cars among themselves. "Mullah Omar had no desire for power," says the former Taliban council member, who says he now supports Hamid Karzai's government. "It was all the fault of the Arabs and Pakistanis, who took advantage of Mullah Omar's innocence and ignorance. Religious men—mullahs do not have much political knowledge. Mullah Omar was not aware of the polit-ical agenda of the Arabs and Pakistanis. He thought they were sincere in helping the cause of Islam."

On the way to the city's main market, I come across the newly painted white walls of the Kandahar Women's Association. A group of thirty-two women gather there every day to learn to read and write in adult literacy classes. They also do sewing and embroidery. The products are sold in the market, and the income goes to the women, as well as paying for the cost of running the centre.

Bebi's husband went missing when the Taliban took over the city. A mother of two, she works with the women's group to make a living. Noriya, who is twenty-one, also lost her hus-band in the war. Ahma-jan, a former teacher and educational administrative assistant, runs the centre. "There are lots of

337

widows in Kandahar," she says. "There are many other young women who would like to study and work. But we don't have enough resources for all." Ahma-jan stayed at home during the seven-year Taliban rule. Now, she wants to organize courses for women in computers, the English language, and hairstyling and makeup. But like many others, she has to wait to receive help from an outside organization—and permission from governor Ghul Agha—to start work.

At Kandahar Airport, an American flag snaps in the air above an EU flag—reminding the Europeans, I suppose, of where they stand in the "war against terror." I am to board a UN flight. After passing through the first gate—heavily guarded by American Special Forces—we arrive at a second. Under a smouldering sun, in forty-eight degrees centigrade heat, we wait our turn. And wait, and wait. After an American security check, we drive to an eighteen-seat passenger plane owned by the World Food Program and flown by South African pilots.

Ordinary Afghans have no access to the airport. It is, after all, *their* airport. But no commercial flights are allowed into Kandahar—only military and diplomatic flights, and flights of the United Nations, the new colonial masters of Afghanistan.

Five lions. That is the meaning of "Panjshir"—the valley north of Kabul Gorge that is legendary for battles against the Russians. For ten years the Soviet military tried to cut across the valley, but failed. The local resistance, under the leadership of Ahmad Shah Masoud, shot down Soviet helicopters, set ablaze the T-72s that came down the Salang Pass and killed or captured any Russian soldier who ventured into the area.

Driving into the valley, I can see why the Russians could never break into this rugged terrain. Our four-wheel-drive Chevy screams as it moves along a mountain road, over a bed of stones. The valley is hemmed in by sheer cliffs, at the bottom of which runs a raging river. The mountain peaks hide in a nest of clouds. Even in midsummer, they are covered with snow.

"The Taliban had only reached this point," says Daoud, an old friend whom I haven't seen in fourteen years. "The Russians came just as far as here. It's called the graveyard of tanks." Hundreds of destroyed, burned and smashed Soviet tanks lie in a massive junkyard, surrounded by a short mud wall. This iron and steel graveyard is deeply unpleasant — man-made, man-destroyed. If the natural beauty of Panjshir makes one believe in God, the detritus of war is evidence of hell.

We stop on a mountaintop, where the road ends at a human grave. It belongs to Ahmad Shah Masoud, whose murder, on September 9, 2001, was probably a coded signal for September 11. Like all other warnings, it was ignored by the White House. As we enter the newly constructed circular stone shrine, decorated with green and red flags, a group of commanders arrives, most of them in military uniforms. Two soldiers place a basket of flowers over Masoud's dust-covered tomb. A man with a thick moustache, dressed in camouflage and army boots, gives a boring speech about Masoud's bravery. Masoud himself would have fallen asleep at the sound of this man's voice. "They all hated him when he was alive," says Daoud, who used to work under Masoud's command as part of a film team. "They wanted him dead. Now they are shedding crocodile tears over his grave." Two lone plasterers are putting the last touches on the outside of the tomb. "Masoud wanted to be buried in his hometown, but not in a cage like this," says Daoud. "If Masoud were alive, he never would have made a deal with the Americans. He refused offers from Arabs and Pakistanis just as he refused the Russians. A foreigner is a foreigner, an invader is an invader, no matter which direction they come from, no matter what their nationality."

On a neighbouring mountainside stands Masoud's home, a two-storey white concrete building overlooking a tiered garden with a swimming pool and an orchard of apple, pear and almond trees, grapevines and flowers. Masoud's wife and children were evacuated after his death. The empty house is now guarded by two gunmen, who follow us everywhere we walk. The man is dead, I want to tell them. What are you guarding?

Near the Panjshir River, young girls make faces at my camera. They want their pictures taken, but shy away each time I press the shutter. A couple of women in bright red and orange dresses peek from behind a wall, next to a garden where a stone house sits above a hill. As a teenage girl, I dreamed about building a stone house in this valley—a home and a family. Those days are long gone. Stones survive the war, not young love. The sun shines for a brief moment through sycamore trees; the shadows of leaves dance like memories.

A bearded man shows up with a basket of fresh gooseberries from his tree. Daoud places the basket in a stream, shaking it from side to side to let water cover all the tiny white and purple berries. I used to compare a moving river to the passage of life. Then someone told me that a river was a mirror of passing love—just leave this country for a few days and you'll understand, he said.

But in the new Afghanistan there is not much time for metaphors. An American Chinook helicopter clatters over the mountain. "A man came to the mosque a couple of weeks ago," says Daoud. "He said he'd had a dream in which Masoud was saying that the jihad is not over yet. He asked everyone to pay attention to what the Americans are doing."

"The jihad is not over yet," says Abdul Latif Matin, regional manager of the UN Mine Clearance Planning Agency. He coordinates the efforts of four thousand Afghan de-miners who are fighting an endless battle against a different antagonist—a hidden enemy of land mines and cluster bombs. Matin takes the bodies of his colleagues to their families. "We Muslims think that de-mining is part of our Holy War," he says. "It is a 'jihad' against the invisible enemies of Afghanistan. We believe if we die, we go to paradise."

Other than land mines—"unpaid soldiers," Matin calls them—the latest threat comes from dangerous yellow-painted canisters that litter the countryside. One of these ominous little creatures sits on Matin's table. It is marked with the code BOMB.FRAG BLU 97A/B 809420–30 LOT ATB92G109–001. This is part of a U.S. cluster bomb, made by arms companies in Minnesota and California. They were dropped in the thousands during America's 2001 bombardment of Afghanistan. Up to twenty percent of the ordnance buries itself in the soil. Each canister turns into a mine.

Two UN-supervised mine clearers have just been killed by cluster bombs. I visit the family of Jawad, who was blown to pieces by a bomblet in July. "My son died because he was trying to help his family financially," his father tells me. Jawad's eighteen-year-old widow cries. Their two-year-old son plays with pictures of his dead father. Jawad with his friends; Jawad in his wedding suit—young, handsome, staring at the camera with a smile; Jawad holding the arm of his bride. They got married during the Taliban rule—in a ceremony inside the house. His wife never thought she'd be made a widow in a time of "peace"—in so-called liberated Afghanistan. She screams over Jawad's grave. "Jawad! Jawad!" she calls. "Why did you leave me like this?" Engraved on the white tombstone, along with his name and dates of birth and death, there are two verses from a Dari poem, found in his pocket when his mutilated body was brought home: "I give my soul, so you'll live/ So offer a prayer over the dust of my grave."

Dyana's family is supposed to have fled to Mazar-e-Sherif. Nominally under government control, Mazar is a shrine city with a turquoise tomb containing the last remains of Ali, one of the four caliphs. That's what Mazar means: "the Holy Grave." Around the shrine, women sit on the curbside, selling cheap men's clothing and equally cheap watches. It is supposed to be beneath the dignity of a woman to sell clothes by the road. But these women, in their all-enveloping burqas, are refugees, protected not by their dignity but by their anonymity. They come from Kabul, from Maimana, from Arghandab. Men bring them tea on the hot streets.

Nasima is a widow from Kabul, driven from her home in Afshar during the 1992–96 fighting between the very men who form most of Afghanistan's current government. For a decade, she has been selling clothes on the street. Only in Mazar would women be doing this. Never in my life have I seen it before. Is something evolutionary happening here? Though all these women are concerned about the future, no one here wants the Taliban back. In fact, they are all very happy that the Taliban are gone. They hope the warlords will also disappear.

So do the women at the city university. I meet with a first-year journalism class. "We wear the burqa because there is no security," says a young student. "Once the weapons are collected and we feel secure, we can go without the burqas." Another woman speaks with equal frankness. "We want an Afghanistan free of war, under the leadership of one central government, where there are no warlords." Girls share classes with boys, walk down the same stairs, use the same library; but before leaving the building, they all have to put on their burqas. I ask myself why Afghans always have to choose between lack of security and lack of freedom. From behind a desk near the entrance to the building, the young women bring out their little plastic bags containing their pale blue burqas—their protectors from the warlords and insecurity. And perhaps from a new Taliban.

Outside the classroom, a group of boys block my camera. "You can't film our women," one of them says. "Why not?" I ask. "Because it's against our religion," says a student dressed in a dark green shirt and black trousers. "Filming Afghan women and showing them in Western countries is against our culture." But I'm an Afghan and I'm a Muslim, I argue. He is disarmed. He can shut a Westerner up, but not an Afghan. I'm impressed, though, that he uses words rather than guns to communicate. Was he educated in one of the Taliban schools? I wonder. Even inside the Taliban school I had a better reception, I tell him.

In March 2000, along with a colleague, the British journalist Robert Fisk, and a dear friend, Siddiq Barmak, I visited two of the Taliban schools in Pakistan. Sheikh Rohat Gul sat victorious, arguing that women were better protected under the Taliban. "I can send you to Afghanistan," he said, "a single woman, and you won't be harmed." It was a guarantee. "So what if I was harmed?" I asked. "The person responsible would have his head chopped off immediately," he replied assertively. Hardly a comforting thought for me, but he was convinced that harsh punishment and strict discipline were the foundations of a moral society. As I filmed him, Sheikh Rohat showed us the safe where he kept his money. Women were like money, he argued. "They are delicate and in need of protection." So what about Malalai? She fought against the British, alongside Afghan men at Maiwand. "Malalai!" muttered the sheikh. He obviously wished I hadn't mentioned her name. He was angry. "She was an exception," he hissed.

As the sheikh spoke, his young students—all men, of course—gathered around him. Their gaze was on the ground, but they nodded their heads in approval at the sheikh's proclamations. As we were leaving, one young man approached Siddiq, telling him to ask me to convert to Islam. His friend was pulling him away, saying it was not the right time. "Ask her, would you?" he said. I was visiting them as a Canadian journalist. "Ask her!" he insisted. I understood what he was saying. But at his insistence, the words were translated to me. I smiled. "Tell him I'm a Muslim, but I don't agree with his interpretation of Islam." The guy must have thought I was insane, or was joking with him. I repeated my response. He was at a loss for words. We left.

I doubt if America's war has changed any of the sheikh's ideas, or those of his students, any more than the new government in Afghanistan has altered the certainties of those young men in Mazar.

Opposite Mazar's shrine stands an office purporting to be a branch of the Afghan Foreign Ministry. It is the personal political headquarters of General Abdul Rashid Dostum. General

Dostum, whose favourite method of punishing thieves among his own men was to crush them under the tracks of his tanks, no longer wishes to be called a "warlord." He wants to be regarded as a "diplomat"—he who refused the duties of vice-president in the transitional government for fear he would be chained to an office in Kabul rather than administering "security" in northern Afghanistan. The Red Cross, the United Nations, and the American security men visit Dostum frequently for discussions. Self-interest means they cannot raise the issue of war crimes with Dostum, who's been accused of the kidnapping, rape and murder of thousands of women in Kabul during the 1992–96 civil war and of suffocating one thousand Taliban prisoners in shipping containers in 2001.

I'm still searching for Dyana, and it's impossible to find anyone in Mazar without the help of one of the warlords. After days of waiting, we are finally taken to General Dostum's fortress of Qalai Janghi, which is guarded by armed Turks. Dostum's brand-new Audi limousine is waiting outside. "This doesn't mean I don't support the current government," he tells me. "But I'd like to see a federation in a future Afghanistan." Which means that General Dostum would like to be the king of northern Afghanistan. Unfortunately for him, he's not the only one with such pretensions. The general shows no interest in helping me find Dyana's family.

There is a refugee camp just outside the city, says a woman on the street. But we need help from a warlord to go there. Ustad Atta is another warlord, a commander with the Jamiat Party who controls most of Mazar. "Ustad Atta is travelling at the moment," says his press officer. "In the meantime we'll help you find the family."

Even if none of the warlords will say so, this power struggle is about smuggling drugs to the former Muslim Soviet republics. The central government in Kabul does not speak of this. Nor do the Americans. Both Dostum and Atta are U.S. allies in the "war against terror."

The historic city of Balkh is about a forty-minute drive from Mazar. I search for clues about Dyana's family in the small town. I visit the main mosque—I have been told the town's religious leader might help. The building is closed for repairs. I walk inside the mosque's garden. Like the mosque itself, the graves scattered in the garden are centuries old. One belongs to an Afghan woman who is perceived as a martyr—a martyr of worldly love. It has a proper tombstone and inscription: "This is the grave of Rabia Balkhi." She was the sister of the king and was in love with her brother's servant. As soon as the king learned of her interest, he ordered that the servant be murdered. A mystic, Rabia wrote poems condemning the world's obsession with heaven and hell, and expressing her anger at the king's inflexibility. She was famous for shouting the following lines in the market:

> I'm going to light a fire in Paradise and pour water onto Hell
> So both veils may completely disappear.

To avoid further embarrassment, the king ordered his sister confined to her palace, where she was killed by the king's executioner. He cut an artery in her wrist and left her to bleed to death. Using her blood, she covered the marble walls of the bathroom with her poems. It was her last statement against the tyranny of her brother. More prominent than Malalai in Afghan literature, Rabia, too, has become a legend. It seems that Afghanistan's glorious past, like most of its innocents, ends up in graveyards.

—

USTAD ATTA'S OFFICE TELLS ME they've found Dyana. They claim she was kidnapped and raped, and that the family now lives in isolation. I am aghast. I cannot imagine this. But I will see Dyana again! "We'll take you there," says the press officer, who is dressed in a suit and tie. "But we must prepare the conditions for the visit first. And there are some costs involved." I agree to pay all their costs, just as long as they take me to her. More days go by. More promises. I'm having doubts. They have shown me nothing to back up their claims.

On the morning of July 11, I receive a phone call from Canada. My worst fears are about to be confirmed. Before leaving for Afghanistan, I had written to Dyana's uncle in Dubai—the one who'd given me the information about the family's move to Mazar. I'd told him I was going to look for Dyana and asked him for her address. After two months, he'd finally received my letter and had responded. "I'm sorry for the late reply to your letter. But I just returned to Dubai after an extended trip to Afghanistan. For a long time, I wanted to tell you the truth about your close friend. But I didn't want to disturb you or your family. Now that you're searching for her and are insisting on knowing, it is painful for me to tell you that your friend Dyana took her life some time ago."

For days, I've been lost in anger and sorrow. Why? I keep asking. Was it a result of my failure to reach out to her? Was it her fault for giving up on life? These questions will disturb me for years to come. In Kabul, I walk on the road that Dyana and I used to take to school, the one where we used to read poetry. I go to the shrine where we used to pull at the locks to see if they would open. I sit staring at the pilgrims—each with a quest, each with a story, each with a hope. "God—help end our homelessness!" whispers a woman. In an odd way, I feel close to Dyana here—I sense her tormented soul, imagine her last moments. What did she say, other than writing that last note to me?

I walk down the road to her old home. I knock on the door, thinking a stranger will tell me what I've been told before—they don't live here any more. But Dyana's sister opens the door. "Mother," she screams, like someone who's on fire. "Mother!" Tears stream down her cheeks. She runs inside the house. I am stunned. A woman walks towards me, in tears, with open arms. "My God!" she cries. I can't think any more.

We sit in the living room—Dyana's mother next to me, reaching towards me to touch my head and hair. "Seeing you makes me feel Dyana's presence," she says. "She's left me heartbroken. She's left me forever." She can't speak for a while. "It's been four years," she says, "and every day of it has gone by like a year for me. I know it was God's will. I pray for her soul to rest in peace, but I can't bring myself to accept her absence. I haven't accepted that, not for a moment. She's with me all the time." She pauses as her younger daughter reminds her that I must be tired and should have a cup of tea. "No, I want to hear," I say. Dyana's sister leaves the room.

"She can't stand it," says Dyana's mother. "They associate you with her so much, it's hard on all of us."

"I'm sorry that I've come like this," I say, "without any warning."

"She'd have been happy to see you. Dyana would have grown wings to fly had she known you were going to be here."

"What happened?" I ask.

"All day she was silent. I asked her if she was in pain. She shook her head. I got upset and asked what shaking her head meant—was it a yes or a no? She said with impatience that it was a no. Her father said no to too many of her suitors, even the one she liked. He didn't think she'd mind. She didn't like her father, you know, but she never disrespected him. She used to read, but then she stopped reading. She said one day that she hated books; she hated everything. I knew she was very unhappy, but I couldn't imagine how unhappy." She wipes her tears.

After writing her last letter to me, Dyana had become reclusive, showing little interest in eating or speaking. Either before or after dinner, she'd secretly hidden pills from her father's pharmacy. Her mother and sisters don't know what kind of medicine it was. "There was morphine, sleeping pills, medicine for blood pressure control, general painkillers, there were stronger medicines for allergies. I wish I knew."

Dyana's mother called her several times the next morning. There was no answer. "I felt something was wrong. I pushed the door open and there she was—in her bed, with her arm hanging over the side." She pauses. "Her father is a broken man now—I'd never seen him cry. He's been mourning her death more than me. We had to move to Mazar—he couldn't work here, and it was as if Kabul were gobbling me up. Mazar was a relief. But we've just come back—we can't stay away from here forever."

A young woman dressed in a long pinkish gown walks into the room, holding a newborn baby. Dyana's elder brother has married. "This is my daughter-in-law," says Dyana's mother. I say hello to her. She is a frail-looking woman, with dark eyes and short hair. Dyana's sister comes in with more tea. How can I sit through this? I've a thousand more questions to ask.

But how much longer can I stay? Then Dyana's mother reaches for the baby. "This is Dyana," she says. The baby is only three months old. "This is my angel, my tiny little angel. See your aunt, see your aunt!" she tells the baby, holding her up towards me. Her features are striking. The baby Dyana moves her head to the right and the left, squeezes her tiny lips together. She's fast asleep. Dyana's mother presses the baby against her chest. Tears run down her face. I have nothing to say, nothing more to ask.

13

THE TOMB

The season of tears is over,
There's no place for official funerals;
Let's laugh.
Let's laugh at seventy years of "Revolutionary October,"
At the poverty of the dead "proletariat."
But before anything else, let's laugh
At the Western peace plans,
At America's humanitarianism,
At us silly chessmen on the board.
Let's laugh
At Lenin's stagnant body and sterilized beard,
At Stalin's moustache.
Though "it's forbidden to touch the dead,"
Let's laugh.

Qahar Ausi, 1991

AT LAST I HAVE COME to Russia—on January 11, 2004. At last, into the land of my enemies, the nation from which that vast army invaded my small country. I walk to the immigration booth, where a boy-soldier, under the watchful eyes of a female officer, stamps my passport. They speak in the language I once refused to learn. The uniforms, the military hats—though the old hammer and sickle has gone—the suspicious looks, the questioning eyes and the heavy architecture are all too Soviet.

There was a time when I used to stare at Russians from far away. Now I'm surrounded by them. One of them is driving me in his taxi to my Moscow hotel. On the long stretch of highway linking Sheremetyevo Airport to the city, large illuminated ads—for JVC, DHL, Kenneth Cole, Kodak—blind the eyes. This is the new globalized Russia. I don't want to talk to the driver. I am moved by both curiosity and contempt. This is the country that helped to destroy mine, and in moments of despair during the war in Kabul, I wished to see this place turn to ashes. Now I've travelled a long way to hear Russians' account of their history, and to talk to Russians who fought in Afghanistan. For kilometres there are only snow-covered trees—the edge of what looks like deep woods—the kind I've seen in Russian movies of the Second World War. And there, to the right of the road, stands the great iron crossbar monument that marks the farthest point Nazi Germany's army reached in that invasion. In the autumn of 1941, the Nazis fought their way to the first tramway station in the Moscow suburbs—and no farther. While many Muscovites embarked on a rampage of looting and burning, their communist leaders and the Red Army held the Germans at bay. The Russians had every right to fight the invaders. So why don't they understand why the Afghans fought *them*, or why Chechens are fighting their army today?

The hotel restaurant has a *Titanic* grandeur about it: heavy decorations, a glass roof and deep crimson seats. A young woman with long black hair, in a pink dress and white gloves, is playing the harp. "It's now or never," goes the tune. "Tomorrow will be too late." The waiters—whose number exceeds that of the guests—serve tea from a silver samovar near a white marble fountain at the centre of the room. The Metropol is a hotel in tsarist style, with high ceilings and marble statues. It is meant to impress, much like the powerful buildings around it—including the secret police headquarters, the former KGB offices that still radiate a particular horror. The methods of punishment and torture developed and practised behind the concrete walls of these buildings were bestowed upon millions of Afghans in the form of a special gift from "mother Russia." Afghans themselves, proud of their training in Russia, supervised the appropriate treatment of prisoners.

My room overlooks the Kremlin's wall; the moonlight is pale on the snow outside my window. I call my father in Ottawa: "You won't believe what I'm staring at this very moment—the Kremlin. I wish you were here to see it with me."

"My dear," comes my father's confident voice from the end of the line, "the Kremlin and I don't get along. We've been going in opposite directions for a long time." I haven't forgotten the days of my father's imprisonment and my mother's tears. How could he forget those days of torture and nights of interrogations that were, ultimately, the result of decisions made behind the Kremlin's walls? Some memories only become sharper with the passage of time. Bad ones have a lasting, bitter taste.

With the infamous yellow *M* of the McDonald's across from the Kremlin in the background—not a place that Mr. Putin would take his lunch while meeting his secret police—a tall

On Arbat Street. Moscow, January 2004.

man is selling old Russian military hats. Here, one can become a Soviet general, commissar or admiral. The Russian hat seller is competing—unsuccessfully—with Boss, L'Oréal, Lancôme, Guess and other Western products displayed in the shopping mall behind him. Not too far away from the lingerie and makeup, the old Russia showcases its gas masks, military water bottles, belts, medals and memorabilia, along with pouches and knapsacks and even a few old military uniforms. All are for sale. Many appear to have been sun-bleached in the mountains of Afghanistan or Chechnya.

Like Afghanistan, Chechnya has become a bleeding wound. "Chechnya is about businessmen, drugs, arms sales and religion—for all sides," says Maria, who's translating for me here. Chechnya, I reply, is about death, destruction, widows, orphans and our failure to learn the lessons of history. It is a place where widows and mothers dress as suicide bombers, burning themselves and others in flames of vengeance and hatred; a place where the throats of foreign journalists are cut so that the outside world will remain immune to its tragedy. "Chechnya" has become Russia's new slogan in the "war against terrorism." In the 1980s, it was "Afghan terrorism"; currently, it's the Chechens who want independence from Moscow; tomorrow, it will be someone else. Chechnya is like a big black hole on the map of Russia.

"When we say war, we think of Chechnya," says Maria. "The Afghan War is history." That is what Tsalko Vallrianovich says when I meet him in his office—the "Inter-Regional Organization of Invalids of Military Service," his business card reads. He gives me a strong handshake. Should there be a picture of this moment? I wonder. This is the first time I've actually shaken the hand of one of the tens of thousands of men who invaded my country. "What was going on in Afghanistan is in the past," he says.

"Is that really true?"

"I was not a top commander. I served as a pilot, for one year—that is what the rotation time was. There are other more interesting things to talk about, like the activities of this organization, a special committee for the wounded veterans of the Afghan War."

He knows I'm an Afghan. Is he testing me?

An orderly man of fifty-seven, neatly dressed in a grey business suit, Tsalko serves tea for me. Originally from Belarus—from a village that ceased to exist after the Chernobyl explosion—he was a major general in the Soviet Air Force. He was sent to Afghanistan in 1981. The Russian military had divided Afghanistan into zones. "I was at the U-zone, near Kandahar Airport. We had certain tasks. They included the escorting of convoys between Kandahar and

Gerishik, checking the roads for the *dushmen,* watching cars during the day. At night, we had orders to shoot anything that moved. We were told that any moving thing was an enemy."

I am struck that he has used a Dari word to describe his guerrilla antagonists in Afghanistan. *Dushmen* means "enemy." "In the spring, my helicopter was attacked by the *dushmen.* I released the bombs. I had no time to think about the fate of the Afghan people below me. I felt sorry for the gardens below. They were beautiful. The claim that Soviet troops attacked peaceful villagers is not true. The peaceful population was dying in the war," says Tsalko. "When we had to bomb villages, it was not our intention to kill innocent people. One day, our base came under attack; we had to cross the road under missile fire to reach our planes. The *dushmen* had a Japanese-made truck with a rocket launcher on the back. Men were firing at us as the truck was moving." Tsalko draws a picture of the truck in my notebook.

"The next day we saw the same truck in a village and destroyed it. In the same raid, about eight houses were hit and about twenty people were killed. Later, we met with local leaders who promised that such cars would not go through their village again. We told them that if our base was attacked again, we'd destroy the entire village." I wonder if he feels sorry for those who died in his attack. "They were victims; they were killed under our helicopters. We gave the families of those who were killed some compensation in the form of food and milk," he says. What a gesture of humanity! The Americans are doing much the same thing in Afghanistan and Iraq now.

Occasionally, Tsalko and his comrades went into the city of Kandahar to buy coats for their wives, gifts of tape recorders. "But to go shopping in Kandahar, you had to have money. Our military salaries were not good enough. Each soldier received 235 coupons—each worth two rubles—a total of less than five hundred rubles that we could use in Afghanistan."

Tsalko had one hundred crews, sixty helicopters and eighteen planes in his brigade. He lost two crews—six men—and four helicopters during his year in Afghanistan. In total, the Russian military lost four hundred crews and six hundred helicopters and planes, he says, an average of sixty helicopters a year. He knew the men who died in his brigade, but he won't utter their names. "They are buried; leave them alone. There is a Russian expression that means: 'Don't touch people who are dead.' There are awful places in Afghanistan," recalls Tsalko. "Over the mountains between Shindand and Chakhcharan, our helicopter had a malfunction. We landed on a cave-like mountain. Taking the helicopter out from there was like hell."

But amid the danger, the beauty of the place struck him. "In spring, around seven or eight in the morning, the horizon coloured and made the lower mountains look like water. It looked as if a sea had lifted Afghanistan up on its waves." Yes, Tsalko says, he would like to return to Afghanistan, but only as a tourist. "If that ever becomes possible," he says. He remembers Afghan friends with whom he has lost contact, in particular a Commander Taher from the Afghan military unit that used MiG 17 jets. "They were intelligent people. But the Afghan government that the Soviet Union supported was hardly representative of all Afghans."

Tsalko insists that the Russian military didn't invade Afghanistan, but "intervened." "It was not an occupation. You've got to understand. We kept all the economic and political structures as they were." What he means is that the

Russians didn't establish a military government. The Afghans were allowed a civilian administration—modelled on that of the Soviet Union. "It was a sort of presence—a support for the local communist government. It was a useless presence, nonetheless. The Soviet policy in Afghanistan wasn't really correct. Without aggressive outside support, the war wouldn't have become so bloody. The war was hardened and prolonged as a result of this. Afghanistan was a political mistake. It was not a military one." Tsalko asks me about the American military presence in Afghanistan today. What does *he* think of it, I ask.

"The Americans have made the same mistakes as the Soviet Union. They provided outside support for the Afghans fighting us, creating and financing Islamic fundamentalism— people like the Taliban. They thought, 'the enemy of my enemy is my friend.' But that old formula doesn't work any more." He pauses. "America created this problem called Afghanistan. Let them solve it." He shrugs his shoulders. "I'm really sorry for what happened to Russia. Afghanistan brought about the collapse of the Soviet Union."

After his return from Afghanistan, Tsalko began to train pilots, preparing others to survive war. "If you dislike life, don't fly," he recalls telling his pupils. He resigned from the military and was elected as a deputy in the last Supreme Soviet parliament before founding his veterans' organization. He lists the results of the war: suicide, sleeping disorders, drug addiction, high divorce rates. "You've heard of the Vietnam syndrome—it could be Afghan syndrome, Chechen syndrome—it's the pressure of battle on your nervous system. You can see its effect in daily life; in the deep sleep that comes around one or two in the morning, you can see very hard battles, you can't escape or run away from them. You wake up shivering. I have nightmares about helicopters on fire, in flames, people shouting; I see them in detail, people dying. These dreams are close to the realities I've seen and experienced."

So why did the Russians invade Afghanistan? "I know quite a few generals who wanted blood—not very intelligent men." Tsalko sighs. The methodical pilot is now a hospitable host. He offers me more tea. "People cannot have relations with weapons," he says. "Victory isn't real in the present. Only in the future will we know what we've done." He leans back on his leather chair with his fingers involuntarily tapping the table.

Finding the southwestern Moscow office of the Veterans of the Afghan War is like going on a winter safari. Instead of open desert and exotic animals, there are clusters of gaunt Moscow buildings, rows of gloomy, square blocks that resemble prison wards. The old Lada car skids and slides ever more dangerously over the ice- and snow-covered road. The suburbs are a world away from the embellished Kremlin and the Metropol. The sun has long gone, and a bitter wind reaches to my bones. No wonder the Germans were forced to retreat; General Winter defeated all of Russia's enemies. Except for the Afghans.

Inside one of the apartments, a tall, strongly built man, Telhushkov Alexander Nickolayevich, greets me warmly. Dressed in a greenish business suit with a tie, he looks like a friendly cartoon character with a big heart and kind eyes. Alexander served as a soldier in Afghanistan for a year and a half in 1985–86. His unit, a special parachute regiment, was based in Kabul.

"Our particular task was to search for weapons and groups of bandits," he recalls. "It was hard work, and I wanted to go home immediately. I wanted to stay alive. The most difficult task was to check the small *qishlok*s [villages, in Dari], which were dangerous and unpleasant places."

He returns with tea, candies and biscuits. He serves politely, and then sits at the end of the table. He remembers an order that sent his unit to one of those small villages he feared. "All the men had abandoned the village. There were only women and children. We didn't touch them," he says, speaking slowly and precisely. They managed to return without incident. How did the women treat the Russians? "They perceived us as the enemies of their husbands," says Alexander. Their translators—mostly Tajik soldiers—made sure they understood.

In one of their searches, in a valley, they were met by fighters, "among them blacks and Arabs." A piece of shrapnel wounded Alexander in the head. "My friends brought me to the base when I was still unconscious." One soldier in his group was killed. "God was quite kind to me." His unit killed six *dushmen* and captured four others, including Arabs. The prisoners were always handed over to the KGB.

"It took me a year before I realized it was all hopeless," Alexander says. "The enemy had American weapons, Stingers, and Chinese guns. They had Pakistani shoes; some of their clothes were better than those of the Red Army. It was obvious that these clothes were European. They had special blankets, sleeping bags. They were courageous, strong, adults in their thirties; they could think for themselves, they were willing to fight. The Soviet army was very young and only followed orders. If the Afghans captured Russians, they shot them in the head or hanged them from trees."

It didn't take long for Alexander to witness the results of such cruelty. A unit of Soviet construction workers had gone to a nearby village to collect gravel for making concrete. The village was near Paghman, about thirty kilometres from Kabul, one of the most beautiful places in Afghanistan. It was to become the site of some of the bloodiest battles during the Russian occupation. "There were thirteen drivers, escorted by thirteen soldiers, one officer and a Russian woman. The atmosphere was relaxed. They stopped to swim. The Russians often travelled under the protection of tanks, but that day, they had decided to go without them.

"An elderly man from the village told us what happened to them next. The villagers were very cruel. First, the children started to throw stones at them, then the adults attacked them, beating them with stones and sticks. The Russians were made to kneel. Then the women from the village started to tug away their hair, scratching the prisoners with their nails. And then the bandits cut off their noses and ears—some were already dead, some were still alive." Alexander pauses, placing both his hands over his face. "Each driver had a gun. Some tried to resist; others surrendered before capture. Some were shot; some had their throats cut. They were all thrown into a small river."

From their headquarters in Kabul, Alexander and his fellow soldiers were sent to rescue the missing men and the woman. "When we arrived, their vehicles were still burning. The bandits had set fire to the cars before leaving. We surrounded the place, but it was too late. We searched for three days for the bodies. What we found were a few remains, which we buried. At first, we didn't know that a woman was with them—the bandits had taken her with them. We started to search for her, but we could find only pieces of clothing and blood. All we saw was the smoke and body parts." Alexander pauses again, resting his hands on the table, then pressing his fingers over his eyes to hide his tears. He doesn't know what happened to the captured woman. "It was the usual practice to sell a woman. Maybe she was sold. The bandits used any opportunity to make some money. Even in this case, we didn't take any revenge."

The attitude of the Afghans towards the Russians varied. "There were districts in Kabul where someone would smile at us. In other districts, people threw stones," he recalls. I can only laugh. My translator, Maria, tells him that I'm an Afghan and that I used to throw stones at the military convoys. All of a sudden, the expression on his face changes. His eyes are fixed on my face; he seems kinder, less formal. He laughs quietly. He speaks faster, realizing that I understand exactly what he's talking about. It is almost as if he'd been waiting for an Afghan to hear his stories.

He tells me that he hated the *dushmen* but admired Ahmad Shah Masoud, though he was an enemy. "Masoud was one of the most advanced military commanders—most efficient," he says. In an attempt at friendship—or so I like to think—Alexander begins to recount the long, amicable relations that existed between Afghanistan and the Soviet Union before the war. He had heard that in 1979, when the Soviet military arrived in Afghanistan, they saw a group of Russians who'd built a camp on a hilltop and were working on a road. The soldiers asked the workers what they were doing there. The workers asked the soldiers, "What are *you* doing here?" The two groups were equally mystified to see each other in a foreign land. One was there to build; the other had come to destroy. And at the end, they both had to leave under treacherous conditions.

Alexander believes that the war set off a chain reaction of vengeance. "It became like a family vendetta," he says.

"Afghans didn't have anything against us, but when their relatives and family were killed, they wanted revenge." Despite that, he doesn't think the Soviets invaded Afghanistan. "It was not occupation, of course," he says, without a shred of doubt in his mind. "We were defending our southern borders." They were told that if the Soviets were not there, the American army would be. And now they are, I tell him.

"America has already succeeded. They supported the *dushmen* against the Soviet Union. They made the Russian army leave. Afghanistan was America's revenge for Vietnam. They lost Vietnam; we lost Afghanistan."

Alexander shows me the Orient-brand watch he bought in Kabul—from a *dokan*, he says. It's been eighteen years, and he's still wearing it. "A souvenir from Afghanistan." I notice that when he is recounting an incident, locked into the memory of the time, he uses Dari words quite naturally, as Tsalko did. A *dokan* is a shop. Like the watch and the memories, Dari and Pushtu words are also their Afghan souvenirs. "The war was not helpful for Afghanistan. We destroyed the country. It was not an occupation, but it was not help either. Brezhnev decided to go to war—maybe he was drunk."

Alexander was twenty when he went to Afghanistan. "I was too young at the time. I wanted to be a hero. I didn't think about the Afghans then. A lot of young men at the time wanted to be heroes. There is a good reason to take young people into the military—they don't think much. But now? I wouldn't go to fight for Russia's southern borders, because it's the soldiers that are killed—for someone at the top who wants money and power as part of a political game." If anything, that's one thing Alexander has learned from Afghanistan. He doesn't want his thirteen-year-old son ever to be a soldier. "I've served in the military for all my family," he says.

Despite our disagreements, I feel Alexander is an honourable man. As I say goodbye, he presents me with a signed copy of a book—photos and short biographies of all the Muscovites who died in the Afghan War—a copy of a book of letters from the soldiers who were sent home, a record of songs composed by Russian soldiers in the Afghan War and a few magazines that his organization publishes. These gifts were to remind me that my countrymen tortured and killed a lot of Russians. Perhaps they were the sorts of things I'd come to collect.

The orange-covered book of letters—published on cheap paper in Moscow in 1991—is an astonishing collection of soldiers' words home. There are a few sketches by a soldier. They include an Afghan mountainside, which looks very calm until I spot the site of an explosion at a cliff on the far left. There are sketches of tanks, an Afghan village, helicopters flying over the mountains. There's a full-page drawing of a dead soldier, a wounded man lying by a wall and a comrade pointing his rifle towards a valley. There are wounded soldiers in hospital beds, even a female nurse. One soldier, Constantine Toroshin, wrote his family in June 1983, describing his work as the "harshest" of all his "past and future military service." The following year, in May, he was in a transport convoy that came under grenade attack. One of the grenades hit Constantine's vehicle, killing him and another soldier.

Viktor Alexeyevich is a man of short stature, lean, with small eyes and a pointed nose. He is the director of the Memorial Museum of Soldiers Who Lost Their Lives in Afghanistan, located in a dingy basement apartment. He presents me with a pink brochure that reads at the top, in English, "Memorial Centre." At the bottom it says: "The Memorial is the only museum of this kind in Moscow and Russia."

But Viktor is more than just a keeper of the memory of those who were killed in the war. He is also a guardian of secrets, his own as well as those of the KGB, in which he was a senior officer—or still is, though he claims that he's quit politics. "Now I pay more attention to mothers and widows, to give them moral support," he says.

As Viktor sits down on a sofa to talk, Maria tells him I'm an Afghan-Canadian. With venom he shouts, "Ah, a mujahid." He studies my notebook and pen carefully. "Are you a mujahid?" he asks, laughing now. To the eye of a Russian secret policeman, every Afghan is a potential enemy. But he knows what went wrong for the Soviets in Afghanistan. "It appears that in the first days the soldiers had the impression that it was their 'international duty' to serve in the country, in order to protect their country's southern borders." He dances around words, tiptoeing in his secret policeman's manner. "They were helping the Afghan people. But day by day, as the Soviet Union got more involved, they realized that the presence of the Soviet army was a mistake by the Soviet government."

A woman shows up with a tray holding white-and-blue cups and saucers, a flask of coffee and toffee candies. Viktor offers his round of hospitality. He begins to sound like the commentaries on the old Soviet radio stations: "Despite their help in building schools and developing roads, the Soviet soldiers met with negative reactions from the Afghans. The Soviet army was forced to be in the war; they had to kill." He points at the photographs of the dead soldiers on the walls around him.

Was he in Afghanistan? His reply is evasive. "It's psycho-
logically difficult for those soldiers who returned, despite the
fifteen years that have passed," he says. "After the war, 9,000
members of the Red Army were invalided; now that number
has increased. It's only normal. About ninety percent of those
who returned have some problem, from drug addiction to
hepatitis to getting involved in the mafia." A total of 500,000
Russians served in Afghanistan over the course of ten years,
with at least 120,000 deployed at any one time.

Eventually he begins to relax; no need to be so much on
guard in the presence of an Afghan. "Let's just say I went to
Kabul with a special unit of the army who captured Amin in
the palace, days before the arrival of the Soviet troops on
December 27, 1979." Did the Soviets go to Afghanistan at the
invitation of Babrak Karmal, who was living in exile in
Moscow at the time? "Amin asked several times for the
Russian intervention, but the Communist Party and the military in Moscow decided not to send troops to Afghanistan."
So why would Hafizullah Amin, who was president at the
time, ask for the arrival of an army that was going to kill him?
I realize this secret policeman knows the answer to a question
that every Afghan would like answered.

"You've studied the history of your country very well,"
Viktor says, sitting up straight. "The chief decision to send the
troops was made by Brezhnev."

"Why did he make that decision?"

"You should ask that question of Brezhnev."

"I would try," I say, "but he is dead. Who killed Amin?"

"On December 12, 1979, a new treaty between the
Afghan government and the Soviet Union was signed.
According to this treaty, the Soviet Union had to give military
support to Afghanistan in the case of a threat from another

country. The United States of America was, for a long time, preparing special troops on the Afghan-Pakistani border. They were in the form of local groups. President Amin was in negotiation with the U.S. government on several occasions. He was playing a double game. He deserved to be killed.

"After the Islamic Revolution in Iran, there was a strong fear of Islamic influences across the Afghan border. But based on the December 12 agreement, it was a wrong decision to send the troops to Afghanistan. There was no direct aggression from Pakistan or Iran. The Soviet government eventually admitted its mistake and started to evacuate its army."

This is extraordinary. Here is a man who may know the secrets behind my country's invasion, but he is afraid to tell me the truth. I repeat, "How did Amin die?"

"I wish to leave this subject alone," he says. But his vanity wins over his prudence. He bursts into self-promotion. "Out of the 500,000 Russians who went to Afghanistan, 499,000 of them don't know how Amin died." He stares at me as if to ask, "Why should you be the one to find out?" Then he says two words: "I know." He wants me to know he was in charge at the time. "There were two stages to Amin's death. At first, when we arrived in Kabul on December 24, 1979, we wanted to help Amin. The Soviet doctors tried to help him. But at the second stage, he felt very badly. He was not willing to talk."

"Were you there when he was killed?"

Viktor has already endangered his position. He retracts, but it's too late. His only way out is the tactic every secret police officer uses to avoid taking the blame. "Leave this subject alone. Just respect the tradition of secret services," he says, getting up. It's probably the fear of having said too much—by his standards—rather than his conscience that's bothering him now.

367

"Was Karmal, one of Amin's rivals within the PDPA, a better candidate to run Afghanistan than Amin?"

"Before the war, Karmal was in Russia. He was a progressive man; he supported the Soviet way of development for Afghanistan. However, during the war, he was not able to unite the people of Afghanistan. About ninety-eight percent of Afghans are poor, with no education; religion is very strong. Besides, the Afghan population was pro-Pakistan, pro-Islam. It was possible for Karmal to change the country, but it should have been done without Soviet involvement."

"Was Karmal responsible for inviting the Russian army?"

"It's impossible to blame one person. Karmal was supported by the young Afghan officers who were educated in the Soviet Union. He's dead now, anyway. Leave him alone."

Ah yes, we must not touch the dead. I had more questions for this strange, disturbing man. "When did the Kremlin realize that the war had gone wrong?"

"The process of realization started around 1984–85. There were lots of factors involved. It was reinforced by the economic and political developments in Russia. The Soviet military started with good intentions, but after a few years they realized that they didn't have the support of the locals. The Afghan army didn't want to fight. If one person was killed, it provoked anger and revenge among the Afghans. Documentary films of how the bandits cut off noses, tortured the Soviet soldiers, went around. About eighty-five percent of Soviet troops were about eighteen years old. They didn't know anything about Afghanistan—that included their officers as well. It was as if a Soviet soldier gave a piece of bread, and in return the bandits took a gun and shot the soldier. So it became a necessity to resolve the problem through peace."

"It took them a long time," I say, "before they withdrew their troops."

"In the Communist Party there were old people who couldn't change their way of thinking," Viktor says. "I understood things from the very beginning." I sense that his vanity is kicking in again. "But I couldn't say it. I had no opportunity to express my opinion. And since 1991, I've been retired from the KGB."

So he claims. Once a secret policeman, always a secret policeman. But Viktor's official resignation from the KGB is a good escape, a way of avoiding responsibility for a war that left over a million Afghans and fifteen thousand Russians dead.

The memorial centre has given Viktor a clean start, this time as a sympathizer for the families who lost loved ones in the war. I suspect he is here to ensure that no one is upset enough about the war to do anything more than celebrate dates of death, spread flowers over graves and join others in expressing sorrow for lost soldiers, for themselves and for their country.

Needless to say, I have only to ask Viktor how he feels about the soldiers on Russia's southern borders today to receive a reply of Putinesque logic: "It's a different time. There is international terrorism that has to be defeated. The Americans are helping get rid of dictatorships, creating democracies. . . ." I tell him he's now beginning to sound like a State Department spokesman. He doesn't like the comment, but he doesn't dispute it. Perhaps, in the new Russia, he's risen above the former KGB standards and come closer to the sleek ideology of the Central Intelligence Agency.

My next meeting is with a mother. It took a long time to persuade her to talk to us of her loss in Afghanistan. She does not know I am from that country. Lubov Zhuravleva has short curly hair, a round face. She is dressed in a black skirt and sweater and keeps her flat black hat on during our entire conversation. A retired nurse, the sixty-nine-year-old looks like the mother character in every Soviet film of communist collectives.

Her large blue eyes, hidden behind thick round glasses, are filled with tears as she shows me pictures of her son, Gannadi Zhuravlev, in civilian clothes, in his military uniform. There is a picture of his grave, a grey bust of the young man staring at the camera. At twenty-two, he died in the western Afghan province of Herat.

"He was a very kind person. He liked animals. His schoolteachers loved him. He'd learned English. In Afghanistan he was studying Spanish. He liked to read, went to exercise every morning as a young boy. He read about history, mostly military history, under his father's supervision. His father is a programmer in the military academy. So Gannadi went to the military college. He used to read under the blanket with the help of a torch; I used to see the light from under the blanket." She orders these thoughts in a proper, formal fashion. For every mother, a child is precious—especially after he's gone.

Gannadi played on his school soccer team. "Once, he went to a game where he was robbed. He didn't have money to come home. He had a habit of giving his things away, but he never asked for anything from others. He had to walk home. I saw the blood in his shoes from his long trek home— it was such a long distance." She wipes her tears. "Once, he tried to defend two girls who were attacked by a robber. He was punched in the eye. He had a bruise."

At twenty-one, Gannadi finished military academy, in 1982, and he was posted to Afghanistan shortly after his graduation.

"He wanted to go there, and he wrote to his commander, showing his enthusiasm to go. He was with the intelligence service. He caught hepatitis in Afghanistan. After treatment, he got leave and came home. He was with us from December 1982 until January 1983." During his stay in Moscow, Gannadi spoke to his father about the war in Afghanistan, not to his mother. But she overheard them speak. "He talked about how they'd investigated an attack. How their group was waiting for *dushmen*." He never wrote about the things he told his father. "He said Afghanistan was good for him. It was 'fun' for him, he'd say. The only thing he'd asked me to make for him was a vest with lots of pockets."

While he was in Moscow, his mother found a talisman— a heavy yellow piece of iron—in his bag. "When I inquired, he said it was given to him by the daughter of a leader of an Afghan tribe. It was symbolic of life. It was for his protection. He said she was in love with him."

Lubov had had a premonition about the death of her only son. "We accompanied him to the airport on his return to Afghanistan. He took sausages and other food for his friends. I felt very strange. The guard let his father go up to the plane to say goodbye to him. I thought it was a sign that he was not going to return. Gannadi participated in twenty-four military operations. He was awarded the special order of the Red Star and a special order from 'the Afghan people,' who thanked him for his services to their country. He was going to come home in July 1983, but he wanted to return after his forthcoming promotion to first lieutenant. He thought it was important for his father."

On August 18, 1983, Gannadi was between a valley and a mountain in Herat, where a platoon of sixteen soldiers were walking, crocodile fashion, watching for the *dushmen*. He was

walking ahead of the soldiers and sergeants, whom he was supposed to follow, not lead. "A land mine blew off part of his left
side. He was alive, but he was badly injured. They couldn't
move him because of the rough track. They sent the information back to headquarters."

At home, Lubov was preparing for the celebration of her
wedding anniversary when a major and a captain showed up.
Her husband was on his way home from work. "Have courage,
your son has been killed," they told her. The *Black Tulip*, the
plane that carried Russian dead from Afghanistan, brought
Gannadi's body back, along with his first lieutenant's uniform.
"They wanted to confirm his rank by giving us his uniform, but
they never confirmed it in writing," says Lubov. That was his
long-awaited promotion. "The body was brought in a zinc coffin. There was a little window in the coffin, but I couldn't see
anything inside." The family asked if they could open the coffin to see their son. "We were prohibited. Officially, Russia was
not at war, so we couldn't demand anything."

Six months after his death, someone from the military
came asking for him. "He's not here," Lubov told him.

"Tell him to come to the local military station to receive
his orders."

She had to insist that her son was dead. The local military
office was supposed to look after Gannadi's tombstone and
dedication, but when Lubov asked them to do this, they
wanted to see documents proving he was actually dead. She
was sent to another office to obtain the documents. "There,
they told me that I already had the documents. I couldn't bear
it any more. I started to cry. Meanwhile, their boss came in. He
saw me there and demanded to know how I'd passed through
the guards to get into the office." Finally, they gave her the
documents, which she presented to the local military office.

They received eighty-seven rubles for the tombstone and the grave. "It was not enough—we paid 7,500 rubles from our savings." They wanted their son to have a proper resting place.

Gannadi was buried in a local public cemetery, with a military funeral. "The officer who accompanied the body said he couldn't leave until we buried Gannadi. So no one would open the zinc box and see his body. But as soon as the first pile of soil was dropped over his coffin, he left." Gannadi's girlfriend promised at his funeral that she'd only marry someone who returned from Afghanistan, and she kept her word. "She told her husband that Gannadi would always exist between them." He agreed. "On holidays, she visits his grave. Her first child—a girl now twelve—was born disabled. Her husband blames her, saying that without love they were destined to have a disabled child."

Gannadi's last letter arrived home weeks after his zinc coffin was laid to rest. In it, he wrote to his parents that he was coming home. "War will never end for me," Lubov says. "I pay attention to anything that I hear about Afghanistan. It's as if he's still there."

Lubov was proud of Gannadi when he was serving in Afghanistan. "I thought he was following certain principles that were right at the time. Our borders had to be defended, otherwise the Americans would be on our southern border."

Originally from Ukraine, Lubov lived under the German occupation. Both her father and brother died fighting to save Russia from fascism. She thought the war in Afghanistan was similar, wanting to believe that her son, too, had died defending his "motherland." But her initial patriotism began to fade when she saw how the army and government treated her son's death. "When the Chechen war started, I realized that it was all just a game. When one political game is over, the government finds another one. The Soviets just delayed the American invasion of Afghanistan." Lubov has no ill feelings towards Afghans. "They are victims. We, too, are victims of political rivalries. The ordinary people don't get to decide anything."

Lubov tells me that her granddaughter is in the hospital for surgery—and is desperately in need of medication that's too costly for the family. "We've managed to buy one ampoule of this hemoglobin for five thousand rubles. She needs at least six for the surgery." I offer a small donation towards her medicine—she is grateful. Then Maria tells her that I'm from Afghanistan—the country where her son died. Lubov walks up to me, puts her arms around me and kisses me three times on the cheek—in the Afghan tradition. And I wonder, of course, if my journey here to the country of the invaders was all about this moment. I never thought I'd live to see the day I'd be in Moscow, crying in my heart, listening to the tragic stories of Russian soldiers. I recall the words of my cousin, who studied in Russia during the war. "The Russian mothers hate us," she said. "They say, 'Afghans have large families— but we have just one son, and he was killed in Afghanistan.'"

The bells of Saint Basil's Cathedral echo hauntingly across the fresh snow that has left a white dusting over the dark stones of Red Square. It's well below freezing; Moscow in January is meant to be taken seriously. But it was the Communist Party, the KGB and the Soviet army generals that took themselves more seriously than anything else. Before them on this square, the tanks, missiles and soldiers paraded in a ceremony of absolute discipline and order. I watched it all live on Afghan television, year after year on the anniversary of the Bolshevik Revolution. It inspired in me both hatred and fear.

Here is the Bolshoi Theatre, the statue of Marshal Georgy Zhukov on his horse, which I saw so many times on Afghan TV that I feel I know him personally. I look at the podium on which Leonid Brezhnev, the man who sent the Russian troops into Afghanistan in 1979, stood with his right-hand military men, always in army uniform, heavily decorated with medals of glory, growing larger in size each year. He didn't seem to breathe; in those television pictures, he seemed to vibrate with power. He had the look of a man possessed—demented or drugged—but invincible. "If only God punishes him for his crimes," my mother used to say. "If only he dies, the world will be at peace," said one of my mother's friends.

He did die, in the end. But the war he had unleashed did not. A bloody wheel had been set in motion. It went on spinning, grinding up more flesh and blood. Unwittingly, he changed the course of history. From a country on a path of development and growth, Afghanistan was turned into a mass of graveyards, suspicion and hatred. Afghanistan is still burning.

The church that Stalin had demolished has been rebuilt. A large statue of the Virgin hangs over its wooden door. And only a hundred metres away are the graves of Stalin and Brezhnev, their grey busts as frightening as the men were in life. In the communist style of perfection, Brezhnev's hair is brushed back in the stone as if it were real. The church is back in business, but Brezhnev and his comrades have turned to dust and stones. Who is laughing at whom? It's hard to say. But Red Square seems to be the house of Russian gods—for here, too, is Lenin's tomb, protected by scores of uniformed men with their long grey Russian coats and stern faces, with their hands pointed in the direction of Lenin's grave. Lenin's tomb—his followers still prefer "mausoleum"—really is a grave.

I walk down the steps to a square underground room, a shrine. But it's unlike any of the Muslim shrines I've visited, where the deprived and dispossessed come to express their frustrations, grievances and helplessness. Visitors pray, talk or cry without fear of being judged. In Muslim shrines, a harmony of colour and art promotes tranquility. Lenin's grave inspires fear. It's about secrecy and silence and an image that is not to be challenged. It is about control—not just control of power but of history itself. No visitor may utter a word. The guards place their index fingers over their lips to remind people not to speak.

A soldier motions to remind me that I cannot stop for more than a few seconds. But I notice how Lenin lies in a dark suit, over red velvet, with one fist clenched, another showing nails that are perfectly shaped and cleaned—they hardly look like the hands of a hard-working revolutionary or someone who held a rifle. In his name, millions have been marching into their graves, carrying rifles, banners and the burden of slavery. Here is the man I've seen in so many pictures—the hair, the funny-looking beard, the face. He looks young for a man of 134. Every now and then, he undergoes a remake, perhaps growing younger year by year. I don't know if I should be appalled at the human frivolity of the body's preservation, or admire the scientific achievement that's become Lenin, or laugh at the insanity.

I cannot believe I'm staring at a man whose dream—the industry that became Russia—affected our lives so tragically: mine, those of my family and of all Afghanistan. And here he is, lying in deep sleep in a cold square, still dreaming. I've seen living people behind bars—jailed for their ideas. This is the first time I've seen a dead man in his marble and glass cell, chained forever, a permanent prisoner of death.

1747   Ahmad Shah Abdali (Durrani), a Pushtun commander in the army of Iranian King Nadir Shah Afshar, seizes power following the king's death and declares his territory an independent country called Afghanistan.

1748   The Afghan empire reaches as far as India and the Arabian Sea.

1772   Timur Shah, Ahmad Shah's son, moves his capital from Kandahar to Kabul.

1803   The British occupy Delhi.

1819 26   Afghanistan is divided into fiefdoms among competing Durrani families in Kabul, Kandahar and Peshawar.

1826   Dost Mohammad Khan establishes the Mohammadzai dynasty in Kabul and begins to unite the country.

1839–42   First Anglo-Afghan War results in British puppet, Shah Shuja, on Afghan throne. A British army of 16,500 men—including Indian troops and followers—is annihilated outside Kabul, the greatest defeat of British arms in history.

1842	Dost Muhammad surrenders to the British, returning to the throne.
1856	Afghanistan remains neutral during the Indian War for Independence (Indian Mutiny) against British rule.
1872	Anglo-Russian agreement on Afghan independence.
1878–80	Second Anglo-Afghan War: The British invade Afghanistan, fearing Russian dominance in Kabul.
1879	The Treaty of Gandamak gives the British control of Khyber Pass.
1880	Abdul Rahman Khan assumes Afghan throne under British protection.
1893	The Durand Line, dividing ethnic Pushtuns, is established by the British as the Afghan-Indian boundary.
1901	Habibullah Khan replaces his father, Abdul Rahman Khan, as king of Afghanistan.
1904	Lycée Habibia, the first Western-style preparatory school, opens in Kabul.
1907	The Anglo-Russian Convention of St. Petersburg declares Afghanistan a buffer state within the British sphere of influence.
1911	Mahmud Beg Tarzi, an Afghan intellectual returning from exile in Ottoman Syria, begins publication of *Siraj ul-Akhbar-i Afghanistan*—the first major Afghan newspaper.

1914	The First World War begins. Afghanistan remains neutral.
1917	Russian Revolution.
1918	Habibullah Khan is assassinated. His son Amanullah seizes the throne. Third (and last) Anglo-Afghan War results in complete Afghan independence from British.
1920–29	Central Asian resistance to the Red Army uses northern Afghanistan as a base and refuge.
1921	Reformer King Amanullah signs Soviet-Afghan treaty of friendship, but the Soviets refuse to return Panjdeh (a part of Afghan territory confiscated by the Russians) to Afghans. The first Afghan constitution is created. Russian military and civilian advisors enter Afghanistan. The British recognize Afghan independence.
1922	The British send an ambassador to Kabul.
1929	Tribal rebellion broadens against King Amanullah and his modernist reforms. He goes into exile in Italy. A Tajik called Bacha-I Saqao (Habibullah) declares jihad against the king and captures Kabul, but is defeated within nine months. General Nadir Khan leads Pushtun war to recapture Kabul.
1930	Nadir Shah opens a medical faculty in Kabul with French professors; it later becomes part of Kabul University. Women are admitted to the university.

The second Afghan constitution recognizes the rights of all Afghans as citizens.

1933   Zahir Shah becomes king following his father's assassination. His two uncles, Hashim Khan and Shah Mahmud Khan, dominate politics until 1953 as consecutive prime ministers.

1939   The Second World War begins. Afghanistan remains neutral.

1942   An American legation opens in Kabul; it's raised to embassy status in 1948.

1945   The Afghan government begins negotiations with a U.S. construction company for agricultural developments in Helmand Valley.

1946   The middle of the Amu Darya (previously the Oxus River) is fixed as Afghanistan's border with the USSR.

1947   Britain withdraws from the Indian subcontinent. Pakistan is created as a Muslim country. The British ignore Pushtun nationalist demands for an independent Pushtunistan.
Afghanistan becomes a founding member of the United Nations and protests Pakistan's entry because of dispute over their mutual border in Pushtun tribal areas (the Durand Line).
Wish Zalmayan (Awakened Youth) is created, laying the basis for the reformist movements of the 1960s.

1948   Liberal elections bring in reformist members of legislature.

1952 The government disbands, closes the free press and arrests opposition leaders.

1953 Muhammad Daoud Khan is appointed prime minister.

In Iran, the nationalist prime minister Muhammad Mossadegh is overthrown with the help of the CIA. Reza Shah establishes Pahlavi control of Iranian politics.

Stalin dies.

1954 Under mutual agreement between the U.S. and Pakistan, American arms are supplied to Pakistan. Kabul views this as a threat to its security.

1955 Afghanistan is a founding member of the nonalign ment movement at the Bandung Conference.

Nikita Khrushchev's visit to Afghanistan results in a US$100-million development loan from the Soviets, secret Russian military aid, and extension of the Afghan-Soviet Friendship Treaty of 1931 for ten years.

The United States refuses to send military hardware to Kabul, which then contracts for arms and military advisors from the communist bloc.

First Five-Year Plan.

1959 Women of the royal family and the families of high officials appear unveiled at Afghan National Independence Day celebrations, ending the practice of police-enforced veiling (the compulsory veil consisted of a modest scarf).

1963   Zahir Shah dismisses his cousin, Daoud Khan, as
prime minister and appoints a Tajik, Dr.
Muhammad Yousuf, in his place.
Zahir Shah makes his first visit to the United
States.
Afghanistan signs Cultural Co-operation Agreement
with the Soviet Union.

1964   The Afghan constitution allows freedom of speech,
and voting rights for both men and women.
Leonid Brezhnev visits Kabul to establish a new
Russian polytechnic institute.
Salang Tunnel and highway opened with Soviet
assistance, linking north and south Afghanistan
with an all-weather paved road.
Afghan-Chinese border demarcated (ninety kilometres) in Wakhan.

1965   The People's Democratic Party of Afghanistan
(PDPA) is established by Nur Muhammad Taraki
and Babrak Karmal as the Khalq Party.
The first elections take place under the new constitution, but without political parties.
Student demonstration forces resignation of Dr.
Yousuf. Muhammad Hashim Maiwandwal becomes
prime minister.
Koubra Nourzai is appointed minister of public
health; she is the first woman in the cabinet in
Afghan history.

1966   Independent newspapers and periodicals begin
publication in Kabul.

Parliament approves political parties law, but King
Zahir Shah refuses to sign.
Natural gas export to the Soviet Union begins.
Khalq Party splits into Parcham and Khalq parties.

1967 Student unrest in Kabul forces the closing of schools.
Second elections under the 1964 constitution.
Babrak Karmal and Hafizullah Amin are elected
from rival factions of the PDPA.

1973 Daoud Khan leads a military coup, declares
Afghanistan a republic and becomes president with
the support of the pro-Moscow Parcham faction of
the PDPA.

1974 Daoud visits Moscow. Soviets pledge U.S. $600
million for Afghan Seven-Year Plan.

1975 Daoud falls out with Brezhnev; he begins to turn
towards Iran and Arab countries for development
funding and support.

1976 The Loya Jirgah approves a republican constitution
and elects Daoud president for a seven-year term.

1977 Mir Akbar Khaibar (a Parcham ideologue) is
assassinated. Daoud arrests communist leaders.

1978
April PDPA coup: the "Saur Revolution." Daoud and his
family are murdered.
August The Khalq Party accuses Parcham Party members
of countercoup plots; a new red Soviet-style flag is
adopted for Afghanistan.
December A twenty-year treaty of friendship and co-operation
is signed between Kabul and Moscow. The treaty is

cited by Moscow as a legal basis for invasion a year later.

1979

January	Small-scale anti-government resistance fighting begins in the eastern provinces.
February	Ayatollah Khomeini arrives in Tehran to establish the Islamic Republic.
December	A large Soviet airborne force occupies Kabul. Amin is killed. Babrak Karmal's Parcham Party takes over the government.
1980	Refugee exodus begins from Afghanistan to Pakistan and Iran. U.S. President Jimmy Carter authorizes the supply of weapons to the Afghan resistance through Pakistan to harass Soviet forces.
1982	Brezhnev dies and is succeeded by Yuri Andropov.
1984	Kabul adopts a stricter conscription (all males over eighteen) to make up for fleeing army deserters. Andropov dies and is replaced by Konstantin Chernenko, who dies a year later.
1985	Mikhail Gorbachev becomes Soviet president. U.S. President Ronald Reagan increases aid to the Afghan resistance.
1986	Gorbachev describes Afghan War as "bleeding wound." The United States supplies the Afghan resistance with Stingers. U.S. aid to the mujahidin reaches $470 million. Muhammad Najibullah, the former head of KhAD, replaces Karmal as president. Kabul launches a policy of national reconciliation.

1988

February   Gorbachev announces an agreement to withdraw
                  Soviet troops. Moscow gives casualty figures for the
                  Soviets in Afghanistan: 13,310 dead, 35,478
                  wounded and 311 missing.

June   An Afghan Interim Government (a coalition of fif-
                  teen mujahidin groups) is formed in Peshawar.

November   Soviets introduce SCUD missiles into Afghanistan,
                  firing more than a thousand in the first year,
                  although their retreat has already begun.

1989   Soviets complete withdrawal of forces under the
                  Geneva Accords. Air bombing mission from Soviet
                  Central Asian bases continues.
                  Ayatollah Khomeini dies.

1990   Mujahidin leaders and commanders declare that
                  jihad will continue until the formation of an Islamic
                  government.

1991   Mujahidin capture Khost in the south and Wakhan
                  corridor in the north. The Kabul regime admits that
                  the local militia of General Rashid Dostum are
                  beyond government control.
                  In September, the U.S. and USSR agree to halt all
                  military aid by end of the year.
                  Burhanuddin Rabbani, one of the mujahidin lead-
                  ers, leads a delegation to Moscow to discuss the
                  end of war. His rivals, Abdul Rasul Sayyaf, Yonous
                  Khalis and Gulbuddin Hekmatyar, denounce
                  Rabbani for "engaging" in an anti-mujahidin con-
                  spiracy with Moscow.
                  Moscow speeds the withdrawal of three hundred

combat experts from Afghanistan, mainly SCUD missile operators.

1992   Mujahidin occupy Kabul on the fourteenth anniversary of the 1978 communist coup. Saudi Arabia, Iran and Pakistan recognize a new Afghan government.

Hekmatyar demands that Dostum's militia be expelled or he will attack Kabul. Two months after their arrival, Hekmatyar's and Rabbani's forces begin fighting each other in Kabul. A number of Western embassies close. Thirty thousand refugees flee Kabul for Nangarhar province.

A new Islamic flag is adopted.

1993   More factional fighting disrupts Kabul, as Pushtun, Uzbek, Tajik and Hazara militias fight for power. In November, the U.S. urges Pakistan to expel Arab "Afghan" fighters.

1994   A UN General Assembly resolution requests an immediate ceasefire between the mujahidin.

The United States declares a state of emergency in Kabul.

Two hundred thousand displaced Afghans are living in Jalalabad.

The International Committee of the Red Cross estimates that seventy thousand Afghans have been killed and wounded in fighting.

In October, Taliban militias emerge and seize the southern city of Kandahar, vowing to oust the mujahidin and introduce Islamic rule. Taliban forces advance to the outskirts of Kabul.

1996	After defeating Hekmatyar's forces at Sarobi and Puli Charkhi, Taliban forces capture Kabul. Former president Najibullah is taken from a UN compound and hanged by the Taliban. Women's access to work, education and health care is prohibited.
1997	Pakistan, Saudi Arabia and the United Arab Emirates recognize the Taliban government. Ahmad Shah Masoud (Rabbani's top commander), Dostum and Abdul Karim Khalili form a coalition to fight the Taliban. A Taliban delegation visits the United States and meets with Assistant Secretary of State Robin Raphel. In March, the Taliban foreign ministry forbids photography and filming.
1998	Two powerful earthquakes in February and June in the northern provinces of Badakhshan and Takhar leave more than nine thousand dead. Taliban forces take Mazar-e-Sherif. Eight Iranian diplomats and a correspondent are murdered, pushing both Iran and Afghanistan to the verge of war. International human rights groups say Taliban fighters massacred between four thousand and eight thousand ethnic Hazaras in Mazar-e-Sherif. In August, the U.S. launches a Tomahawk missile strike on suspected Saudi dissident Osama bin Laden's bases in the southern province of Khost. The UN evacuates most expatriates. Taliban forces seize the central province of Bamiyan.

1999

October   The UN imposes an air embargo and financial sanc-
              tions to force the Taliban to hand over Osama bin
              Laden.

2000

December   UN resolution imposes air and arms embargo,
              restricted-travel sanctions, and freezing of funds of
              Osama Bin Laden and his associates.

2001

March   The Taliban blows up the giant Buddha statues in
              Bamiyan Valley.

September 9   Ahmad Shah Masoud, the leader of the main
              opposition to the Taliban, is killed by assassins
              posing as journalists.

September 11 Attack on the United States.

October 7   The U.S. and Britain launch air strikes against
              Afghanistan after the Taliban refuses to hand over
              Osama bin Laden, who is held responsible for the
              September 11 attacks.

November   Opposition forces, with aid from the U.S. military,
              seize Mazar-e-Sherif and within days march into
              Kabul.

December 5   Afghan groups agree in Bonn on a deal for an
              interim government.

December 7   The Taliban's last stronghold of Kandahar falls, but
              Taliban leader Mullah Omar remains at large.

December 22   Pushtun royalist Hamid Karzai is sworn in as head
              of a thirty-member interim power-sharing
              government.

2002

January   The first contingent of foreign peacekeepers arrives
                 in Kabul.

April 18   Former king Zahir Shah (age eighty-seven) returns
                 to Afghanistan after twenty-nine years in exile in
                 Italy.

May   The UN Security Council extends the mandate of
                 the peacekeeping International Security Assistance
                 Force (ISAF) in Afghanistan until December 2002.
                 Turkey prepares to take over command of the five-
                 thousand-strong ISAF from Britain by the end of
                 June 2002.

June   The Loya Jirgah elects Hamid Karzai as interim
                 head of state. Karzai picks members of his adminis-
                 tration, which is to serve until 2004.

July   Vice-President Haji Abdul Qadir is assassinated by
                 gunmen in Kabul.

September   Karzai narrowly escapes an assassination attempt in
                 his hometown of Kandahar.

2004

October   First presidential elections won by Hamid Karzai.

NOTES

CHAPTER TWO

1 (p. 30) One of its founders, Sarwar Joya, a poet and a writer, had spent twenty-two of his forty-two years in prison; other members, including Abdul Ali, were frequently questioned and detained by the government.

2 (p. 30) Other major ethnic communities include Hazaras, who are also Shia but speak a variant of Persian called Hazaragi; and Uzbeks, who are Sunnis and speak Uzbeki.

CHAPTER THREE

3 (p. 66) General Omerzahi, at the time a senior intelligence officer who was told to report on Khaibar's funeral, claims in his book *Kabul Nights* that Khaibar's death was wrongfully blamed on the government. He suggests that Khaibar was killed by a group of unidentified gunmen, possibly his own friends, such as Babrak Karmal, who replaced him as leader of the People's Democratic Party of Afghanistan (PDPA). Sultan Ali Kishtmand, a long-time member of the PDPA, argues in his recent memoirs that Hafizullah Amin, a PDPA member accused of having ties to the CIA, was involved in Khaibar's murder. There are more speculations than evidence surrounding Khaibar's death.

4 (p. 70) The Mohammadzai are a clan of the Pushtun tribe who had been providing the country with rulers since the 1930s.

5 (p. 70) Daoud Khan served as prime minister from 1953 to 1963

under Zahir Shah. He wanted the Afghan throne, but the king secured an oath of allegiance from his eldest son to replace him, effectively blocking Daoud Khan from achieving his ambition.

6 (p. 71) Bhabani Sen Gupta, *Afghanistan: Politics, Economics and Society* (Boulder: Lynne Rienner Publishers, 1986), 28.

7 (p. 95) According to Archer Blood, the United States' chief of mission in New Delhi—who served for several months in Afghanistan in 1979—Amin had approached the Americans for aid when he was serving as foreign minister in Taraki's administration. Amin was trying to take advantage of Afghanistan's officially non-aligned status, hoping that American help would negate Pakistan's support for anti-communist Afghan opposition groups. But the Americans were too preoccupied with the Iranian Revolution and the burning of the U.S. embassy in Pakistan to pay much attention to Afghanistan.

8 (p. 96) Borovik's compelling book is called *The Hidden War: A Russian Journalist's Account of the Soviet War in Afghanistan* (New York: Grove Press, 1990).

CHAPTER FOUR

9 (p. 104) Nasri Haqshenos, *Tahwlot Seyosi Jihad Afghanistan*, Volume 1 (Delhi: Jayyed Press, 1998), 55.

CHAPTER FIVE

10 (p. 136) Mir Gholam Muhammad Ghobar, *Afghanistan dar Maseer Tarekh* (Tehran: Inteshorat-e Jamouree, 1995), 638.

11 (p. 137) Abdul Raouf Binava, *Pashtani Mermoni* (Kabul: Pouhana Rana, 1944), 159.

12 (p. 137) *The Second Anglo-Afghan War 1878–1880*, Official Account (London: John Murray, 1908), 516.

SELECT BIBLIOGRAPHY

Beevor, Antony. *The Fall of Berlin 1945* (New York: Penguin Books, 2002).

Binava, Abdul Raouf. *Pashtani Mermoni* (Kabul: Pouhana Rana, 1944).

Borovik, Artyom. *The Hidden War: A Russian Journalist's Account of the Soviet War in Afghanistan* (New York: Grove Press, 1990).

"Crisis of Impunity: The Role of Pakistan, Russia and Iran." In *Fueling the Civil War* (Human Rights Watch, Volume 13, No. 3, July 2001).

Dupree, Louis. *Afghanistan* (New York: Princeton University Press, 1980).

Farhang, Mir Mohammad Siddiq. *Afghanistan dar Panj Qaaran Ahkheer,* Volumes 2 and 3 (Kabul: [publisher unknown], 1994).

Ghobar, Mir G. Mohammad. *Afghanistan dar Maseer Tarekh* (Tehran: Inteshorat-e Jamouree, 1995).

Griffin, Michael. *Reaping the Whirlwind: The Taliban Movement in Afghanistan* (London: Pluto Press, 2001).

Gupta, Bhabani Sen. *Afghanistan: Politics, Economics and Society* (Boulder: Lynne Rienner Publishers, 1986).

Haqshenos, Nasri. *Tahwlot Seyosi Jihad Afghanistan,* Volume 1 (Delhi: Jayyed Press, 1998).

"Humanity Denied: Systematic Violations of Women's Rights." In

Afghanistan (Human Rights Watch, Volume 13, No. 5, October 2001).

Keshtmand, Sultan Ali. *Yaddoshtahi Seyosi wa Roydodahi Tarekhi: Khoteroat Shakhsi* (Najeeb Kabeir, 2002).

Kushoan, Mohammad Qaawi. *Khoteroat Seyosi Sayeed Qasim Reshtya* (Kabul: [publisher unknown], 1992).

Magnus, Ralph H., and Eden Naby. *Afghanistan: Mullah, Marx, and Mujahid* (Boulder, CO: Westview Press, 1998).

Maley, William. *Fundamentalism Reborn? Afghanistan and the Taliban* (London: Hurst & Company, 1998).

Marsden, Peter. *The Taliban: War, Religion and the New Order in Afghanistan* (London: Zed Books, 1998)

Moluro, Kobra Mazhari. *Pashtani Lekwali aw Shoheroni* (Kabul: Dawlati Matboha, 1987).

Nuzhat, Nazeifallah. *Aushoub Begonagan* (Kabul: Inteshorat-e Maiwand, 2001).

Omerzahi, General. *Shab ahi Kabul: Khoteroat yak Afsar Nezomi* (Peshawar: Sabah Ketobkhona, 1995).

Rashid, Ahmed. *Taliban: Islam, Oil and the New Great Game in Central Asia* (London: I.B. Tauris, 2000).

The Second Anglo-Afghan War 1878–80, Official Account (London: John Murray, 1908).

Tears, Blood and Cries: Human Rights in Afghanistan since the Invasion, 1979–1984 (New York: Helsinki Watch, 1984).

ACKNOWLEDGEMENTS

IN WRITING THIS BOOK, I am indebted to Afghans, Russians, Pakistanis, Iranians, Canadians, French and Americans.

I'm grateful to the help and encouragement of friends and colleagues. My special thanks go to Hassan Abdul Rahman, Riaz Akhtar, Daoud Arefy, Qahar Ausi's family, Siddiq

Barmak, Sorour Bani Hashemi, Marisa Berenson, Murray Brewster, Fulvio Caccia, Andrew Campbell, Ms. Cox, Hamid Dabashi, Farhad Darya, Kim Elliott, Saifullah and Hassibullah Fazel, Tammy and Sandro Giuliani, Nader Hashemi, Mushfiq Hashimy, Alia and Murray Hogben, Afra Jalabi, Rafi Khan, Rahat Kurd, Maja Lees, Christopher Levenson, Paul Mackereth, Ian Mccallum, Mohsen Makhmalbaf, Irina Mekkawi, Partaw Naderi, Andaleeb Qayyum, Emran Qureshi, Brenda and Richard Ricker, Reza Sadeghi, Lena Saidi, Tamim Sediqui, Ahmed Shebaro, Nada Sparks, Maria Strizhevskaya, Dave Tait, Brenda Winter and Lila Yalda.

At CBC, my thanks go to Nazim Baksh, Tony Burman, Geraldine Connelly, Jack Schoon and Daniel Schwartz.

My thanks go to Wali Karzai, Gul Agha Serzai, Rashid Dustam, Ustad Attah, and the staff at the Afghan embassies in Rome and Ottawa, in particular Hamidullah Nasser-lia and Mirwais Salehi.

Above all, I thank my family: my mother, Jamila, my father, Habibullah, my sister, Mejgan, and my brother, Hassib; thanks also to Abdul Ali Sarwar, my uncles Ghafour and Asad, my uncle Wahid, his wife, Samera, Aunt Najmeya, my grandmother, and their families, all of whom appear in the pages of this book. Also Robert Fisk, who does not need me to say how much he contributed to this story.

Lastly, my gratitude goes to my agent, Helen Heller, my editors Anne Collins and Pamela Murray at Random House, and Sue Sumeraj and Gena Gorrell.

Needless to say, I alone am responsible for all the views expressed in this book. Any mistakes are mine.

INDEX